DISROBED

DISROBED

THE NEW BATTLE PLAN

TO BREAK THE LEFT'S

STRANGLEHOLD ON

THE COURTS

MARK W. SMITH

CROWN
FORUM
NEW YORK

Published in the United States by Crown Forum,
an imprint of the Crown Publishing Group,
a division of Random House, Inc., New York.

www.crownpublishing.com

Crown Forum and the Crown Forum colophon are
trademarks of Random House, Inc.

Library of Congress Cataloging-in-Publication Data
Smith, Mark W., 1968–
    Disrobed : the new battle plan to break the Left's stranglehold on the courts / Mark W.
    Smith.— 1st ed.
    Includes bibliographical references and index.
      1. United States. Supreme Court.   2. Political questions and judicial power—United
    States.   3. Conservatism—United States.   4. Right and left (Political science)   I. Title.
    KF8748.S537 2006
    347.73'2—dc22   2006004993

ISBN-13: 978-0-307-33925-6
ISBN-10: 0-307-33925-4

Printed in the United States of America

Design by Joseph Rutt

10 9 8 7 6 5 4 3 2 1

First Edition

To my mother, Joan Smith, and
to the memory of my father, Warren B. Smith

Also to the memory of General Joseph Warren,
who gave his life for American liberty
at the Battle of Bunker Hill, June 17, 1775

CONTENTS

PART I

WHY WE LOSE

ONE

"IS THIS IT?"

I was still in bed when the cell phone and the BlackBerry came to life. I tried to ignore the ringing and whizzing sounds and catch some more sleep, but the noise wouldn't stop. It wasn't just a few calls and e-mails, but a whole stream of them pouring in at once. I realized something must have happened—something big.

That "something big" became clear once I checked the BlackBerry: President George W. Bush had just announced his nominee to replace Justice Sandra Day O'Connor on the U.S. Supreme Court—his White House counsel, Harriet Miers. And as one of the urgent e-mails instructed me, I had a conference call about Miers in just moments—a call with the White House team defending the president's pick.

Who on earth is Harriet Miers? I thought.

Only days earlier I had attended the formal swearing-in ceremony of Chief Justice John Roberts in the East Room of the White House, and through my work as an officer of the Federalist Society, the nation's most prominent conservative legal organization, I knew the members of the White House team advising the president on Supreme Court nominations. Still, the Miers pick surprised me.

When the conference call began, I listened intently as the group, made up of reputable conservatives and led by former Republican National Committee chairman Ed Gillespie, made the case for Miers. They emphasized her loyalty to the president and her accomplishments as an attorney in Texas. But then something strange happened: They stopped talking, when it seemed they had only begun their case.

Maybe I was still groggy. I had jotted down only a few notes—generic comments about the nominee's view that "the role of the judiciary should be limited" and her vow to "strictly apply the laws and the

Constitution." Surely there was more to say for Harriet Miers's qualifications, a stronger case to make? I had yet to hear anything about Miers that convinced me that she was a committed conservative. I had publicly supported the Roberts nomination and expected to do the same for this one. I naturally began searching my mind for ways to phrase the case for Miers in the inevitable television debates I'd be engaged in with liberals. Then I realized, Forget the Left, what would I say to my friends on the Right about the pick? I struggled to convince *myself* that this was a good conservative candidate.

So finally I piped up with a question.

"Is this it?"

The point was, when you're talking about the highest court in the land, the president must compile a formidable case for his nominee. The White House team hadn't done it. And as I now listened to them repeat the same few talking points, it became clear—as it soon would to the rest of the conservative movement—that there really wasn't more to the case for Harriet Miers.

I left the call unconvinced and a bit confused. After conservatives had spent years waiting for an opportunity to change the balance of the Supreme Court, was Miers really the best pick? Not at all.

And so, like many other conservatives, I breathed a sigh of relief when Miers withdrew her name from consideration and the president nominated a judge with unquestionably strong conservative credentials—Samuel Alito—in her place. A bullet dodged, perhaps. But relieved as we all were, no one on the Right should make the mistake of celebrating this near-miss as a victory for the conservative cause or for the country. We should be worried—deeply worried.

Think about it: How could someone like Harriet Miers come so close to sitting on the Supreme Court at a time when a Republican resides at 1600 Pennsylvania Avenue and the GOP solidly controls the U.S. Senate? The disturbing answer is this: The guidelines conservatives use to select judges, and the language we use to describe the role we want courts to perform, are so broad and vague as to be essentially meaningless; they apply to Miers just as much as they do to Supreme Court justices Antonin Scalia, Clarence Thomas, John Roberts, and Samuel Alito.

In fact, as much as I admire and respect Chief Justice Roberts and Justice Alito, I cannot celebrate their confirmations in themselves as major victories for conservatism—and neither should you. Even with Roberts, Alito, Scalia, and Thomas sitting on the Supreme Court, we have only *four* conservative justices out of a total of nine. And that's at most: As conservatives have learned the hard way, supposedly conservative jurists have a way of "evolving" to the left once they ascend to the bench. That's no accident—and you'll see why in this book.

In any case, conservatives can't make the mistake of believing that a mere two appointments to a single court—even to the Supreme Court—will magically fix all the problems in the courts and stop the Left's legal assault on America. The deeply uncomfortable but undeniable truth for conservatives is one the Harriet Miers saga highlighted: *We still don't get it when it comes to the courts.*

In the days after the White House conference call—even after Miers withdrew—I kept coming back to the question I had asked Ed Gillespie's team: *Is this it? Is this* the way the conservative movement is going to address the courts after being outgunned and outmaneuvered by the Left for some seventy years, ever since liberals began dominating the judiciary? Is *this* the strategy—mouthing platitudes about "respect for the rule of law" and "judicial restraint" and "strictly interpreting the law"?

Is this it?

Sadly, I concluded, yes, it is.

And the nation will continue to suffer if conservatives don't come up with an entirely new—and radically different—battle plan for the courts and American law.

This book is that battle plan.

THE SECRET WEAPON

THESE DAYS CONSERVATIVES rail against the courts, and with good reason. Liberals win victory after victory after victory in the judiciary—advancing a radical agenda that could never win approval in the democratic process. Consider: Today's law permits the starving of a woman in Florida but not of a dog; permits aborting an unborn child but criminalizes the destruction of spotted-owl eggs; permits the consideration of race in law school admissions but does not allow wardens to consider the racial composition of prison gangs in making decisions about cell assignment; considers minors too immature to be executed for murder but more than capable of deciding whether to have an abortion without consulting parents; grants more legal protection to the "right" to abortion—which is mentioned nowhere in the Constitution—than to the right to property or right to bear arms, both of which are identified in the Constitution; and forbids laws banning virtual child pornography but permits federal laws criminalizing the running of political advertisements in the months leading up to a federal election.

American courts have gone so far as to increase taxes, ban nativity scenes in public parks during Christmas, mandate the approval of gay marriage, declare the recitation of the Pledge of Allegiance in public schools unconstitutional because it contains the phrase "under God," prevent public schools from inviting clergy to give nondenominational prayers at graduation ceremonies, compel states to provide free taxpayer-funded public education to illegal immigrants, restructure election districts, resolve presidential and gubernatorial elections, and second-guess presidential decisions about how to fight a war.

And the Left continues to achieve extraordinary success in the courts even now, despite the sharp right turn the nation has taken over the past quarter century; despite Republican control of the White House, both houses of Congress, and most state legislatures and governorships; despite the fact that Republican presidents have appointed most of America's federal judges; and despite the fact that for the past thirty years at least seven of the nine Supreme Court justices have been Republican appointees—something that should temper the enthusiasm of conservatives who rejoice in the mere ascension of John Roberts and Samuel Alito. Conservatives rightly recognize that what Alexander Hamilton once called the "least dangerous branch" of government has instead become the *most* dangerous branch.

Something is wrong here—something is very wrong.

In the popular Harry Potter books and movies, the game Quidditch revolves around the Golden Snitch—a small, winged ball that zips around the playing field. Basically, when a player captures it, the game ends and his team wins.[1] The courts have become the Golden Snitch of American politics: If one party captures the courts, that team wins. The party then has the ultimate power: to strike down laws that the elected branches enact and to shape American society for decades to come. And the frightening truth is that the Left has held the Golden Snitch for some seventy years, despite the Republicans' success at the polls.

No conservative who is being honest with himself can deny how badly we're getting beaten in the courts. The question, then, is: *Why* do we keep losing? How does the loony Left, discredited virtually everywhere and in countless respects, keep using the legal system to advance its radical social and political agenda seemingly at will? The conservative movement includes many sincere, intelligent, earnest representatives committed to keeping liberal judges from destroying "the land of the free and home of the brave." Yet we've made little progress in our fight to stop the left-wing judicial assault.

I've spent years in the legal and political trenches fighting for the conservative cause—as vice president of the New York City Federalist Society, as a practicing attorney, as an author, and as a legal and political commentator on television and radio. I've worked closely with many of the Right's most able legal and political minds and spoken at length with them about how we can fix this urgent problem. I've attended more law conferences, speeches, and lectures than I care to count in hopes of helping the Right fight back. And I've long wanted to believe that the solutions the conservative movement usually advances would finally begin to pay off, for many of these proposals come from conservatives and legal experts whose opinions I deeply respect. Indeed, for many years and in countless media appearances I have argued passionately for many of these same ideas. But the lessons of history—underscored by the eye-opening Harriet Miers experience—have led me to conclude, reluctantly, that a new approach is required.

The plain truth is this: The Right will never thwart the liberal legal assault until we abandon our own self-defeating tactics. That's right, *self-defeating*. Our current strategy (such as it is) is to pillory liberals for their underhanded (albeit highly effective) tactics in the courts—judicial activism, inventing rights and principles found nowhere in the Constitution, ignoring legal precedents when it suits their needs, relying on foreign precedent to justify desired outcomes, suing to achieve in the courts what they can't achieve through the democratic process, and much more. And after we attack, criticize, and harangue the Left, we propose this alternative: *Everyone should play by the rules—the rule of law.*

In essence, all that proposal amounts to is this: *Hey, guys, this isn't right. Let's cut it out.*

Yes, that's it. You've heard it all before, though not quite in those terms. Instead, you hear it phrased in terms of the Right's favorite legal catchphrases. Think back to the Supreme Court nominations of John Roberts and Samuel Alito. How many times did you hear Republican politicians and conservative commentators—judges, academics, editorial writers, syndicated columnists, television and radio hosts—call for "judicial restraint," "judges who strictly interpret the law," "judges who won't legislate from the bench," "an end to judicial activism," "judges who respect the rule of law," or some variation thereof?

It all sounds great, and indeed conservatives should be credited for having a clear conception of how the Framers intended the judiciary to work—that judges should *not* be "politicians in black robes" with the power to determine how we all live our lives. In fact, I think we can all agree that it would be ideal if the judiciary really did play the role in society conservatives say it should.

But I'm here to tell you: It ain't happening. Yes, I would love to embrace the Constitution and use its text to resolve all questions of constitutional law. I would love it if judges stopped focusing on political outcomes—upholding laws whose objectives they support while striking down laws of which they disapprove. I would love it if courts hadn't spent the past seventy years inventing certain rights and taking others away from Americans. I would love it if left-wing legal organizations stopped filing lawsuit after lawsuit after lawsuit until finally they get the political outcome they want. Like it or not, though, all of these things are realities of twenty-first-century American law and politics. Simply wishing they didn't exist will not make them disappear. Sorry, conservatives, we're not in Kansas anymore.

And even if somehow, magically, we could click our heels and get every one of the thousands of judges in America—many of them proud liberals with lifetime appointments—to stop legislating from the bench, what would that buy us? Not enough, because this step does nothing to address the seventy years of liberal legal precedents now on the books. In essence, the conservative proposal of judicial restraint is purely a defensive measure. It would try to lock in the status quo—and the status quo is a legal system that skews radically to the left. As conservatives, we must finally admit to ourselves that not only is our approach to the courts fanciful, it's not even *desirable*. We can't remain blindly committed to the same losing strategy.

So what do we do? We must stop playing defense against the courts and instead go on offense by *using* the courts. We must take back the law from liberal judicial activists and thwart the loony Left's assault on America. Fortunately, there's a secret weapon we can use to do that. And the weapon is lying right in front of us, hiding in plain sight, ours for the taking. It's a secret only in the sense that the conservative movement refuses to consider it as an option. In fact, it's a weapon that the Left has wielded against us for decades, and with startling results.

The weapon? Judicial activism.

Yes, judicial activism—the very thing conservatives decry at every turn.

Wait, does this mean I've become a feel-good liberal, torn up my vast-right-wing-conspiracy membership card, turned my back on the Federalist Society, and become Air America's seventy-ninth listener? Not at all. As you'll see in this book, conservative attacks on judicial activism have missed the point: The problem with the courts is not judicial activism per se, but *liberal* judicial activism. Judicial activism is nothing but a tool; what matters is for what purposes the tool is applied—for good or for bad.

Radical as it may sound to conservatives who have been taught that judicial activism is an inherent evil, our secret weapon—*conservative* judicial activism—in fact offers us the greatest opportunity to preserve and protect the rights, freedoms, and ideals that the Constitution was designed to protect and that America's Founders cherished. Even those committed to ending judicial activism altogether must realize this point: No strategy conservatives adopt, other than engaging in judicial activism ourselves, will end judicial activism by the Left.

Conservatives now have a golden opportunity not just to thwart future liberal gains but actually to convert America's courts into allies of the Right and the American way of life. Now is not the time to settle for half measures. Embracing such strategies as "judicial restraint" may have made sense in a previous era when the conservative movement was confined to the margins of American political life, but we are now in a position to start governing, not just reacting to the Left. Times have changed, and the Right's tactics should, too.

There is no guarantee that conservatives and Republicans will continue to dominate the political scene as we have in recent years. We must not hesitate any longer to capture the courts—the last liberal stronghold.

MYTH VS. REALITY

IF CONSERVATIVES WANT TO thwart the liberal assault, the first thing we must do is to abandon the illusions we have clung to for so long. One of the great virtues of conservatism is that it teaches us to be realists, to look at the world as it truly is, not as we wish it to be. Unfortunately, conservatives do not take this approach to the courts. Here, it seems conservatives and liberals have switched roles. Conservatives have become utopians when we assess the courts. And liberals, who typically engage in wishful thinking, take a cold-eyed look at the courts and use the judiciary skillfully—ruthlessly—to achieve a precise political and social agenda.

This bizarre role reversal must stop. Conservatives must accept the reality of the modern law, even when the truth is uncomfortable. Not only must we accept this reality, we must adapt our strategies to it. Otherwise the conservative political agenda and the American way of life will keep getting destroyed—legal case by legal case—in the courts.

That means we must stop clinging to dangerous myths like these:

MYTH: Courts should exercise judicial restraint.
REALITY: Judicial restraint will never be a reality—and even if it could be reality, we don't want it now.

Sure, we'd all like to rein in judges and get them to act within the narrow confines of the role the Founders expected them to play. But how in the world could we ever make this happen? There are upwards of 19,000 judges in the federal and state court systems, according to the reference work *The American Bench: Judges of the Nation.* Many of these judges hold lifetime tenure. Appointing judges who honor judicial restraint (which is harder to do than it sounds, as you'll see) does nothing to stop the liberal activists *already* on the bench from pushing the left-wing agenda. Besides, as noted, even if we could miraculously convince every judge in America that he must never overstep his authority and must simply "follow the law," we'd have done nothing to get rid of all the existing liberal legal precedents—to which judges who believed in "judicial restraint" would be inclined to defer. Think of it is this way: Conservatives find themselves deep in a hole after seventy years of liberal judicial activism; merely putting down the shovel by achieving judicial restraint might ensure that we didn't dig ourselves deeper, but it wouldn't lift us *out* of the hole.

MYTH: Judges should be apolitical.
REALITY: Judges don't—and can't—check their ideology at the courtroom door; they often, by necessity, function as politicians wearing black robes.

Thanks to Bernard Goldberg, bloggers, the Media Research Center, the Fox News Channel, and the rest of the new media, most Americans have finally abandoned the myth of an unbiased media and accepted the notion that even earnest and honest reporters are not truly *objective.* Now we must reject the myth that judges are apolitical and unbiased. Just like all journalists—indeed, just like everyone else on the planet—judges come to the table with prejudices and biases that do not get checked at the courtroom door. We mustn't pretend otherwise. What economist and author Thomas Sowell said of people who disagree on political issues applies equally to judges who arrive at different judgments: "they are reasoning from fundamentally different premises" and "have different visions of how the world works."[2] Any judge's starting premises and worldview will naturally enter into his reflections on the complex legal and political questions he confronts every day. Is it mere coincidence that in hotly contested political cases, Supreme Court justices Stephen Breyer and Ruth Bader Ginsburg often line up on one side and Justices Scalia and Thomas line up on the other? And do you harbor any serious doubts about how Hillary Rodham Clinton or Jesse Jackson would rule as judges presiding over hot-button legal cases?

MYTH: Judges should just follow the law.
REALITY: Deciding what the law is ain't always easy.

Conservatives frequently criticize liberal judges for acting "lawlessly" or "imperially." Usually such accusations ignore a key fact about law at the highest levels and especially in the most politically charged constitutional cases: the law is often ambiguous and leaves

room for multiple reasonable interpretations. Sure, intelligent, serious people can debate various rulings and the reasoning behind
them, but there's often no way to prove definitively that only one interpretation is legitimate. It's not as if we can just feed all the details
of a case into a computer and have it spit out the correct answer. If
the law was clear-cut, we wouldn't see so many cases endure appeal
after appeal, sometimes all the way to the U.S. Supreme Court. And
we'd see a lot more unanimous court rulings than we do. Even the
Right's favorite Supreme Court justices, Scalia and Thomas, disagree
with each other on occasion.[3] And even the Constitution, a brilliant,
clearly worded document, leaves ambiguities. Remember, Thomas
Jefferson and James Madison fought about the meaning of the Constitution back in the eighteenth century.[4] If Jefferson and Madison
couldn't always agree on the Constitution's meaning, should we
realistically expect different from today's sitting judges or political
leaders?

MYTH: Judges should defer to the elected branches.
REALITY: Judges make law all the time, and often we want
them to.

It's easy to get exercised about the fact that five unelected judges
sitting in Washington, D.C., can overturn laws passed democratically.
Appallingly, liberal judges have often ignored the wishes of the people
to follow the objectives of the leftist elite. For example, in 2003 the
Supreme Court overruled the Texas state legislature and struck down a
law banning homosexual sodomy. Conservatives were up in arms over
the ruling. But two years later we were equally horrified when the court
approved an eminent-domain law in New London, Connecticut, that
enabled the city to seize private property and sell it to private developers simply to generate more tax revenue. In the first case, the Supreme
Court overruled "we the people," but in the second case the court
deferred to the democratic process. And both cases rightly angered
conservatives.

The problem, then, was not an activist court; what angered us
was the specific *outcomes* of the cases. Conservatives thus cannot
call for such simplistic solutions as asking judges to defer to "we the
people." Like liberals, we should support judges' ability to make law

that invalidates undesirable action by elected branches of government. We only disagree with liberals on *when* judges should exercise that power.[5]

> **MYTH:** Judicial activism tramples on the rule of law.
> **REALITY:** Judicial activism *is* the rule of law.

Conservatives regularly appeal to the "rule of law" in condemning judicial activism. It's another nice sentiment that ignores reality. We must remember that in many cases judges themselves are the ones who define what the rule of law is. Justice William Brennan, one of the heroes of the Left, liked to impart a simple lesson: "What is the first rule of the Supreme Court? You have to get to five."[6] Five justices, that is—a simple majority.

The Left gets it.

We don't.

But we must.

THE BATTLE PLAN

THESE FIVE MYTHS are only a sampling of the illusions preventing conservatives from adopting a winning strategy in the courts. We'll visit more later. The key point is this: If we don't open our eyes to the sometimes harsh reality of our situation, liberals will continue to use the courts to foist their policies, programs, and vision of society on all Americans.

And once we open our eyes, we'll see exactly how the courts can become our ally in the war against the loony Left. To see real change, we can't be content simply to pick up the weapon of conservative judicial activism, important as that is. We must rethink our entire approach to the courts, judges, and American law. We must abandon *everything* we thought we knew, since we've been operating under illusions and false assumptions for far too long. And we need all-new tactics, a whole new battle plan that is more intelligent, more aggressive, and more constructive.

Disrobed provides that battle plan. In addition to embracing conservative judicial activism, conservatives can and must:

- *Pick "Judicial Reagans."* Our first priority is to select solid and reliable *conservative* judges.

- *Embrace litmus tests.* We must recognize that the often-disparaged litmus test represents the *only* way to ensure that we get reliable right-wing judges, not more David Souters.

- *Understand "Judicial Darwinism."* We need to recognize that many judges "evolve" to the left once they arrive on the bench (as so many Republican appointees have), and then deploy strategies to encourage judges to "evolve" to the right.

- *Enjoy better living through litigation.* We must use well-timed and well-placed lawsuits to advance conservative social and political priorities.

By now conservatives recognize how deep the problems run in the courts. Still, sometimes we make the mistake of thinking that these problems are far removed from our everyday lives. The law, in fact, affects virtually everything we do, and the left-leaning legal system poses a devastating threat to the "unalienable rights" referenced in the Declaration of Independence—indeed, to the American way of life.

We must not miss this opportunity to fight back, at last, against liberals' attempt to remake America according to their vision—a vision at odds with that of the Founding Fathers and most Americans.

The good news is that this is a fight every conservative can support and even join. For all the focus on the Supreme Court, we must realize that the Left is waging war throughout the entire legal system. And all of us can affect how our courts respond to the left-wing social and political crusade, especially at the state court level; thirty-nine states hold some form of judicial elections, meaning that most of us have a direct say in what kinds of judges are deciding the issues that matter most to our communities.

I, for one, shudder to think what this country might look like if we allow liberals to continue to dominate the courts as they have for the past seventy years. Conservatives have been fighting a losing battle for years now. The battle plan I put forward here might sound radical, but it's really not. The battle plan merely acknowledges the reality of the current legal system and culture—the things we've been afraid to admit to ourselves. And the battle plan fully exploits that reality for the Right.

Be prepared to set aside your comforting assumptions about the courts. Trust me, the Left would be delighted to see conservatives stick with the same old misguided assumptions and failed strategies. But we should give them neither solace nor quarter. If we adopt this bold new battle plan, American conservatives can finally thwart the loony Left's political and social agenda in the courts while advancing the conservative cause and the American way of life.

BLUE COURTS, RED STATES, AND JUDGES GONE WILD

In the movie *Devil's Advocate,* Al Pacino plays the Devil himself, posing as the senior partner at a New York City law firm. When the firm's hotshot attorney, played by Keanu Reeves, finally realizes his boss is Satan, he demands to know, "Why lawyers? Why the law?"

"Because," the Devil declares, "the law, my boy, puts us into everything. It's the ultimate backstage pass. It's the new priesthood, baby."

If American lawyers are the "new priesthood," then guess who the bishops, cardinals, and popes are? Judges!

There's a huge problem with this: Judges have gone wild (and it's not the kind of thing you'd want on videotape).

Some people still consider the judiciary the "least dangerous" branch of government. But think about how much the law affects our everyday lives. It affects getting married, obtaining a divorce, bearing children, starting a business, accepting or quitting a job, hiring or firing employees, voting, buying a gun, receiving health care, downloading music, buying or selling a home, taking a shower, preparing a will, paying taxes, flushing toilets—you name it. This is why Harvard Law School professor Mary Ann Glendon describes modern America as "undoubtedly one of the most law-ridden societies that has ever existed on the face of the earth."[1] We tend to think of the law simply in terms of the fast-growing pile of federal, state, and local statutes and regulations. Yet judges play an enormous role in determining how those laws affect ordinary Americans by "interpreting" the meaning of laws in a never-ending stream of court cases. As Tunku Varadarajan of the *Wall Street Journal* has explained, "The courts—more so than the legislatures—now determine the way we live."[2] Their tentacles extend everywhere.

Long ago, courts became policy-making bodies, with judges eager to "answer any conceivable question which any conceivable litigant might choose to ask," in the words of Yale law professor Grant Gilmore.[3] Like the camel that put its nose in the tent, judges began by interfering only a little, but by now they insert themselves into virtually all aspects of American law—and, indeed, American life. As constitutional attorney Mark Levin pointed out in his best-selling book *Men in Black*, "Judges have taken over school systems, prisons, private-sector hiring and firing practices, and farm quotas; they have ordered local governments to raise property taxes and states to grant benefits to illegal immigrants; they have expelled God, prayer, and the Ten Commandments from the public square; they've endorsed severe limits on political speech; and they've protected virtual child pornography, racial discrimination in law school admissions, flag burning, the seizure of private property without just compensation, and partial-birth abortions. They've announced that morality alone is an insufficient basis for legislation. Courts now second-guess the commander in chief in time of war and confer due process rights on foreign enemy combatants. They intervene in the electoral process."[4]

Levin's recounting indicates the most disturbing element of all: These judges who insert themselves into all aspects of American life actively push a left-wing agenda. It's not just Levin who has noticed. Countless commentators and politicians sound clarion calls about the dangers of liberal judicial activism. Judge Robert Bork decries the "political seduction of the law." Tom DeLay rails against the "runaway judiciary."[5] The *Wall Street Journal*'s editorial pages present piece after piece identifying the dangers of "activist courts." Pat Buchanan declares that a "judicial dictatorship" has foisted a "social revolution" on the American public.[6] Sean Hannity of Fox News speaks out against jurists who "rule by judicial fiat."[7]

We absolutely should be outraged by the growing influence the courts wield over our lives. Since the middle of the twentieth century liberal judicial activists have lorded over American law the way *Tyrannosaurus rex* ruled the prehistoric era. Back in the 1830s Alexis de Tocqueville wrote, "If I were asked where I place the American aristocracy, I should reply without hesitation that . . . it occupies the judicial bench and the bar."[8] Tocqueville's observation was most prescient. If he could have been frozen (like Ted Williams's head) and thawed out now (like Austin Powers), he'd see the incredible power that the aristocracy of liberal judges and the elite legal culture has stolen for itself.

ABANDONING TRADITIONAL AMERICAN RIGHTS AND VALUES

ONE OF THE MOST famous speeches in modern political history is Senator Ted Kennedy's scathing denunciation of Judge Robert Bork after President Ronald Reagan nominated Bork to the Supreme Court in 1987. "Robert Bork's America," Kennedy intoned melodramatically, "is a land in which women would be forced into back-alley abortions, blacks would sit at segregated lunch counters, rogue police could break down citizens' doors in midnight raids, schoolchildren could not be taught about evolution."

Kennedy's characterization of Bork's America was disingenuous and completely misleading (though in those days before we had the new media to counter the liberal spin, few knew it). But we could rephrase Senator Kennedy's speech to accurately characterize what left-wing judges want to do to this country: "The America in which liberal judges rule is a land in which the unborn are legally and routinely killed, the phrase 'under God' has been removed from the Pledge of Allegiance, Islamo-fascists who attack Americans receive taxpayer-subsidized attorneys, local councilmen may steal your home and give it to land developers to build a shopping center, law-abiding citizens cannot own a gun to defend their families against criminal predators, criminals are coddled, Heather can have two mommies, lawyers serve as the toll takers on the highway of life thanks to the proliferation of laws and regulations, big-government and socialistic schemes trump tried-and-true free market capitalism, and the Fourteenth Amendment's equal protection clause guarantees a minimum wage to the poor."

The American judiciary issues a never-ceasing line of rulings that are totally out of sync with ordinary Americans and the values they hold dear. Supreme Court justice Antonin Scalia has said, "It is literally true, and I don't think this is an exaggeration, that the Court has essentially liberated itself . . . from the traditions of the American people." While Americans support free markets, free trade, property rights, and the realistic right to self-defense and to individual autonomy, the courts rule against these values time and time again. Judges far too often support the Left's radical social, political, and economic agenda. Scalia cited two prominent examples: In recent decades the Supreme Court invented the right to abortion and the right to homosexual sodomy, even though each supposed right was "so little rooted in the traditions of the American people that it was criminal for 200 years."[9]

THE SLIPPERY SLOPE OF GAY MARRIAGE

THE MESSAGES COURTS send can have a huge impact on public policy debates. Gay marriage is a disturbing example. Throughout the 1990s, a lawsuit wound its way through the court system of the State of Hawaii. The case challenged Hawaii's law limiting marriage to a man and a woman. Numerous legal opinions called into question the constitutionality of prohibiting gay marriage. Though a 1998 constitutional amendment enacted by state voters precluded the recognition of gay marriage, the Hawaii legal challenge sparked a nationwide debate over gay marriage. In 1997, a group of lesbians and gays sued the People's Republic of Vermont, claiming that marriage is a fundamental human right that should not be denied to gays or lesbians. The Vermont Supreme Court agreed, concluding that the Vermont law limiting marriage to a man and a woman violated the state constitution. The court then directed the state legislature (that's right, the court *told* the state legislature) to enact either statutes permitting gay marriage or laws creating a domestic partnership for gays that would grant them the same benefits under Vermont law as married couples. The Vermont legislature rolled over; it created civil unions for gays and lesbians.

Such decisions send powerful messages to other courts and even to society. In 2003, the U.S. Supreme Court struck down as unconstitutional a Texas state law outlawing same-sex sodomy. The decision in *Lawrence v. Texas* found that the Texas state legislature had acted irrationally in permitting heterosexual sodomy but not same-sex sodomy. Soon thereafter, in late 2003, the Massachusetts Supreme Court tossed aside the Commonwealth's definition of marriage as a legal union between a man and woman—a definition that had stood since well before the Boston Tea Party. Following the earlier *Lawrence* decision, the court called that definition "irrational." So in a single decision, four judges eliminated a three-hundred-year-old law irrespective of the views of the other 6.5 million Massachusetts residents about the divisive issue of gay marriage. Thanks to four people in robes, gay marriage is now legal in Massachusetts and may soon become legal in many other states.

Think about that progression: A multiyear lawsuit in Hawaii generates national publicity over gay marriage, then a court in the tiny state of Vermont directs the state legislature to enact civil unions, and a few years later the Massachusetts Supreme Court foists gay marriage on the nation. (And then a Republican president embraces civil unions as a preferable alternative to gay marriage.) So in just a few years, without proponents winning a single democratic vote by "we the people," gay marriage went from being a pipe dream to a reality—all because a handful of judges decided to make it so. Never mind that the American people continue to overwhelmingly oppose gay marriage; it's no accident that gay marriage referendums were voted down in all eleven states where they were on the ballot in 2004. Courts are forcing Americans to embrace gay marriage whether we like it or not.

The Left, by circumventing the democratic process to create the "right" to gay marriage, is simply following the playbook it used to enact another "right"—the right to abortion. As President Ronald Reagan explained in 1983, "Our nationwide policy of abortion-on-demand through all nine months of pregnancy was neither voted for by our people nor enacted by our legislators—not a single state had such unrestricted abortion before the Supreme Court decreed it to be national policy in 1973."[10] As usual, Reagan was right.

THE U.S. SUPREME COURT IS CONSERVATIVE? HA!

REPUBLICANS CONTROL THE White House and both chambers of Congress, not to mention the majority of governorships and state legislatures. Conservatism has been on the ascent since the election of Ronald Reagan in 1980. Even President Bill Clinton's achievements were *conservative* policy victories: budget surpluses, "the era of big government is over," welfare reform, and the North American Free Trade Agreement (NAFTA).

So, now that conservatism is on the rise and the nation has turned rightward on so many major issues, is the Left's judicial agenda still such a problem? You might think the crisis in the courts is passing. Think again.

Our legal system keeps shifting further and further to the left. Sure, the courts might not be smashing American traditions at quite the rate they did in the 1950s, '60s, and '70s. But by reaffirming astonishing liberal legal precedents time and again, and periodically adding new ones, the courts ensure that American law continues to tack leftward.

Even those judges who are lifelong Republicans and sympathetic to the conservative cause continue to be captured by decades of wrong-headed liberal legal decisions and practices. For example, in *Planned Parenthood v. Casey,* Republican-appointed justices Sandra Day O'Connor, Anthony Kennedy, and David Souter provided the swing votes in favor of upholding *Roe v. Wade,* which prohibits state and federal legislators from passing laws to protect the unborn. These Republican judges did so not because they necessarily agreed with the original *Roe* decision but because they felt bound to follow *Roe* as a legal precedent. In their opinion they wrote, "Liberty finds no refuge in a jurisprudence of doubt. Yet 19 years after our holding that the Constitution protects a woman's right to terminate her pregnancy in its early stages . . . that definition of liberty is still questioned." Thus their earnest and admirable allegiance to the rule of law results in the reaffirmation of those liberal precedents already on the books—precedents that betray not only the original vision of the Constitution but also traditional American values.

Scores of decisions like *Casey* should disabuse anyone of the notion that the Supreme Court tilts right. Still, the Left loves to perpetuate the myth that the Court follows a right-wing agenda, usually relying on the fact that seven of the nine justices were Republican appointees (which should send Republicans running for the Prozac). For instance, the *New York Times* editorial page, that reliable barometer of liberal opinion, complained that the 2000 election was "decided by a conservative Supreme Court," and then a few years later gloated that "even today's conservative Supreme Court could see that" laws banning homosexual sodomy belong "in history's dustbin."[11]

In reality, to call the Supreme Court "conservative" is a rhetorical ploy by the Left and the mainstream media. Under William Rehnquist, who served as chief justice from 1986 until his death in 2005, the supposedly conservative Supreme Court repeatedly supported the liberal agenda. Let's mention just the lowlights.

In *Dickerson v. United States* (2000), the Supreme Court forcefully rejected the opportunity to overrule the *Miranda v. Arizona* decision, in which the Supreme Court invented from whole cloth the requirement that police must inform criminal suspects of their constitutional rights before questioning them.

In 2003, the Court upheld affirmative action policies in higher education—which is to say, it approved of universities' engaging in racial discrimination—in the name of advancing educational diversity. But, as Justice Clarence Thomas observed in his dissent, the very same Supreme Court had, back in 1996, given zero deference to the Virginia Military Institute's educational mission or judgment to maintain its student body as all-male.[12] Go figure.

A few days after the "conservative" court blessed race discrimination in higher education, it struck down the Texas law forbidding homosexual sodomy.

In 1996, the "conservative" Supreme Court said a state couldn't prevent local governments from enacting laws outlawing discrimination against homosexuals. In the process it struck down a statewide law that had been approved directly by Colorado voters—showing just how much respect these "conservative" justices have for the democratic process and the will of the people. The Supreme Court, in *Romer v. Evans,* said the Colorado amendment was unconstitutional because it had been adopted out of a "desire to harm a politically unpopular group" and was "born of animosity toward the class that it affects." Gee, I wish every time a state enacted yet another tax law or business regulation, the Supreme Court would strike it down, saying it reflected a "desire to harm a politically unpopular group" known as productive Americans (also called "rich people").*

The "conservative" Rehnquist Court did not always ignore the will of the people. Sometimes it deferred to them even when doing so contravened the text of the U.S. Constitution. For instance, in the 2005 case *Kelo v. New London,* the court ignored a key part of the Fifth Amendment's takings clause in order to permit local governments to

---

* Come to think of it, the Democratic Party platform is almost entirely "born of animosity toward the class of persons affected." It is dedicated to punishing Americans for building wealth (think estate tax), private-sector workers and business owners for being hardworking and productive (think progressive income taxes), companies for producing pretty much anything (think environmental regulations based on alchemy), and children for being unborn (abortion). By the Supreme Court's rationale in *Romer,* perhaps the entire Democratic Party is unconstitutional. Hey, maybe the *Romer* decision wasn't so bad after all!

trample on our property rights. The clause says clearly that private property shall not be taken for *public use* without just compensation. But in *Kelo*, the city of New London exercised the power of eminent domain to seize private property and sell it to *private developers*. So basically, thanks to our oh-so-conservative Supreme Court, local councilmen may vote to award your home to some other dude on the grounds that anything he built on its site *might* generate more local property tax revenues than your modest dwelling.

Kelo was, in fact, just one of three cases in 2005 in which the Supreme Court expanded the government's powers at the expense of individual property rights. And believe it or not, *Kelo* is not the most egregious example of how the Supreme Court runs roughshod over property rights. Thanks to the Court, the government can regulate your property so much that its value could be substantially reduced and still you would not receive any compensation; in some instances the government can take your property completely.[13] Likewise, rent control schemes preventing landlords from charging "too much" for their property are viewed as constitutional.[14] John D. Echeverria of the Georgetown University Law Center's Environmental Law and Policy Institute noted the obvious in 2005 when he said, "In terms of the outcome, over the last several years, the takings argument has failed in the Supreme Court in each instance. . . . That looks like at the least the beginning of a trend that is highly favorable for the government side."[15]

The Rehnquist Court also thumbed its nose at the Bush administration—obviously a conservative thing to do—by declaring several war-on-terror initiatives unconstitutional. Specifically, the Supreme Court hewed to the desires of the antiwar Left by granting the captured Taliban fighters in Guantánamo Bay access to American courts (the very same courts the Taliban fighters wished to destroy). The Court also told the president that of course the judiciary gets to second-guess his decision about who is an enemy combatant seeking to destroy the United States. (I guess we screwed up by not giving those Nazis captured on Omaha Beach the opportunity to make their case by serving subpoenas and lawsuits.)

Under Rehnquist, the Supreme Court supposedly started a "federalism revolution" to return power from the federal government to the states. In reality the Court has placed only the narrowest limits on federal power. Even when the Court concluded that Congress had acted beyond its enumerated powers—such as when it struck down parts of the Gun-Free Schools Act and of the Violence Against Women Act—the decisions were largely symbolic and had little effect on Americans. More recently the Court has actually expanded the federal government's power. Notably, in 2005 it authorized Congress to override state laws permitting the medical use of marijuana. Liberal justice Ruth Bader Ginsburg crowed, "Federalism this term was the dog that did not bark."[16]

Far from advancing conservatism, the Supreme Court in recent years has *at best* put its finger in the dike, keeping a potential flood of liberal legal precedents from gushing out. But if all you're doing is maintaining the status quo in American law, you're preserving a *left-wing* status quo, established by some seven decades of liberal judicial activism. And as we've seen, the court has not merely been defending the status quo; it has kept pushing the law to the left.

This not only has to stop—the trend must be *reversed*. Starting right now.

HOW DID WE GET HERE?

JUST HOW DID American law become so gosh darn liberal? After all, we didn't just wake up one morning surrounded by Blue State courts. How did the courts go from protecting economic liberties (agreeing that the "business of America is business") to blessing every imaginable and wacky government program coming down the pike? How could they ignore certain rights clearly protected in the Constitution and yet invent certain "rights" nowhere even hinted at in the Constitution? How did we go from the nation's founding document, the Declaration of Independence, referring specifically to the "Creator," to a world where religion is being expunged from the public square?[17]

Sadly, today American law does far too little to uphold the very rights this country was founded upon. The most famous passage from the Declaration of Independence tells us: "We hold these truths to be self-evident, that all men are created equal, that they are endowed by their Creator with certain unalienable Rights, that among these are Life, Liberty and the pursuit of Happiness." The Founders weren't just paying lip service to these rights. In fact, they declared their independence from and fought a war against the world's most powerful nation because England had violated those unalienable rights. Then they debated, drafted, and ratified the U.S. Constitution and Bill of Rights to create a framework to protect those rights.

One of the most fundamental individual rights was the right to "property," which the Founders considered to be a natural liberty even preexisting government. This right extended far beyond owning land and goods. "Property" included the right to one's body, to self-defense, to exercise one's religion, and to engage in the panoply of human actions. James Madison, the primary author of the Constitution, made this point in his 1792 essay "Property," explaining that "a man has a property in his opinions and the free communication of them. He has a property of peculiar value in his religious opinions, and in the profession and practice dictated by them. He has a property very dear to him in the safety and liberty of his person. He has an equal property in the free use of his faculties and free choice of the objects on which to employ them. In a word, as a man is said to have a right to his property, he may be equally said to have a property in his rights."

Believing, along with political philosopher John Locke, that all men were entitled to their body and to the fruits of their labor, the Framers wanted the Constitution to guarantee the right to property. In fact, one of the main reasons—if not *the* main reason—they scrapped the Articles of Confederation (essentially, the nation's first constitution) was that the Articles provided inadequate protections to the "unalienable right" of property. Individual states frequently abused private property rights of people in other states by practicing economic protectionism. So, as constitutional lawyer Mark Pollot points out, the Framers of the Constitution installed more than twenty provisions that "directly or indirectly concern themselves with the protection of property and economic rights."[18] The Framers viewed the right to contract as so critical to American liberty that it is one of the few individual rights actually mentioned in the U.S. Constitution itself, as opposed to in the Bill of Rights, which was ratified two years later to alleviate concerns that the Constitution's checks and balances might not do enough to prevent the new government from violating fundamental individual rights.

In addition to those checks and balances, the Framers made sure that the federal government was granted only "enumerated powers"— that is, the powers specifically set forth in the Constitution. The Tenth

Amendment drove the point home, stating, "The powers not delegated to the United States by the Constitution, nor prohibited by it to the States, are reserved to the States respectively, or to the people."

The Framers created a judiciary as part of the Constitution's checks and balances—specifically, to help check the elected branches and make sure America didn't simply trade in the tyranny of the British king for the tyranny of the "mob," or a democratic majority. But the Constitution itself said little about the judiciary. It required only a single court—a "Supreme Court"—and authorized Congress to create "inferior" courts as needed. The Constitution granted the courts no real powers, not even the now commonly accepted notion of "judicial review," which gives courts the power to void the actions of the elected branches of governments.

No, the Supreme Court gave *itself* this extraordinary power. In 1803, Chief Justice John Marshall, writing for the Supreme Court in *Marbury v. Madison,* found that the Court had the power to declare unconstitutional, invalid, and unenforceable any laws inconsistent with the Constitution itself. Marshall stated, "It is emphatically the province and duty of the judicial department to say what the law is." Hence the power of judicial review.* Even back then, critics complained about an "imperial judiciary." So great was the outcry about the decision in *McCulloch v. Maryland* (1819) that Chief Justice Marshall wrote an anonymous letter to the *Philadelphia Union* to defend the Court's decision.[19] Could you imagine Chief Justice John Roberts writing an anonymous letter to the editor of the *Wall Street Journal* defending a particularly controversial ruling?

Despite the early power grab, the judiciary by and large was nowhere near as imperial as the one we know today. This is not to say the courts didn't overreach at times or make mistakes—look at the infamous *Dred Scott* decision upholding slavery. But on the whole, they

---

* Even before *Marbury,* the Supreme Court hinted that it might possess the power to strike down laws passed by the legislature. In the case of *Calder v. Bull* (1798), the Court did not invalidate the law in question (an act passed by the Connecticut legislature), but one justice wrote, "I cannot subscribe to the omnipotence of a State Legislature, or that it is absolute and without control," while another said, "If, then, a government, composed of Legislative, Executive and Judicial departments, were established, by a Constitution, which imposed no limits on the legislative power, the consequence would inevitably be, that whatever the legislative power chose to enact, would be lawfully enacted, and the judicial power could never interpose to pronounce it void."

respected rights and the American way of life that liberal judges have since tossed aside.

In 1921, Supreme Court justice George Sutherland declared, "It is not the right of property which is protected, but the right to property. Property, per se, has no rights; but the individual—the man—has three great rights, equally sacred from arbitrary interference; the right to his life, the right to his liberty, and the right to his property. The three rights are so bound together as to be essentially one right. To give a man his life, but deny him his liberty, is to take from him all that makes life worth living. To give him liberty but take from him the property which is the fruit and badge of his liberty, is to still leave him a slave."[20] This was hardly a radical position. The courts up to then had frequently struck down laws and regulations that interfered with economic rights, property rights, and contract rights. They functioned as a real, albeit not perfect, check on undue government interference in the economy.

For example, in 1895 the Supreme Court struck down the federal income tax as unconstitutional, explaining, "Whenever a distinction is made in the burdens a law imposes or in the benefits it confers on any citizens by reason of their birth, or wealth, or religion, it is class legislation, and leads inevitably to oppression and abuses."[21]

In 1897 the Court voided a Louisiana law that prohibited anyone from purchasing insurance on Louisiana property from companies not licensed in the state, ruling that the law violated the Fourteenth Amendment's due process clause, whose right of "liberty," the Court said, included the freedom of contract. (Later, liberal judges would take a shine to the Fourteenth Amendment by interpreting it to justify such rights as those to abortion and to homosexual sodomy.)

In the 1905 case of *Lochner v. New York*, the Supreme Court voided a state law that prohibited bakers from working as many hours as they wished. Amazingly, Lochner, a bakery owner, had been convicted of a *criminal offense* for allowing his employees to work more than sixty hours per week or ten hours per day (apparently he didn't get the memo explaining that working around cupcakes and pastries so much constituted an ultrahazardous condition). The Court said the law violated the bakers' "liberty of contract."

In 1908, in *Adair v. United States*, the Supreme Court again explicitly defended the freedom of contract, decrying "arbitrary interference with the liberty of contract which no government can legally justify in a free land."

In the 1915 case *Coppage v. Kansas,* the Court declared the right to contract to be "essential" and said, "If this right be struck down or arbitrarily interfered with, there is a substantial impairment of liberty in the long-established constitutional sense."

If there was any doubt that the right to contract was a fundamental right enshrined in the Constitution, in 1923 the Supreme Court removed that doubt. Voiding a federal minimum-wage law for women in the case of *Adkins v. Children's Hospital,* the court declared, "That the right to contract about one's affairs is a part of the liberty of the individual protected by [the Fifth Amendment's due process clause] is *settled by the decisions of this Court and is no longer open to question"* (emphasis added).

Don't you wish today's Supreme Court sounded like that? What happened to the idea that the government should leave people alone and not interfere with their fundamental property and economic rights? Well, unfortunately for the American people, not long after, the wheels of American constitutionalism started to fly off and truly fundamental American rights were subverted while "rights" fancied by Europhiles, self-proclaimed sophisticates, and big-government New Dealers moved to the fore. Though the Supreme Court had declared a robust judicial protection of individual economic rights to be "settled" and "no longer open to question," the liberal judicial revolution revealed that the Court's only precedent regarding precedent is to not follow precedent—especially if ignoring precedent produces the desired policy result.

The real change came with the Great Depression. The stock market crash of 1929 started a series of massive and undesirable government interventions into the economy. The federal government shrank the nation's money supply, allowed banks to fail, raised taxes, shut off free trade, and generally punished all productive Americans—including, or perhaps especially, the employers who could have provided jobs. (Liberals have never understood the truism that you can't have employees without first having employers.) These unnecessary interventions turned a typical recession into the Great Depression, as a wealth of evidence now proves. (The evidence is ably summarized in historian Jim Powell's book *FDR's Folly.*) President Herbert Hoover, a Republican, started this government activism, but Franklin D. Roosevelt, a Democrat, accelerated it after he took over the White House in 1933, launching a barrage of new federal programs, trade protectionism, and tax hikes.

Roosevelt and his New Dealers were "progressive" thinkers heavily influenced by socialism and various other utopian schemes predicated on the notion that "government knows best." With the economic emergency of the Great Depression, they saw their chance to turn over control of the economy, and the nation, to a bunch of government regulators. These nanny state do-gooders, however, had to circumvent the fact that the Constitution protected individual rights and provided the federal government only with certain enumerated powers. They also had to address the problem of the courts: In the early years of the New Deal, the Supreme Court followed then well-established precedents to declare many federal statutes unconstitutional on the grounds that Congress had no authority to enact them.[22]

The New Dealers debated whether to amend the Constitution formally, using procedures outlined in Article V, but decided against it. Amending the Constitution was difficult politically (by the mid-1930s only eleven amendments had been ratified beyond the original ten, the Bill of Rights).[23] The New Dealers chose the easier, politically expedient option: using the courts to get what they wanted. President Roosevelt turned to the courts after his landslide reelection in 1936, proposing to pack the Supreme Court with six New Deal–friendly justices. Roosevelt claimed that the additional justices would help the Supreme Court's older justices handle their workload, when in fact his scheme was obviously political: to ensure he had a Court majority that would rubber-stamp New Deal measures. Even the heavily Democratic Congress rejected the proposal.

FDR lost that battle, but he won the war. He was rescued by what became known as the "switch in time that saved nine." The "switch" was made by Justice Owen Roberts, who had voted against New Deal measures throughout Roosevelt's first term. Suddenly, in the 1937 case of *West Coast Hotel Co. v. Parrish,* he changed his vote to favor big government, giving the New Dealers the fifth and deciding vote they had coveted. Roosevelt used the remainder of his presidency to appoint nine justices (all New Dealers supportive of big government) to the Supreme Court, putting an indelible (and costly) stamp on American law for decades to come.

After these dramatic changes, there was no going back to the limited government Americans had known for a century and a half. As FDR desired, the Supreme Court eviscerated the idea of enumerated powers, essentially announcing that Congress could enact virtually any law it desired. The Court also destroyed the idea that the Constitution protected individual property and economic rights, concluding that courts should defer to the elected branches on such issues.[24] In time, the Supreme Court began to afford property rights and other traditional American rights less constitutional protection; in effect it became easy for the government to defend virtually all economic regulations as constitutional. In contrast, the Supreme Court began actively protecting "personal rights" such as speech from government regulations.[25]

In other words, the Supreme Court drew a bright, and unjustified, line between so-called personal rights and individual property rights: Property and economic rights were relegated to second-class status, while certain manufactured "personal rights" favored by the Left became "fundamental." Never mind that this artificial distinction ran counter to what the Founders had intended and to the Supreme Court's own unequivocal declaration, made only a few years earlier, that the right to contract was "no longer open to question." Once the Court set up this framework, the judiciary could then do what it has done for the past seventy years—permit just about any and all economic laws to stand while striking down any social laws with which a court disagrees.

THE LEFT-WING SOCIAL AGENDA

HAVING TOSSED ASIDE constitutional restraints, the courts became a dominant institution in American life. After the 1930s, courts propped up big government at almost every opportunity. As federal appeals judge Janice Rogers Brown has explained, "The economic convulsions of the late 1920s and early 1930s passed away," but the "doctrinal underpinnings of *West Coast Hotel* and the 'switch in time' did not. Indeed, over the next half century it consumed much of the classical conception of the Constitution."[26] And the American people have paid the price, sacrificing fundamental American liberties and self-government.

Just look at how liberal justices decided when to use the power of the courts—and when not to. In *Williamson v. Lee Optical* (1955), for example, the Supreme Court upheld an Oklahoma law preventing opticians, as opposed to licensed optometrists or ophthalmologists, from fitting lenses to eyeglasses. In short, the Court rejected any suggestion that opticians or their patients had a right to enter into a voluntary economic transaction without the blessing of the state. In his opinion, Justice William O. Douglas concluded, "The day is gone when this Court uses the [Constitution] to strike down state laws, regulatory of business and industrial conditions, because they may be unwise, improvident, or out of harmony with a particular school of thought. . . . 'For protection against abuses by legislatures the people must resort to the polls, not to the Courts' " (emphasis added).

Yet it was the very same Justice Douglas who a decade later wrote the majority opinion in *Griswold v. Connecticut,* striking down laws that restricted the sale of contraceptives. Apparently, in the eyes of Justice Douglas, only economic conservatives needed to "resort to the polls" when government regulators curtailed their liberties; social liberals could absolutely resort to the courts "for protection against abuses by legislatures." Justice Douglas and the rest of his left-wing cronies on the high court obviously took to heart Emerson's line that "a foolish consistency is the hobgoblin of little minds."

Liberal justice William Brennan approved of this same double standard. As constitutional scholar Bernard Schwartz explained, Brennan practiced "judicial deference in the economic realm" but "believed that the Bill of Rights provisions protecting personal liberties imposed more active obligations on the judges. When a law infringed upon the personal rights the Bill of Rights guaranteed, Brennan refused to defer to the legislative judgment that the law was necessary."[27]

Why should Justice Brennan defer to government actions in the economic realm but not in the social or personal realm? What about the constitutional guarantees to the right to keep the fruits of your own labor? Did the Framers of the Constitution jettison the original Articles of Confederation to guarantee the "fundamental" and "unalienable" rights to abortion and buggery and the right to be free from hearing the words "under God" uttered in the Pledge of Allegiance?

The answer seems to be yes, at least according to the liberal jurists who dominated American law for the second half of the twentieth century. Not content to justify the "progressive" campaign to rapidly expand the federal government, the courts embraced the Left's social agenda as well. In this new crusade for "social justice" (a euphemism for socialism and other harebrained liberal schemes), judges received public cover in the form of hosannas from the nation's left-wing establishment—the *New York Times,* the *Washington Post,* the rest of the mainstream media, and elites in the legal profession and political realm. Together, the judiciary and the left-wing establishment revolutionized the country's social structures and traditions.

THE SLIDE LEFTWARD

WHY DID THE LEFT choose to advance its radical social agenda through the courts? Because liberals knew they couldn't enact their social reforms via the democratic process. Americans opposed the Left's agenda. Only a small elite corner of the population supported these policy preferences, so liberals used the courts to thrust their unpopular radical agenda on an unwilling American electorate. And the effort succeeded.

The Supreme Court's social activism began in earnest after President Dwight D. Eisenhower installed Earl Warren, former California governor, as chief justice of the United States. As more liberal justices joined the Court in the 1950s, the Warren Court engaged in, as Robert Bork puts it, the "wholesale subordination of law to an egalitarian politics that, by deforming both the Constitution and statutes, reordered our politics and our society."[28]

Revolutionizing criminal justice became a priority of the Warren Court. Liberal justices such as Warren and William Brennan supported the movement to view criminals as victims of racism, society, mental illness, economic injustice, the lack of a puppy as a child, whatever. This radical change in perception about the "root causes" of crime—from a view that individuals are responsible for their conduct to a view that society is responsible for criminal conduct—unhinged the criminal justice system. The Court made policing, prosecuting, and imprisoning criminals more costly and difficult. In the 1961 case of *Mapp v. Ohio,* for example, the Supreme Court invented the "exclusionary rule," which barred the use at criminal trials of evidence the police seized improperly—even if the evidence clearly established the defendant's guilt. Then, in 1966, the Warren Court invented the now-famous "Miranda rights" ("You have the right to remain silent," etc.) in *Miranda v. Arizona,* turning police into criminal defense attorneys by requiring them to "advise" arrested suspects of their various individual rights. Say, maybe we need *Miranda* warnings for property owners? "You have the occasional right to your property unless a puddle (also known as a wetland) sits on it or unless a large private developer is able to persuade your local township otherwise."

Finally, in 1972, the Supreme Court (now under the leadership of Chief Justice Warren Burger, a Republican) declared the death penalty as practiced in the United States unconstitutional. It didn't matter that the death penalty had existed in America from day one, that the U.S. Constitution expressly contemplates the death penalty (the Fifth Amendment provides that one "cannot be deprived of *life,* liberty, or property without due process of law"), or that the majority of Americans supported the death penalty.[29]

Likewise, the courts eventually ignored the Constitution and the popular will in taking up the liberal fight on abortion, gay rights, criminal rights, school prayer, pornography, the death penalty, and other social issues. In supporting the Left's attack on religion, for example, the Supreme Court paid little attention to the portion of the First Amendment that forbids the government from infringing on the "free exercise" of religion. (Like the secular Left, the Supreme Court has fixated on the amendment's prohibition against the "establishment of religion.") Nor did the Court seem to care that the Declaration of Independence mentions that unalienable rights come from a "Creator," that our coins read "In God We Trust," or that the Supreme Court itself opens every session with a marshal bellowing, "God save this honorable court." So in a 1963 case, the Warren Court ruled that starting a school day with a reading from the Bible violated the law even when kids could be excused upon parental request.[30] In other words, the Supreme Court waited more than 150 years after the ratification of the Bill of Rights to discover these apparently long-standing unconstitutional conditions.

Nowadays, with the Supreme Court upholding overt racial discrimination by the government, outlawing the laws of numerous states that permitted the execution of brutal murderers who failed IQ tests or were under eighteen years of age, striking down laws forbidding homosexual anal sex, allowing the gruesome procedure known as partial-birth abortion (which borders on infanticide), and banning some public displays of the Ten Commandments, there can be little doubt that the Left has achieved many of its biggest political victories in the courts.

SEIZE THE COURTS!

JUSTICE ANTONIN SCALIA put it well when he wrote, "What secret knowledge, one must wonder, is breathed into lawyers when they become Justices of this Court, that enables them to discern that a practice which the text of the Constitution does not clearly proscribe, and which our people have regarded as constitutional for 200 years, is in fact unconstitutional? . . . Day by day, case by case, [the Supreme Court] is busy designing a Constitution for a country I do not recognize."[31]

The conservative movement certainly shares this frustration, so eloquently articulated by Justice Scalia. Conservatives must fight back against this liberal judicial assault. The time to change American law is now, after substantial conservative electoral victories, especially in presidential and Senate races.

Despite the many judicial appointments Republican presidents have made in the past half century—going all the way back to Dwight D. Eisenhower's presidency and continuing through Nixon, Ford, Reagan, the elder Bush, and now George W. Bush—conservatives continue to be on the outside of, and on the defensive in, America's legal system.

It's not as though voter outrage over liberal judicial activism is new. Back in 1968, Americans elected Richard Nixon as president in no small part because he ran an aggressive campaign focusing on the liberal Warren Court. More recently, in 2000, Hispanic Americans in Florida outraged by a federal court's ruling in favor of Bill Clinton's effort to return the six-year-old Elián González to Cuba may have tipped the election to George W. Bush; Bush won Florida, the decisive state, by only 537 votes. In 2004, Bush benefited from an outpouring of pro-Republican support in key swing states after the Supreme Court, in *Lawrence v. Texas,* struck down Texas's statute prohibiting same-sex sodomy. The decision angered Americans even more when the Massachusetts court relied on *Lawrence* to discover the "right" to "gay marriage" (but not the "right" to other oxymorons such as "jumbo shrimp," "recorded live," or "French deodorant"). For example, in Ohio— the decisive state in 2004—the voters overwhelmingly approved a ballot referendum to recognize marriage as a union between one man and one woman (not between one man and three women, or two women, or three perfectly coiffed metrosexuals).

Why have conservatives failed to fix the courts so far even when the American electorate sends such strong signals about the need for reform? Though we may understand that we have a severe problem with the courts, we still fail to grasp the true *nature* of the problem. So we've stuck to the same losing strategy. We've allowed liberals to hijack the judiciary to achieve their agenda. Now conservatives *must* recognize and adapt to the realities of the modern American legal system; if we misdiagnose the real problems we face, we'll never fix the courts. We need to be honest with ourselves about our relationship to the legal system, how the system actually functions, how the Left has so successfully gamed the courts for political gain, and how the Right has a terrible record in thwarting the Left's judge-created political advances.

Conservatives can finally undo seven decades of liberal legal decisions antithetical to the ideals of the American founding and the American way of life. We must seize this tremendous opportunity to recapture the courts and fundamentally alter the direction of American law—lest the American ideal be lost for another seventy years.

How do we do it? Forget old-school tactics. We need some new-school ones. And we can get them by stealing some pages from the Left's playbook.

PART II

THE SECRET WEAPON

THREE

SHOGUN

What the Right Can Learn from Japan's Warriors

We conservatives face a choice in the courts: modernize our approach and stand a chance to change the nation for the better, or continue on our current idealistic path while getting steamrolled by the loony Left.

The fight for American law will not be won using archaic, ineffectual weapons. Conservatives must embrace modern tactics and weapons to succeed on the modern legal battlefield. And where exactly can we find such tried-and-true tactics and weapons? Why, from the Left—yes, you read that correctly, the Left. To show what I mean, let's go to the history books before considering how the Right can capture the Left's legal weapons, ammunition, and, indeed, armada.

As a nod to those jurists who love multiculturalism and relying on foreign precedent, we turn to the rising sun of Japan for a history lesson. In the sixteenth century, Japan's ruling elite, the Tokugawa shoguns, grew worried about the Western influences brought to Japan by traders and missionaries. To preserve their existing social and political hierarchy, the shoguns sealed the nation to foreigners and entered a few-hundred-year period of almost complete isolation. The Japanese went so far as to ban a developing weapon of war—guns. Why? Because the sword-wielding shogun warriors knew that with guns, lower-class enemies could threaten their dominance. Then, in the mid-nineteenth century, four American warships under the command of Commodore Matthew Perry appeared in Tokyo Bay. Perry's demonstration of America's modern military prowess presented Japan with a stark choice—trade with and adapt to the Americans and their modern technology or refuse to adapt and get colonized by the Americans' cannons and modern weaponry.

The Japanese (being no dummies) chose the former, realizing that they could no longer protect through isolation the traditions and ideals of the shogun warriors. They not only opened up trade with the Americans but also began building a modern army and arsenal based on Western technology and weaponry—an arsenal that less than a hundred years later sank much of the American navy at Pearl Harbor.

Conservatives today find ourselves in a position similar to the one the Japanese were in when Commodore Perry's ships cruised into Tokyo Bay. Like the Japanese then, we face a stark choice—embrace modern weapons, strategies, and tactics or get bombarded by a powerful enemy (in this case, *continue* to get bombarded) deploying cutting-edge weaponry and tactics. The shoguns realized that they could no longer hide, that the enemy's weapons were superior and would inevitably defeat them. Today, instead of battleships sailing into Tokyo Bay, judicial activism has sailed into American law. Conservatives must recognize the reality and inevitability of judicial activism. We can't continue to seek refuge in utopian fantasies of judicial restraint, strict constructionism, originalism, and such.

The Right should embrace modernity and win rather than embrace an idyllic past and keep losing.

THE LEFT RESHAPED SOCIETY WITH
LIBERAL JUDICIAL ACTIVISM

THE LEFT USED judicial activism to reshape American constitutional law, thereby altering the American political and social landscape in a manner completely foreign to fundamental American values. Liberals have used the courts as their legal armada, while conservatives refuse to engage in judicial activism to advance their agenda. The Left takes full advantage of lawsuits, even largely frivolous ones, to set the tone of political debate on key topics in American law and politics. For example, liberals have sued to challenge abortion laws and won, sued to challenge antisodomy laws and won, sued to stop school prayer and crèches and won, sued for the "right" to gay marriage and won, and on and on. In case after case, on political issue after political issue, liberal elites have tilted the law, and society with it, in their favor and away from the constitutional text, the Framers' intent, the expressions of the will of the American people, and even the American way of life.

Let's face it: Conservatives haven't simply been getting beaten in the courts—we've been getting crushed. Can you think of one major court win for conservatives in recent years? I'm not talking about a win in the sense of a court decision thwarting some liberal advancement—I'm talking about a court ruling that removed from the American political debate an issue and awarded it to the Right's position. You probably can't think of one, because there hasn't been any of real importance. The Right's biggest legal victory in recent memory probably came in the Supreme Court case of *Bush v. Gore,* but that doesn't count. Why? Because that did nothing more than prevent Al Gore from using the Florida state courts to steal the electoral votes from a state in which George W. Bush never trailed. In other words, the decision only stopped a lower court from practicing liberal judicial activism. It did not advance the conservative agenda; it simply stopped the liberal agenda in this one specific instance. That's not a victory; it's merely avoiding a loss.

Want other examples? How about the Supreme Court's decision thwarting a New Jersey state law requiring the Boy Scouts to send young boys into the woods on overnight camping trips with gay scoutmasters, or the one preventing Massachusetts laws from requiring St. Patrick's Day parades to permit gays to march? Hardly "big" wins, since they accomplished nothing more than thwarting further advances of the radical gay agenda.

Where is the conservative equivalent of *Roe v. Wade*—that is, a Supreme Court decision favoring the Right that removes a particular policy debate from the democratic process? There are countless examples of liberal decisions taking hot-button issues off the table and resolving them in favor of the Left. *Roe v. Wade* ruled on abortion in favor of the liberal position and made it "settled law." *Lawrence v. Texas* eliminated laws criminalizing same-sex sodomy, and the Left used it to foist gay marriage upon Massachusetts residents. Decisions have even undone restrictions on pornography, including virtual child pornography. Other court decisions have banned school prayer, the recitation of the Pledge of Allegiance in classrooms, prayers at high school football games (even when the prayers are voluntary), and certain displays of the Ten Commandments on public grounds (though not in the Supreme Court). But there is no decision that has removed a political issue from the democratic process and resolved it in favor of the conservative position.

For example, where is the major Supreme Court ruling relieving law-abiding residents of New York City from onerous gun laws requiring a many-month wait and hundreds, if not thousands, of dollars in fees to buy a gun for the home? Where is the major Supreme Court ruling striking down a major government boondoggle on the grounds that it was an unauthorized usurpation of power under Article I of the Constitution? Where are those court decisions declaring rent control laws unconstitutional? And where are those decisions requiring failing public school systems to adopt school choice programs?

WE'VE CEDED THE BATTLEFIELD

FOR DECADES NOW, the Left has achieved great political triumphs through the courts even though Republicans have had chances to put our stamp on the courts. Republicans have held the White House for all but twenty years in the past half century and thus have appointed the vast bulk of America's federal judges. Still, the Left continues to dominate the Right in the courts. Just think of the Democrats as the New York Yankees—they of the amazing twenty-six World Series titles—and the Republicans as the Chicago Cubs, who haven't won a championship ring since 1908.

So why *does* the Right keep losing in the courts? Because conservatives have ceded the battlefield to the Left by refusing to take the offensive in the courts. Rather than trying to win political battles over hot-button issues in the courts, the Right seeks only to prevent the Left from winning. With a defensive mind-set, conservatives continue to advocate judicial restraint, an approach that has failed us miserably for decades. Why do we think it will work now? It won't. Conservatives saying that judicial restraint will fix the courts is no different from Charlie Brown swearing that *this time* Lucy will not pull the football away or J. Lo thinking that *this* husband is "the one."

Like it or not, judicial activism is here to stay. Advocating judicial restraint now, given the current state of American law, is akin to trying to fight a modern war with seventeenth-century weapons—as effective as the Polish cavalry, on horseback, charging armored Nazi Panzer tanks.[1] Or to playing professional football while refusing to use the forward pass because, well, that wasn't part of the original game and it's just not how the game should be played. Allowing the Left to pillage our cities with the weapons of judicial activism while we stand there offering the flowers of judicial restraint is a path to dismal failure. A new tactic is required.

STOP BEING UTOPIANS!

As CONSERVATIVES, WE pride ourselves on being hard-core political realists—on being rational, knowing history, understanding economics and human nature, and looking at the world as it really is, not as we might wish it to be. The Right, after all, takes a reality-based approach to life, society, and politics.

Think about conservative perspectives on welfare, guns, and the war on terror versus liberal views. Liberals believe that massive government handouts can eliminate poverty, but conservatives understand that, in the real world, welfare encourages people to sit home and eat Doritos. Liberals wishfully think that a world without guns leads to a world without violent crime, but the Right knows that Cain killed Abel without guns, and that guns deter criminals from preying on the law-abiding and innocent. Liberals think the United Nations can end wars by getting diplomats in native garb to "hug it out" in Turtle Bay, but conservatives recognize that the UN sat idly by during the genocides in Cambodia, Rwanda, and the former Yugoslavia and failed to prevent wars in Africa, the Balkans, Korea, Vietnam, Afghanistan, and the Middle East. During the Cold War, liberals raced around with T-shirts asking us to "visualize world peace" while conservatives, led by Ronald Reagan, built bigger weapons systems, tried to deploy the Strategic Defense Initiative, called the Soviet Union evil, and then destroyed it all without firing a shot.

Simply put, conservatives view the Left as a bunch of wild-eyed utopians beholden to harebrained schemes and fantasies that can work only in the imagination of some nebbishy sociology professor with too much time on his hands. We rely on cold, hard facts.

But in the debate over the courts, it's the conservatives who become the wild-eyed utopians and the liberals who operate as realists. The Left long ago recognized that courts are political institutions that can be used to further a political agenda. The Right, in contrast, refuses to accept the inevitable. Failing to recognize that the courts long ago became politicized, we embrace flawed notions such as judicial restraint, originalism, strict constructionism, and textualism. Conservatives demand a return to a prelapsarian world in which courts play only a limited role in American government and politics. But that is pure fantasy. We can never and will never get back to that world. Sure, it would be lovely if courts didn't practice judicial activism, but we must accept the courts as they really are—political institutions with extraordinary power to invent rights not mentioned in the Constitution, to overturn democratically enacted laws, to make law and to change society.

Not only must we accept this reality, we must adjust our strategies to it. Otherwise we'll keep getting destroyed in the courts.

THE LEFT GETS IT; THE RIGHT DOESN'T

WHAT MAKES LIBERALS realists when it comes to American law? The Left is results-oriented, while the Right is process-oriented.

Look at how liberals evaluate judges. The judges they praise the most are the ones who have handed them policy victories. You almost never hear the Left praising a judge's legal reasoning or interpretative methods, except perhaps as an afterthought; all that matters are the *results* of the judge's decisions—the political ramifications of those rulings in the real world. For example, National Public Radio's Juan Williams hails Justice Thurgood Marshall for promoting "preferences, set-asides, and other race-conscious policies" as the "remedy for the damage remaining from the nation's history of slavery and racial bias." Former U.S. solicitor general Drew Days applauds Marshall's "use of the law as an instrument of social change," while Janet Reno, former U.S. attorney general, applauds the justice's "deep appreciation of how both the law and the Court's decisions actually affected real people in an uncloistered world."[2] Similarly, A. M. Keith, former chief justice of the Minnesota Supreme Court, salutes Justice Harry Blackmun for bringing "a human dimension to his decisions" and for setting "our ultimate sexual and social relationships, bodily integrity, and personal choices outside the legitimate scope of governmental intrusion."[3]

The Left's emphasis on the political and social policy results of particular legal decisions came to the forefront during the Senate confirmation hearings for John Roberts. Senator Dick Durbin pressed the nominee for his views on a Supreme Court decision that required state taxpayers to pay for free public schooling for the children of illegal

immigrants. Needless to say, nothing in the Constitution actually requires state taxpayers to provide free education to the kids of illegal
immigrants—yet the Supreme Court interpreted the Constitution to
say exactly that.[4] Still, Senator Durbin explained to Roberts, "Whether
we're talking about millions of uninsured people or millions of Hispanic children, I would think that it would be a basic value, you'd
say this is good for America for people to have insurance and bad
for them to be denied; it is good for America to see children with
education rather than to see them in the streets, ignorant. It seems so
fundamental."

Durbin's statement reveals a fundamental fact conservatives must
recognize: Liberals view the role of judges in American law as render-
ing decisions that will be "good for America"—from their perspective,
of course.

Roberts's response, typical of mainstream conservative legal thought,
indicated a much different sense of the role of the law and the courts:
"Senator, I don't think you want judges who will decide cases before
them under the law on what they think is good—simply good policy
for America. There are legal questions there."[5] (Here he was echoing
the dissenting opinion in the case Durbin cited, in which Chief Justice
Warren Burger wrote, "Were it our business to set the Nation's social
policy, I would agree without hesitation that it is senseless for an en-
lightened society to deprive any children—including illegal aliens—of
an elementary education. . . . However, the Constitution does not constitute us as 'Platonic Guardians' nor does it vest in this Court the authority to strike down laws because they do not meet our standards of
desirable social policy, 'wisdom,' or 'common sense.'")[6]

Roberts's response is all well and good—admirable, even—but it
ignores the reality that many judges do believe it is their job to decide
what is "good for America." The Durbin-Roberts exchange reflects the
crux of the conservatives' problem: The liberals use courts as a policy-
advancing tool, while conservatives delude ourselves into thinking that
judges and court cases do not set public policy. The Left uses the courts
to wage an offensive war seeking to win political battles for radical liberalism; the Right refuses to even pick up the weapon of judicial activism. The Left sees every lawsuit as an opportunity to move the law
and society leftward; the Right (perhaps with the exception of advocating the reversal of *Roe*) merely seeks to thwart future liberal gains.

That needs to change. As the Japanese did in response to Commodore Perry's warships in the nineteenth century, conservatives must respond quickly and forcefully to the far more advanced Left. Liberals are the ones with the mighty armada, the powerful weapons; we must make them our own. Here's what we need to know to do it.

LIBERAL LESSON NUMBER ONE: COURTS AND JUDGES ARE POLITICAL

CONSERVATIVE CRITICS FREQUENTLY ACCUSE liberal judges of acting "lawlessly" or "imperially." Sometimes the charges are fair, but in a number of cases the critics overlook a simple fact: Serious, intelligent people can reasonably disagree about what the law means or how it applies in a particular case. Just because a judge reaches a conclusion that differs from the one you reached does not mean that the judge's interpretation is indisputably incorrect. That's not liberal relativism; it's just reality when it comes to interpreting law at the highest levels.

In fact, on the toughest cases—often the most politically sensitive cases—it's far from easy to decide what the law really is and how it should be applied. When cases reach appellate courts and especially the U.S. Supreme Court, the relevant laws and earlier precedents are often ambiguous and even downright confusing. The very fact that lawsuits make it all the way to the Supreme Court often reflects the law's indeterminacy; if it were clear how the law should be applied, the two sides would never have to battle through appeal after appeal. There are no Supreme Court cases interpreting the meaning of those big red hexagonal signs reading "STOP" that sit on many of America's street corners. And it's not as if Supreme Court justices can just look at all the evidence and arrive at the same, indisputably correct answer; after all, few cases are decided unanimously, and a substantial number are decided by a 5–4 margin. Even the justices whom conservatives usually hold up as the model for judges—Antonin Scalia and Clarence Thomas—disagree with each other in plenty of cases.

Hey, even the Founders differed on the meaning and purpose of the Constitution and how it applied to particular controversies. If Thomas Jefferson and James Madison couldn't agree, is it reasonable to expect that all modern-day judges will suddenly, after more than two centuries of debate, resolve these differences? Those on the Right who demonize judicial activism need to understand that there's often no one correct answer to difficult legal questions—that in constitutional law, there are lots of legitimate ways to skin a cat.*

Interpreting the Constitution is a bit like interpreting the Bible, the Talmud, or the Koran: Scholars take a variety of positions on the meaning and importance of the text, and have done so for centuries. Say a judge is dealing with a First Amendment case. Should the judge read the relevant clause of the First Amendment only or should he read the First Amendment as a whole? Or should he read the amendment within the context of the entire Bill of Rights, or within the context of the overall Constitution? Should he look at the text only, or also try to determine what the Founders' motivations and purpose were by looking at their debates and writings? If the latter, which Founders should he consider, and which debates and writings? Who were more important, the drafters of the Constitution or the state legislators who debated and ratified it? Should he defer to prior judges or view their opinions as anachronistic? On and on it goes.[7] And all this comes up even before you get into the factual niceties of politically charged cases.

In short, a blithe appeal to the "rule of law" cannot resolve complex cases of the kind that the highest courts must regularly address. A judge is forced to choose among various reasonable, competing interpretations of the exact same text or precedent. A judge's biases, ideology, background, and priorities are always going to enter into the equation as he attempts to decide from among a variety of options—and this isn't necessarily a bad thing for conservatives or the country.

Yup, that's right, biases and ideology are hugely important. The Right doesn't get this, or at least refuses to acknowledge it. For example, Republican Senator John Thune said during the John Roberts confirmation hearings that he thought a judge could separate his views from the meaning of the law. Thune explained that "judicial activism" occurs when judges "rely on their personal views rather than the Constitution when deciding cases of great importance."[8] Similarly, Senator Orrin Hatch has argued that judges "must *interpret* the law, not legislate from the bench," and that a "judicial activist, on the left *or* the right, is not, in my view, qualified to sit on the federal bench."[9]

But the Left does get it: For instance, in early 2006 Harvard law

---

* Disclaimer: No cats were injured in the writing of this book, and the author has made a contribution to a local cat shelter to cleanse any moral guilt felt by his exploitation of the "skin a cat" cliché.

professor and noted liberal Alan Dershowitz said, "Almost all justices vote almost all of the time in accordance with their own personal, political and religious views. That is the reality, especially on the Supreme Court, where precedent is not as binding, and where cases are determined less by specific facts than by broad principles. Although presidents, senators and judicial nominees loudly proclaim that justices should merely apply 'the law' in a neutral manner, every experienced lawyer understands that the best predictors of a justice's actual votes are his or her personal, political and religious predilections. . . . Good lawyers check the biographical material about judges even before they read their cases."[10] Dershowitz is right.

No doubt about it, judges are political actors. They regularly deal with complex, politically charged cases, and sometimes they are required (or choose) to *make* law rather than merely "interpret" it. In any given case, judges must somehow make sense of all the conflicting claims in order to reach a decision; that decision will inevitably be informed by the judges' own ideology, priorities, and, yes, biases. Like anyone else, judges do not function in isolation from society; they read the newspapers, watch TV, have friends and colleagues, and fight over Xbox 360s while shopping for Christmas or Hanukkah or Kwanzaa (circle the one you prefer). As Judge Robert Bork explains, there is "strong reason to suspect that the judge absorbs those values he writes into law from the social class or elite with which he identifies."[11]

Conservatives might fool themselves into believing that interpreting the Constitution is a legal act, not a political one, but as Justice Scalia observes, Supreme Court decisions are often geared toward policy results, not law. In his dissent in *Lawrence v. Texas,* Scalia wrote, "It does not surprise me, and should surprise no one, that the Court has chosen today to revise the standards of stare decisis set forth in *Casey.* It has thereby exposed *Casey*'s extraordinary deference to precedent for the result-oriented expedient that it is."[12]

Is it really so terrible to think of judges as political actors? It's not as if anyone really thinks judges are all-knowing demigods imbued with the truth of law at birth. The Founders certainly didn't harbor any illusions about judges. They knew judges were shaped by experience and ideology just as much as elected politicians are. Jefferson put it well when he wrote, "Our judges are as honest as other men and not more so. They have with others the same passions for party, for power, and the privilege of their corps."[13] The passions, emotions, and selfish desires of powerful men will be no different whether they wear suits to work or don black robes; they will be no different whether they seek personal financial profit, academic tenure, elected office, or a prestigious judicial appointment.

And, last but not least, a bit of common sense is in order. If judges and courts are not political, then why on earth would anyone be spending millions of dollars running political ads in favor of or against Supreme Court nominees such as John Roberts and Samuel Alito? And why would presidential candidates be asked about the types of judges they would nominate if elected to the White House?

Judgeships at the highest levels are important political positions, plain and simple. We do ourselves no good to pretend otherwise. And embracing conservative judicial activism simply means making sure that conservative priorities get a fair hearing in the courts while giving us the best chance to stop future liberal bastardizations of American law.

LIBERAL LESSON NUMBER TWO: JUDGES MAKE LAW

THE OLD *SCHOOLHOUSE ROCK* song about "how a bill becomes a law" might still be accurate, but it's foolish to believe the simple story that Congress makes the laws, the president executes and enforces those laws, and the courts interpret the laws. While this explanation works for sixth graders, it constitutes nothing more than "civics for suckers" for voting adults who want to understand how American politics and law work today.

Too many conservatives have bought into a "civics for suckers" mentality, unfortunately. In denouncing judicial activism, we declare that judges shouldn't make the law. We are fond of stating that "Americans should be governed by 'we the people' and not 'they the judges.' " That's rhetorically persuasive on a talk show—I know, I've used it myself—but it fails to address the complexities of the situation.

Just for starters, consider exactly what courts do in our political system. Liberals and conservatives alike concede that, through the power of judicial review, courts may declare popularly enacted laws unconstitutional (even though the Constitution itself fails to mention anything about judicial review). Nor does anyone call for pure democracy.

In the words of Harvard law professor Laurence Tribe, a noted liberal, the democratic process "leaves political minorities vulnerable to the will of the majority."[14] The Framers recognized the dangers of a pure democracy and did not want to create a system that left Americans vulnerable to the tyranny of the mob. They needed to permit majority rule while also protecting minority rights; reconciling the two needs became known as the Madisonian dilemma. If 51 percent of the electorate voted to take the property of the other 49 percent, presumably most of us would cheer a court striking down the democratically enacted law as unconstitutional.[15]

Professors Erwin Chemerinsky and Catherine Fisk of the prestigious Duke University School of Law neatly debunked the myth that judges do nothing more than "apply" or "interpret" the law. "Judges do make law and always have," they stated flatly. Indeed, "it's their job" to make law, the legal scholars insisted. That's something "everyone knows about the legal system." Chemerinsky and Fisk are both proud liberals. It just goes to show you that liberals don't delude themselves about the courts as the Right does. And in this case they have plenty of evidence to support their view. "Almost all tort law (governing accidental injuries), contract law, and property law are made by judges," the professors pointed out. "Legislatures did not create these rules; judges did, and they continue to do so when they revise the rules over time."[16]

America's Founders recognized the importance of judges making the law when they embraced the writings of the prominent English legal scholar William Blackstone, the author of *Blackstone's Commentaries*. Like the writings of natural-law philosophers such as John Locke, the writings about English common law—a fancy way of referring to the law that judges make—factored heavily into the Founders' approach to creating the new federal government. And it's not just in common law that prior decisions, called precedents, play a prominent role; in constitutional law, many judges and legal scholars cite precedent as a major factor in their decisions. Even Justice Alito acknowledged that legal precedents were entitled to due weight. But as it happens, even though liberals have overturned many precedents in the past seventy years on their way to remaking American law, they're starting to find religion now; they want to make sure conservatives understand that *Roe v. Wade* and other Supreme Court decisions they like established firm legal precedents.

To think that judicial restraint could be a reality in modern American courts reflects a misguided belief that the courts stand apart from the political process. As fine a legal mind as Judge Robert Bork has fallen for this fantasy. Bork is a brilliant jurist who should have been confirmed to the Supreme Court, but he got it wrong when he warned in *The Tempting of America* that the nation should not allow the law to be seduced by politics. It's a fine thought, but unfortunately, that horse has left the barn—the law was seduced by politics long ago. We're not going to get that horse back in the barn, so we need to figure out how to deal with the situation as it exists.

Indeed, conservatives will never take back the courts—or more important, American law—if we fail (or refuse) to recognize that judges are intimately involved in the process of making laws that affect each and every one of us. And if we don't reclaim the courts, we will fail to achieve a fundamental goal of modern-day conservatism—preserving and advancing the American way of life.

LIBERAL LESSON NUMBER THREE:
THE RULE OF FIVE IS THE RULE OF LAW

WE NEED TO PROTECT *the rule of law.* That's a line we hear all the time from critics of judicial activism. But think about it: What is the "rule of law," exactly? In practice it's often judges themselves who define the rule of law. Indeed, the rule of law is sometimes nothing more than the rule of five—five justices, that is.

The Left figured this out ages ago. Liberals have long understood, for example, that the U.S. Supreme Court is "primarily a political institution," as a book honoring liberal icon Justice William Brennan put it.[17] Brennan himself taught a simple lesson in his constitutional law seminars, asking, "What is the first rule of the Supreme Court? You have to get to five."[18] All that matters, in the end, is the scoreboard.

Perhaps "getting to five" sounds like a crude method of jurisprudence, but conservatives will keep getting killed in the courts if we don't focus on the results of court cases the way the Left does. Rather than focusing on methods of interpretation—such as originalism or strict constructionism—the Right should focus on the desired result: advancing the American way of life. Conservatives accomplish nothing by consistently being in the minority in key legal decisions. Look at Justice Scalia. His opinions are invariably eloquent, intelligent, insightful, and witty. In fact, his most famous and eloquent opinions have been collected in a wonderful book, *Scalia Dissents*.[19] That's an honor bestowed on few Supreme Court justices. But as much as his dissenting opinions make for edifying reading, ultimately they matter little. They are, after all, *dissents;* they do not represent the law of the land. Better to be part of the rule of five than in the noble minority.

By failing to appreciate this basic reality, we play into the Left's hands. Why? Because whenever the Left places five justices on the Supreme Court who hold typical liberal leanings, such as those expressed by Democratic Senator Durbin, we will see a never-ending parade of decisions that advance the left-wing cause. But if we cling to judicial restraint, the Right will never make similar gains for the conservative cause, even when we have five conservative justices on the court. Sure, the Right may hold the line against a whole host of liberal lunacies and keep gay marriage and the like from becoming law. But holding the line is different from pushing the law to the right. It does not repair the wreckage that is constitutional law. It may prevent the situation from getting worse (at least temporarily), but it doesn't make it better. That's not good enough, not after decades of liberal judicial activism.

And worst of all, as soon as liberals have five votes again, guess what—the law will immediately lurch further leftward.

DON'T BRING A KNIFE TO A GUNFIGHT

FACING REALITY—recognizing that courts are indeed political institutions, that judges do in fact make law as de facto legislators, and that, at the end of the day, the rule of five is actually the rule of law—is an essential first step to taking back the courts and in turn American law. Recognizing reality will allow us to defend traditional American freedoms and values. And it will enable conservatives to pick up our secret weapon—conservative judicial activism.

Right now all we try to do is disarm ourselves in the courts by trying to ban judicial activism. This approach is naive and self-defeating. The Right must remember the adage "Don't bring a knife to a gunfight." To do nothing but cry out for judicial restraint is to bring a knife to a gunfight. It's a losing proposition that must be rejected.

And why wouldn't conservatives embrace judicial activism? The tools used to accomplish the Left's social engineering projects are not inherently liberal or anti-American tools, any more than warships were inherently American or anti-Japanese in the time of Commodore Perry. Judicial activism and lawsuits are apolitical tools; it's just that they have been wielded almost exclusively by the Left. Nothing about these tools precludes conservatives from seizing and wielding them too. Indeed, the fact that the Left has been the only side to benefit from judicial activism should be regarded as nothing but a historical oddity—and not an inevitability.

It's time for conservatives to correct our mistakes. The only way to overturn the precedents, statutes, and laws enacted by liberals—and to create *conservative* precedents as well—is to learn from what the Left has done.

The time has come to turn the Left's guns against it. Anything short of an all-out offensive assault using the courts as a weapon in today's political wars with the Left will fail. It's the best way to put American law back on course.

FOUR

JUDICIAL ACTIVISM IS NOT A FOUR-LETTER WORD

Why Conservatives Must Abandon Wishful Thinking About the Courts

Judicial activism has become a dirty word to conservatives. At first glance, that's no shock.

Conservatives are understandably gun-shy when it comes to judicial activism. After all, it's liberals who have wielded this weapon to fundamentally change the American political and social landscape. Decades of liberal judicial activism have eliminated, with the mere swipe of a pen, long-standing constitutional protections for property owners, business owners, and gun owners, while simultaneously inventing constitutional "rights" favored only by the nation's liberal elites.

But conservatives misdiagnose the essential problem in the courts. The problem is not judicial activism—it's *liberal* judicial activism.

In reality, judicial activism is an apolitical tool. Consider: Arsenic ice cream is bad; ice cream is not bad. Similarly, liberal judicial activism is bad; judicial activism is not bad. As a tool, and nothing more, judicial activism is neither good nor bad, although it can certainly be *used* either for good or for bad.

With judicial activism, the question is how the tool is applied. Sure, it can be judicial activism when a court strikes down a parental notification law for teens seeking abortions, but judicial activism could also be used to strike down restrictions on gun rights or property rights. Conservatives will have wasted a golden opportunity if we continue to advocate judicial restraint when the courts are well positioned to become a valuable ally of the conservative movement and the nation.

But to make the judiciary a partner in advancing the conservative cause and the American way of life, the Right must rethink its approach to the courts, judges, and American law. Rather than merely attacking the courts for their left-wing slant, conservatives need a more intelligent, constructive approach—one that not only thwarts liberal advances but also generates wins for the Right.

Conservatives must first recognize that we have been in search of a false idol this whole time. In a classic example of not seeing the forest for the trees, we have committed ourselves to defending certain institutions and doctrines when in fact what we should be defending are the liberties, values, and rights those institutions and doctrines were designed to protect and advance. We've dedicated ourselves to maintaining certain artificial means rather than the greater goal—preserving American freedoms and the American way of life.

Conservatives have lost sight of what is most important. We must rethink our approach to the courts and judges, and recognize that they can be our allies.

THE ONGOING AMERICAN EXPERIMENT

WHILE MANY CONSERVATIVES do not hesitate to vilify activist judges, our devotion to concepts such as judicial restraint, strict constructionism, and originalism reflects a certain respect for the institution of the judiciary. Or, perhaps more accurately, we consider judicial activism an affront to the democratic process and the elegantly crafted system of government that the Framers designed.

I am certainly an admirer of the Founders, and I believe we should devote our efforts to preserving the great nation they created. Without doubt, they designed a fine system of government whose well-known system of checks and balances has, by and large, functioned effectively for more than two centuries. The "American experiment" has been a remarkable achievement.

But the Founders themselves viewed the government they created as just that—an experiment. This is critical to remember, for today there is a great deal of confusion about what it is we should admire about the Framers. The Framers did not love, or even like, government. They feared government. Nor did the Framers love the system of government they created because they thought the system had unique and intrinsic value (though it has proven to be the best form of government available to us). No, they perceived the governmental system's value in the ends it served. Their primary interest was to design a system that would protect the fundamental freedoms bestowed by the Creator as unalienable individual rights. The Declaration of Independence identified those rights, and the Framers spent years designing an appropriate government to try to preserve them. Law professor Scott Gerber explains that the Constitution is "a political document in the noblest sense. It establishes a framework of government through which certain underlying philosophical principles are to be advanced. And those philosophical principles are the natural-rights principles of the Declaration of Independence. To ignore this fact is to ignore the reason we are a nation."[1]

Keep in mind that some thirteen years elapsed between the signing of the Declaration of Independence in 1776 and the ratification of the Constitution in 1789. In between, the Framers created—and discarded—another system of government entirely, the one codified by the Articles of Confederation. The Framers undid the Articles once it became clear the system wasn't functioning effectively, and in particular when they realized the government wasn't protecting the core values, freedoms, and principles America was built around. They weren't afraid to make adjustments to their experiment. The Founders regarded government as a necessary evil and weren't afraid to change it in pursuit of their larger goal of preserving fundamental American liberties.

In another sign that the Founders did not consider any particular form of government to be sacrosanct, the Declaration of Independence states that if a government becomes more a danger to liberty than a boon, the people can rebel: "When a long train of abuses and usurpations, pursuing invariably the same object evinces a design to reduce [the people] under absolute despotism, it is their right, it is their duty, to throw off such government, and to provide new guards for their future security."

CONSERVATIVES SHOULD NOT BE BEHOLDEN TO ANY INSTITUTION, DOCTRINE, OR THEORY

JUST AS THE FOUNDERS did, conservatives today must remember that we are fighting for a larger goal: preserving the American way of life and American liberties. We thus must change our perspective on the courts. We should not advocate a policy of judicial restraint in deference to the institution of the judiciary or in the name of protecting it. Rather, we must use the courts as a vehicle to advance a greater cause—preserving individual freedoms. The Founders did not hold sacred the courts themselves, or any other part of government. We must not either.

Unfortunately, Americans commonly confuse the mechanisms of government with the greater ends. It's not just with the courts. In the spring of 2005, when Republican senators discussed employing the "nuclear option" to block filibusters of President Bush's judicial nominees, many on the Left—and even some on the Right—deplored the tactic because it would run counter to the "traditions of the Senate."

Hogwash. The traditions of the Senate, or of any other government institution, can and must be discarded when they cease to function effectively or to advance the interests of the American people. The Senate, like the courts, is merely an institution; yes, it has served us well for more than two centuries, but to believe that is unchangeable—or that the Founders themselves would have refused to make adjustments—is ridiculous. If the Framers were willing to discard an entire system of government (as they did with the Articles of Confederation), they certainly wouldn't be so beholden to largely arbitrary traditions. Nor would they consider the institutions themselves sacrosanct.

The same thing goes for political doctrines such as federalism. Conservatives regularly praise the system of federalism. But when push comes to shove, it's not always a particularly good system. Consider this: George W. Bush arguably ignored federalism when he went to the U.S. Supreme Court to stop the Florida Supreme Court's activism. How many conservatives think it would have been better for the nation to have had the judicial activism of the Florida Supreme Court win the day in the interest of deferring to the states?

Conservatives should not support separation of powers or federalism or any legal doctrine for its own sake. Liberals never handcuff themselves in this way. Forget about separation of powers; the Left turns to whichever branch of government is in the best position to advance the liberal cause. For example, when Democrat Bill Clinton sat in the White House with a Republican-controlled Congress, liberals deferred to executive power and executive privilege. After Paula Jones sued Clinton, Democrats vociferously argued that a president should not have to defend against a lawsuit until out of office, as if the president were above the law. In contrast, when Republican Richard Nixon was in the White House, the Democrats who controlled Congress made it a point to highlight Congress's power to exercise oversight of the president, and to push Nixon to resign. In fact, in 1973, a Democratic-controlled Congress overrode President Nixon's veto of the War Powers Resolution in order to restrict the powers of the president. Liberals pursue their political objectives first and foremost.

Besides, why would conservatives be so deferential to the courts when the judiciary has changed in ways the Framers never would have envisioned? Conservatives cannot try to imagine the courts as they existed two centuries ago. Nor should we hesitate to use the courts to achieve the same goals the Founders had in mind. After all, the judiciary is just another institution, just another tool the Founders bequeathed to us to protect fundamental freedoms.

CLICKING YOUR HEELS FOR JUDICIAL RESTRAINT IS NOT AN OPTION

WELL, WHY WON'T JUDICIAL restraint work? From a pragmatic perspective, conservatives need to understand that the judiciary simply won't practice judicial restraint because that means practicing *self*-restraint. After all, one of the Supreme Court's earliest and most important decisions found that the ultimate arbiter of the meaning of the Constitution is . . . the Supreme Court. As law professors Erwin Chemerinsky and Catherine Fisk put it, "One of the most fundamental doctrines of American law—the authority of courts to declare laws unconstitutional—is entirely made by judges. Nowhere does the text of the Constitution mention the power of judicial review, and it may fairly be debated whether the Framers of the Constitution intended to create such a power."[2] Thomas Jefferson made the same point almost two centuries earlier. Writing on the question of "whether the judges are invested with exclusive authority to decide on the constitutionality of a law," Jefferson stated, "Certainly there is not a word in the Constitution which has given that power to them more than to the Executive or Legislative branches."[3]

In the two centuries since, judges have continued to grant themselves greater powers and further influence. Even conservative judges, who exercise judicial restraint far more than their liberal counterparts do, make clear that courts may not be limited by the legislature. For example, in the case of *Dickerson v. United States* (2000), Chief Justice William Rehnquist led the Supreme Court in voiding a federal statute permitting a federal judge to ignore the Supreme Court's *Miranda* decision, which requires that those arrested be read their rights before being allowed to confess to crimes. In essence, Chief Justice Rehnquist reminded us that in disputes between the courts and Congress over what the Constitution means, the courts win!

WHY ORIGINALISM, STRICT CONSTRUCTIONISM, AND TEXTUALISM WON'T WORK

IF JUDICIAL ACTIVISM is a no-no to most conservatives, how are judges supposed to act on the bench? Many people on the Right endorse a series of overlapping legal doctrines—originalism, textualism, and strict constructionism. Unfortunately, taken together or separately, these doctrines will fail not just conservatives but the nation as a whole. We need to debunk the myth that these doctrines can advance conservatism and the national interest.

Let's look at each of these methods of legal interpretation. According to the theory of *textualism*, judges read the text of the law first and try to give the words an ordinary and reasonable meaning based on what the language meant when enacted. So, for example, the phrase "well regulated militia" in the Second Amendment would be interpreted by using dictionaries and other sources defining these words in the late eighteenth century. A textualist would generally be uninterested in the intent of the drafters of a law, focusing instead on the ordinary meaning of the law's text. *Originalism* is a doctrine whereby a judge tries to advance the general intent of the drafters of the Constitution. An originalist asks what the Framers intended by a provision and then asks whether a particular interpretation today is consistent with that intent. *Strict constructionism* is a related concept that was popularized by Richard Nixon during his 1968 presidential campaign.[4] The term generally means that judges should not engage in judicial activism or legislate from the bench, but should look at precisely what the Constitution says.

Many conservatives view these doctrines as the necessary counter-weight to judicial activism, but the doctrines share at least four fundamental flaws making them undesirable for conservatives.

Flaw #1: The Law Can Never Be Perfectly Clear

THE FIRST MAIN FLAW is that each of these doctrines presupposes a world in which the laws, constitutional or otherwise, are so clearly and unequivocally defined that they cannot be subject to materially different interpretations. But the language contained in the Constitution is as close to perfect as we can hope to achieve as a nation, and sadly, it utterly failed to achieve its ultimate goal—maintaining the federal government as a government of limited, enumerated powers as opposed to the leviathan it has become.

Look at the rather unambiguous evidence that the Framers wanted to constrain the size and scope of the federal government. The Tenth Amendment provides, "The powers not delegated to the United States by the Constitution, nor prohibited by it to the States, are reserved to the States respectively, or to the people." In addition, Article I of the Constitution sets forth a list of specific powers given to the federal government. Chief Justice John Marshall, the man who is considered the George Washington of America's judges, wrote in *McCulloch v. Maryland:* "This government is acknowledged by all, to be one of enumerated powers. The principle, that it can exercise only the powers granted to it, . . . is now universally admitted."[5] And if that were not enough to establish that the federal government was always intended to be a very limited one, there is Thomas Jefferson, who wrote, "Our tenet ever was . . . that Congress had not unlimited powers to provide for the general welfare, but were restrained to those specifically enumerated; and that, as it was never meant that they should provide for that welfare but by the exercise of the enumerated powers, so it could not have been meant they should raise money for purposes which the enumeration did not place under their action."[6]

Despite all that—the clear language of the Tenth Amendment, historical documents from the time, the structure of the Constitution itself, and even Supreme Court opinions from America's most influential justice—the federal government today is by all measures a behemoth, not the limited government originally intended.

Bear in mind, too, that "there is not a word in the Constitution" about judicial review (to use Jefferson's language), but that hasn't stopped judges from grabbing power and completely rewriting American law. If the clear language of the U.S. Constitution failed to prevent the federal government from growing into a leviathan or prevent federal judges from acting in ways divorced from the constitutional text, then exactly what language would fix the problem? No law Congress can enact, no constitutional amendment the states can ratify, no decision the U.S. Supreme Court can issue—even if the language seems unambiguous—can stop liberal judicial activism. I would love it if the perfect sentence could be devised to protect us eternally from encroachments on our rights and the expansion of state power—or from liberal judges willing to ignore clear constitutional text—but that will not happen. To think otherwise is naive and self-defeating.

Flaw #2: Not Everyone Will Follow the Rules

THE SECOND FLAW of these doctrines is that they assume everyone will play by the same rules. We know this can't work either, because we have seen how the Left has played by a completely different set of rules and legal principles despite being bound to follow the exact same Constitution, statutes, and laws as conservatives. In other words, liberals "cheat" for their side in politically charged cases, and always will.

For example, the late Supreme Court justice Thurgood Marshall, a self-avowed critic of the Founders for their acceptance of slavery, regularly departed from the text of the Constitution in his decisions. In fact, Marshall reportedly described his judicial philosophy as "I do what I think is right and let the law catch up with me."[7] Similarly, the personal notes of Harry Blackmun show that he reached key conclusions on *Roe v. Wade* before the case was ever argued. His notes read: "A fundamental personal liberty is involved here—right to receive medical care," and "Much precedent for this sort of thing—*Griswold* et al." So he had already decided the case involved a "fundamental personal liberty" protected by the Constitution; he just hadn't figured out what it was yet. It seems his main task from there was deciding how to rationalize his conclusion that a "fundamental" right was at stake. Blackmun apparently decided what he wanted the outcome to be, then reasoned backward to find a legal justification for it. These are the kinds of games liberal judges play. No language can thwart such efforts.

Conservatives must recognize the dangers to conservatism and the American way of life that come from having one set of judges interpreting the law without regard to political outcomes while a second, equally (if not more) powerful set of judges is out to achieve particular policy objectives. How can the conservative view of law, life, and politics prevail when nobody in black robes vigorously defends and advances that view? To allow only the Left to deploy the courts as an offensive weapon is a self-defeating strategy for the Right.

Flaw #3: The Constitution Can't Explain Everything

A THIRD MAJOR FLAW is this: While doctrines such as textualism and originalism sound good in theory, they don't help us with many of the political-legal questions now posed to the courts. Even conservatives must acknowledge that many important legal issues arise today for which the Constitution provides incomplete or unsatisfactory answers.

The Constitution says nothing about the Federal Reserve system, NASA, the Federal Aviation Administration, the Federal Deposit Insurance Corporation, the Air Force. Can conservatives undo these bureaucracies and programs because they are "unconstitutional"? The First Amendment's protections of free speech say only that *Congress* "shall make no law . . ." Does this mean conservatives should agree that state legislatures can do whatever they want to curtail free speech? Nothing in the Constitution gave President Thomas Jefferson the authority to agree to the Lousiana Purchase. Do we have to turn over all that land to America's casino owners? Of course not.

University of Chicago law professor Richard Epstein, one of the country's leading conservative legal scholars, has explained why textualism alone has never worked and will never work in practice. "Jurists have universally held that the initial text sets the first leg of the journey, but does not provide a road map for the entire trip," Epstein wrote.[8]

And let's be honest: Even we conservatives pick and choose those aspects of the Constitution we prefer. On abortion, for example, conservatives embrace the concept of textualism, arguing that the right to abortion does not exist as a matter of constitutional law because it is not expressly mentioned in the Constitution. Since abortion is not a matter of constitutional law, many pro-lifers say that issues associated with abortion should be kicked to the legislative and executive branches. But does that mean conservatives always feel constrained to support only those individual rights found in the text of the Constitution? Absolutely not. In fact, many rights that Americans take for granted are mentioned nowhere in the Constitution.

Should conservatives support the right of parents to have children and then raise them as the parents see fit? Nothing in the Constitution mentions the "right" to get married, have children, or raise children in accordance with the parents' values. Yet why would conservatives object to a court protecting these rights? We wouldn't want laws prohibiting a man and woman from marrying each other or a married couple from procreating. Parents should be able to raise their children as they see fit, even though there is no textual basis to conclude that parents have any kind of right to do so (or even to get married and have children in the first place).

The point: Courts do and should protect certain rights and liberties found nowhere in the Constitution. Conservatives should not always blanch at these efforts.

Flaw #4: Unfortunately, These Doctrines Are Minority Views

A FOURTH FLAW of such doctrines is that, sadly, they don't carry nearly enough weight to matter in today's legal world. As much as we might admire originalism, strict contructionism, and textualism as judicial theories, the truth is that they have been relegated to the fringes of the modern-day legal system. Supreme Court Justice Antonin Scalia, the country's leading originalist, has said that originalism is "such a minority position in modern academia and in modern legal circles that on occasion I'm asked . . . , 'Justice Scalia, when did you first become an originalist?'—as though it is some kind of weird affliction that seizes some people: 'When did you first start eating human flesh?' "[9] Scalia isn't exaggerating. At Harvard, one of the most prestigious law schools in the nation, originalists simply don't exist. Harvard law professor Charles Fried has said that an originalist on the faculty would be like "a Flat Earther in a geography department." An originalist, he suspected, "would have a hard time getting appointed" to the faculty.[10]

I suppose it's not all that surprising that originalists and strict constructionists are so marginalized. Liberals can easily set a political trap for advocates of such doctrines. Want to appeal to the understanding and desires of eighteenth-century white men? Okay, then the Left will slam you with accusations of wanting to bring back sex discrimination, flogging for minor crimes, racial discrimination, even slavery. Liberals love to portray conservative jurists as backward, racist, sexist, whatever—and the attacks seem to work. Never mind that it was a Republican president who freed the slaves, while the Democratic Party remained "pro-choice" on the issue of slavery. And never mind that segregationists in the South were called Dixiecrats because they were Democrats.

Liberals have it both ways with the Framers, too. When they're not bashing conservatives for rigidly sticking to the policies of dead white slaveholders, they're casting themselves as the true legatees of the Framers. So conservatives gain no advantage by claiming to be the defenders of the Constitution or the Framers' legacy. For instance, liberal Supreme Court justice Ruth Bader Ginsburg has explained that the "framers of the Constitution allowed to rest in the Court's hands large authority to rule on the Constitution's meaning."[11] During the Alito hearings, Senator Ted Kennedy put down his drink just long enough to embrace the wisdom of the Framers, stating, "We need justices who can examine this issue objectively, independently, and fairly. And that's what our founders intended."[12] Abner Mikva, who served as White House counsel to Bill Clinton, writes that liberal lion William Brennan "never thought of himself as making it up as he went along. He thought that the splendid ambiguities that the Founding Fathers deliberately put in the Constitution . . . gave the Court full authority to do what is necessary and come up with the right result." *Result* is the key word, of course. Mikva added, "This judicial activist did not reach for feel-good results, but instead found a doctrine and precedent to justify his progressive decisions."[13]

In the end, conservatives don't gain much from trying to stand on interpretative principle in constitutional matters. Conservatives should instead fight for the principles and ideals the nation was founded on.

And we should do so using every arrow found in the quiver of modern American law.

TOSSING OUT THE OWNER'S MANUAL

HERE'S ONE WAY TO think of the whole question of judicial restraint versus judicial activism: If you buy a car today, it comes with an owner's manual that tells you the basics about how to operate the car, where the lights are, how to open the trunk, what the dashboard warning lights mean, and so on. That owner's manual presumes the car will remain in one piece. It does not tell you how to repair the computerized fuel injection system or the antilock brakes if those break down. Indeed, if the car became completely disassembled, the manual would be useless except maybe for providing the toll-free number to a service center. In other words, once the car is lying in a thousand pieces on the garage floor, you have to throw out the owner's manual. Its guidance has become useless and obsolete.

Doctrines such as originalism, strict constructionism, and textualism were the owner's manual to the Constitution. But the Constitution is now lying in thousands of pieces scattered throughout thousands of Supreme Court decisions. These traditional methods of interpreting the Constitution can't fix the problem now facing conservatives in the courts. Their instructions might have been relevant before, but they are inadequate to cope with the current state of constitutional affairs. Like the car, the Constitution and the legal system the Founders designed have been almost completely disassembled; two centuries of legal decisions and political practice, along with decades of aggressive liberal judicial activism, have torn them apart. The law currently being interpreted is not an unadorned Constitution but the constitutional text plus more than two hundred years of legal decisions, political history, and institutional inertia that radically altered the original meaning of the Constitution.

Indeed, all that judge-made law is now more influential than the Constitution itself. As University of Texas law professor Lino Graglia puts it, "Consider, for example, that there was a time when the assignment of children to public schools on the basis of race was constitutionally permissible, a time when it was constitutionally prohibited, and a time, the present, when it is sometimes constitutionally required.

That covers all the possibilities, yet in all that time, the Constitution was not amended in any relevant respect."[14]

It's time to throw out the owner's manual. If we ever expect to push back against the liberal judicial assault, we need something new—something more.

That something new is conservative judicial activism.

"LET'S HUG IT OUT"

Embracing Judicial Activism

Here's my strategy on the Cold War: We win, they lose.
— PRESIDENT RONALD REAGAN

Whether in sports, politics, or war, the same thing holds true: the best defense is a good offense. Merely trying not to lose, instead of actively trying to win, is a certain prescription for defeat and even disaster. If you don't engage in offensive maneuvers and tactics, you will surely lose. You must bring the war to the enemy.

This reality applies equally to the fight for the judiciary. By advocating judicial restraint and other constrained constitutional theories, conservatives have fixated almost entirely on not losing in the courts. Meanwhile, liberals play to win. Thus they win policy debates through the courts—and conservatives lose.

Remember this basic principle of negotiation: If you want something, you should ask for it, and probably even ask for more than you want. Certainly if you ask for less than what you desire, or you don't ask for something at all, you'll never get what you really want.

Conservatives repeatedly fail to recognize this basic idea as it applies to the courts. We do not routinely ask the Supreme Court to strike down gun regulations or other noxious statutes, laws, and regulations that liberal legislators have forced on Americans. Nor do we ask explicitly for judges who will support conservative policy outcomes. Instead, conservatives simply ask judges to respect and follow the "rule of law." This is a fundamental strategic mistake by the Right. The conservative movement has relegated itself to defending ground already held (and that's not much ground).

For example, Sandra Froman, president of the National Rifle Asso-

ciation, writes that "a federal judge should be either a strict constructionist or an originalist." Why? Because a strict constructionist "interprets the plain meaning of the words of the Constitution and laws as
they are written," while an originalist (who "is even better") looks at
"the plain meaning of the Constitution or laws at the time they were
written. So the Second Amendment, as well as the entire Constitution
and Bill of Rights, would be construed according to its meaning in
1789."[1] But why should the NRA rely only on code words such as
"originalist" and "strict constructionist" when the real goal is to nominate and confirm judges to the bench who will vigorously defend the
right to own, carry, and use firearms?

Should conservatives really be surprised that we haven't gotten
what we want in the courts? More concerned with playing fair than
with winning, the Right relies on high-minded rhetoric that ignores the
reality of today's judiciary. Or, perhaps afraid of speaking as bluntly as
the Left does, too many on the Right speak in code, relying on eu-
phemisms. When you speak in code, don't be astonished when you
don't get what you want.

An example of this miscommunication came with the nomination
of Harriet Miers to the Supreme Court. I believe President Bush did
what he thought was right and what he thought the people who elected
him wanted—that is, appoint a reliable conservative to the court. But
he discovered that, lo and behold, Miers didn't satisfy conservatives'
criteria, and he had to scramble to fix the situation. Why? Because
those criteria were never clearly articulated. Bush himself had vaguely
characterized his priorities, saying things such as "We stand for judges
who faithfully interpret the law instead of legislating from the bench."
A statement like that doesn't mean much in practice, since, as demonstrated, judges are required to make the law all the time, and many
rights we want judges to defend—the right to self-defense, to marry, to
associate freely with like-minded individuals, or to raise your child as
you see fit, for instance—can't be found by "strictly interpreting" the
Constitution.

Conservatives will be hard-pressed to deny the Right's failure in the
courts to date. So why in the world would we cling to a losing strategy?
Conservatives are at war—at war with liberals over the nature of
American society. The fight for the courts is a critical battle in the overall war effort.

We must change our tactics. We need to go on the offense immediately. Fortunately, we have the secret weapon to do this: conservative judicial activism.

Many conservatives view judicial activism as though it's the Death Star from the *Star Wars* films—they want to destroy it forever. Remember, though, the good guys destroyed the Death Star in *Star Wars,* but then the Empire rebuilt it in *Return of the Jedi.* So too will those on the Left reengage in liberal judicial activism as soon as they regain political power. We need more than a temporary fix, which is all we would get from judicial restraint, strict constructionism, and other legal doctrines popular with conservatives. The only way to thwart liberal judicial activism is to engage in conservative judicial activism.

Conservatives should not be afraid to take the offensive, because doing so will benefit the country. Not only will conservative judicial activism keep the Left from making further advances (an essentially defensive achievement), it will also allow conservatives to protect and advance American rights and freedoms: the right to property, the right to realistic self-defense, the right to live your life free from capricious government interference, and the right to life for the unborn.

Going on offense in the courts does not mean abandoning the Founders; in fact, it is the best way to defend the very freedoms and values for which the Framers fought. It is simply a different means—a better means—to a greater end.

DISRAELI WAS RIGHT—AND SO WAS HILLARY'S MENTOR

BENJAMIN DISRAELI, THE GREAT conservative British statesman, noted that "political life must be taken as you find it."[2] American conservatives need to take that lesson to heart and adapt to the battlefield conditions we encounter in the courts. Liberals definitely have. Hillary Clinton's mentor, the radical organizer Saul Alinsky, explained, "As an organizer I start from where the world is, as it is, not as I would like it to be. That we accept the world as it is does not in any sense weaken our desire to change it into what we believe it should be—it is necessary to begin where the world is if we are going to change it to what we think it should be. That means working in the system."[3]

Working within the modern judiciary requires adopting the tactics the Left has used to fully exploit the power of the courts. If conservatives hope to change the system and the nation's laws for the better, engaging in judicial activism is a necessity. We've seen why judicial restraint and originalism won't work, and the reality is that unless conservatives engage in decades of conservative judicial activism, you can kiss goodbye any prospect of those currently fringe doctrines becoming the mainstream in American law.

LEARNING FROM HISTORY

THINK ABOUT HOW Ronald Reagan defeated the Soviet Union. He did not do so by embracing the advice of the radical Left (to preemptively surrender) or of slightly more moderate liberals (negotiate arms reductions but don't do anything to offend the Commies). No, Reagan embraced a strategy of *winning* the Cold War—aggressively moving forward with a large military buildup until the Soviets cried out, "*No más*" (wrong language, I know, but Republicans want to court the Hispanic vote). Reagan refused to embrace a policy of "restraint" toward the Soviets.

When it comes to the courts, the Right must embrace this exact same strategy of winning rather than settling for the status quo. Conservatives skeptical of judicial activism need to recall that before the Soviet Union collapsed, the United States had to scare the bejesus out of the Soviets with a major arms buildup. Had Jimmy Carter continued in office and kept prioritizing "stability," "understanding," and, yes, "restraint," who knows what would have happened? The Soviet Union might still be targeting American cities with nukes and American men would be deprived of the opportunity to watch Maria Sharapova and Anna Kournikova play tennis (or at least model).

Another history lesson reminds us that fighting for victory is the best way to prevent disaster. Upon returning from the Munich conference in 1938, British prime minister Neville Chamberlain (himself a naive conservative) told the British people that by negotiating with Adolf Hitler he was "bringing peace with honor." Chamberlain proudly added, "I believe it is 'peace for our time.' Go home and get a nice quiet sleep." We know how that turned out. The American Right cannot make the same mistake and think that embracing a doctrine of judicial restraint will buy "peace for our time." It won't.

PUTTING DOWN THE SHOVEL ISN'T GOOD ENOUGH

WE MUST CONFRONT the fact that seventy years of liberal legal precedents are in place. Accepting the cold reality will allow us to change the entire conservative approach to the courts and the law.

The first piece of advice given to someone buried in debt is "Put down the shovel!" If you've dug yourself into a hole, you need to stop digging deeper. This is good advice as a first step, but it is *only* a first step. Sure, you won't make the hole any deeper, but just stopping digging won't lift you *out* of the hole.

Those conservatives who earnestly advocate judicial restraint are in effect asking the judiciary to put down the shovel. They implore the courts to stop inventing new liberal rights and precedents. For example, William Kristol of the *Weekly Standard* has said President Bush should "make the case for judicial restraint and constitutionalism," while Bush himself, when he nominated Harriet Miers to the Supreme Court, honored judicial restraint by explaining that Miers would "strictly interpret the law." Unfortunately, judicial restraint—simply stopping the courts from inventing new liberal precedents—does nothing about all the left-wing precedents already on the books.

And if conservatives lose power, liberals will again be well positioned to advance their agenda through the courts. As soon as liberals regain power, they will start almost exactly from where they were earlier, since a policy of judicial restraint will have done nothing to overturn seventy years' worth of troublesome liberal precedents. The Left won't need to concern themselves with fighting old fights, since abortion, gay rights, and other issues they had previously "settled" through the courts won't have been affected. Liberals will be right back where they were, happy to dig conservatives into an even deeper hole.

Advocating judicial restraint may have been an appropriate tactic while the Left dominated the government, but to do so now, when Republicans wield so much political power, is not only self-defeating for the conservative movement but also harmful to the country.

THE LEFT'S THEORY OF PRECEDENT:
WE WIN, YOU LOSE—PERIOD

CONSERVATIVES MUST UNDERSTAND THIS about judicial activism—
either we use it or the Left will use it against us. This is a critical point:
Nothing the Right can do, other than engaging in activism ourselves,
will suffice to end judicial activism by the Left. Judicial activism and
legislating from the bench can't be eliminated. Deal with it.

The conservative movement has fallen into a trap set by the Left:
Many of us believe we are engaging in judicial activism when we advocate
a position that is contrary to legal precedent or when courts strike down
democratically enacted laws. This is one of several archaic objections
conservatives often raise against judicial activism: that it violates legal
precedent and the "rule of law." Like a lot of conservative ideas about
the courts, this sounds nice and principled, but it has almost no relevance to the actual system we're forced to work within. Sure, liberals
speak out against the threat to precedent and "settled law," too—but
only when *liberal* precedents are at stake. The Left doesn't give a hoot
about precedent set by conservative courts. Remember, in 1923 the
Supreme Court said definitively that the right to contract "is settled by
the decisions of this Court and is no longer open to question." But
today, courts happily sign off on laws that violate this once "well-
established" right.

The Left's highly selective concern for precedent became perfectly
clear as President George W. Bush began nominating judges. Suddenly
we heard Democrats and left-wing activists expressing horror that
"extreme" right-wing judges might overturn "settled law." Remember
Senator Dick Durbin's pointed questions during John Roberts's confirmation hearings about the Supreme Court decision that required states
to pay for free public schooling for the children of illegal immigrants?
In that same colloquy, Durbin, an advocate of taxpayer-funded public
education for illegal immigrants, explained that it would "be a jolt to
the system in America if we decided that we would no longer offer education to these children." Of course, Durbin and his liberal buddies
on the Supreme Court didn't seem to care about the jolt to the system
that came from forcing states to pay for these educations in the first
place. Nor did liberals seem to care about the jolt to the system that
came when the Massachusetts Supreme Court imposed gay marriage

on Americans, or when abortion restrictions all across American were struck down overnight, or when school prayer was outlawed. Nor did liberals worry about the jolt to the system when the Supreme Court revolutionized the criminal justice system in favor of criminals.

Liberals have a simple rule when it comes to precedent. If the precedent helps the Left, it's "well established" and "etched in stone"; that's when we hear liberals sanctimoniously defending the doctrine of stare decisis (which means to stand by that which is decided). If, however, the precedent helps the Right, it is considered "unsettled"; in fact, you can count on the Left screaming, "It's alive!" and fighting to overturn the precedent. That's especially true if a case was decided by a 5–4 vote, even though plenty of decisions favoring the liberal side, including a string of cases in the 1930s that paved the way for the New Deal expansion of government, were decided by 5–4 rulings.

Let's illustrate the Left's hypocrisy: In 1973, the day after the Supreme Court decided *Roe v. Wade* (a 7–2 ruling), the *New York Times* ran this headline: "Supreme Court Settles Abortion Issue."[4] More than three decades have passed and still no retraction from the *Times*. In contrast, how did the *New York Times* describe a rare victory for the Right in *Adarand v. Peña* (1995), a decision that effectively struck down a race-based affirmative action program for government contractors? The paper reported, "In a decision likely to fuel rather than resolve the debate over affirmative action, the Supreme Court today cast doubt on the constitutionality of Federal programs that award benefits on the basis of race."[5] The point: A legal win for the Left is immediately heralded as a precedent for the ages, while a win for the Right is considered merely a temporary mistake by a misguided Supreme Court in need of greater wisdom.

Today, many liberals dub as "extremist" anyone who dares suggest that *Roe* or any other liberal Court decision is unfounded in American law. Before President Bush nominated John Roberts to the Supreme Court, the *New York Times* editorialized, "Some of the president's supporters on the far right really want him to name a radical ideologue who would work to upend well-established legal doctrines and take away basic rights that Americans have come to cherish."[6] The *Times* didn't explain why, if we Americans cherish those "rights" so much, we can't simply maintain them through the democratic process. Nor did the *Times* mention that many of the "well-established" doctrines were considered radical or baseless when the decisions were originally handed down, and that the judges plowed ahead regardless of contrary precedent or hostile public sentiment.

It's fascinating to look at exactly when the Supreme Court chooses to place a premium on precedent. In 1992's *Planned Parenthood v. Casey*, for instance, the Court upheld *Roe v. Wade* and the right to abortion—even while three of the justices voting to uphold *Roe* refused to state that *Roe* was correctly decided in the first place. Writing together, Justices Sandra Day O'Connor, Anthony Kennedy, and David Souter stated, "We do not need to say whether each of us, had we been Members of the Court when the valuation of the state interest came before it as an original matter, would have concluded, as the *Roe* Court did, that its weight is insufficient to justify a ban on abortions prior to viability even when it is subject to certain exceptions." The three justices simply concluded that *Roe* was too well established to overrule. Score a win for abortion (and the cultural elite of New York and San Francisco). But in 2003 the same Court had no problem jettisoning precedent in *Lawrence v. Texas*. That ruling rejected the Court's 1986 decision in *Bowers v. Hardwick*, which found that the Constitution did not provide a fundamental right for homosexuals to engage in sodomy. Apparently hundreds of years of laws forbidding sodomy were not sufficiently well established. In the ruling, the Court explicitly rejected the notion that it had to honor precedent, saying stare decisis is not "an inexorable command." Most relevant were the "laws and traditions in the past half century," the court argued.[7]

How can you can reconcile the Supreme Court's embrace of precedent in *Casey* with its rejection of precedent in *Lawrence*? Only by realizing that in each case the Court embraced the Left's worldview.

And gay rights is not the only issue on which the courts overturned seemingly settled laws. The Pledge of Allegiance has been voluntarily recited since 1943 (with the the words "under God" added in 1954), yet somehow this was not sufficiently "settled" to prevent federal judges from concluding in the twenty-first century that its use in public schools, with the words "under God," was unconstitutional. For a century, nativity scenes were featured in public parks and buildings in celebration of Christmas; then, somehow, such displays became unconstitutional. The Boy Scouts always had kept homosexual Scout leaders from taking young boys into the woods, but then state court judges ruled this practice illegal, and four U.S. Supreme Court justices agreed. One wonders whether the Declaration of Independence itself, with its express reference to "the Creator," would withstand scrutiny from some judges.

The Supreme Court has spoken, and the message is clear: *Precedent shmecedent—we'll change the law if we want to.* Basically, the Supreme Court's approach to precedent is, well, that it need not follow precedent, especially if precedent represents a barrier to reaching a desired outcome in a particular case.

And liberals' view of precedent? If it helps them, they follow it—and win. If it hurts them, they ignore it—and win. At least those on the Left are consistent—they just want to win political battles using the courts. So should conservatives, starting now.

THE NEW LIBERAL TRAP: SUPERPRECEDENTS

OH, BUT NOW LIBERALS are terrified that the Right will finally clue in and realize how valuable the courts can be to advancing a political agenda. That's why, during the Supreme Court confirmation hearings of John Roberts and Samuel Alito, we heard liberal senators piously talking about *Roe v. Wade* and other favorite decisions as settled precedents. In fact, it was during the Roberts hearings that the nation heard a relatively new idea being floated—the idea of *super*precedents.

Superprecedents? Yup. Actually, it was a Republican—the prochoice senator Arlen Specter—who first used the term during the Roberts hearings. Specter asked Roberts whether the judge agreed that *Roe v. Wade* constituted a superprecedent—or, as the senator put it, a "super-duper precedent." The Left quickly embraced this idea, attaching the label of *superprecedent* to rulings "so deeply embedded in the fabric of law they should be especially hard to overturn," in the words of George Washington University law professor Jeffrey Rosen. "Since the Roberts hearings," Rosen points out, "prominent liberal academics have seized on the idea as their best chance in a generation for countering the claim of conservative 'strict constructionists' that any precedent should be overturned if it is inconsistent with the original understanding of the Constitution."[8]

It's a novel theory—and completely made up. But it helps the Left keep their prior legal victories in place. Liberals actually encourage conservative talk about judicial restraint, since it has made conservatives a feeble opponent in the courts. That has made it easy for liberals to run roughshod over long-standing precedents and effect the social and political changes they desire. Encouraging the Right's rhetoric about judicial restraint apparently is no longer enough for liberals; now they disingenuously champion "superprecedents" in order to preserve their prior victories in the courts. Conservatives must not get suckered by the Left's ruse.

In fact, when conservatives fall for the liberal argument that to engage in judicial activism is to violate the rule of law and legal precedent, we succumb to what I call the "left-wing ratchet effect." Think about it: Liberal judges have spent decades pushing the law to the left, by recognizing abortion, criminal, and gay rights, for instance. So what happens when conservative judges merely maintain the status quo? They are preserving the *left-wing* status quo. That is totally unacceptable. Even assuming that conservatives could reform the system so judges simply interpreted the law rather than made it up, what happens when the liberals get back into power and recapture the bench? They will, of course, push the law even more to the left. If the clear language of the Constitution failed to constrain results-oriented liberal judges (which it has), then what exactly will stop those on the Left from reembracing the same liberal judicial activism that served them so well for the past seventy years? Nothing. Conservative judges must actively undo left-wing decisions to prevent our laws from skewing further leftward.

ASKING THE GENIE FOR THREE WISHES

THE GENIE OF JUDICIAL activism is out of the bottle. It's not going back in. Liberals, assuming they have enough votes on a court, will never embrace originalism or judicial restraint. Not only do conservatives need to beat the liberals, but we must also fight back against a powerful legal culture of politicians, attorneys, judges, law schools, and interest groups, all of whom have a vested interest in creating ever more powerful courts willing to stick their noses into more and more aspects of life. Sure, liberals may occasionally talk a good game about the virtues of judicial restraint, but don't believe them for a second. These are mere interludes between bouts of liberal judicial activism, giving the Left's legal soldiers a chance to clean their weapons and rearm for their next chance to move American law—and with it American society—leftward.

Whenever given the chance, liberal judges will issue liberal decisions regardless of what the Right says or does. And there will always be left-wing judges; the judiciary is not something you can remake overnight, since there are thousands of judgeships, many of them granting lifetime tenure. (Remember the simple fact that Republicans have controlled the White House for all but twenty years of the past half century and we're *still* dealing with liberal judicial activism.)

So why do we keep trying to stuff the judicial activism genie back in the bottle? It's never going to work, and it's absurd to think it will work if only we keep pushing. Conservatives should take a new tack. Let's ask the genie of judicial activism to grant us some wishes— because the Left will sure as heck keep asking the genie for wishes.

It calls to mind an old lawyer joke. Three people from the same law firm—a paralegal, an associate, and a partner—are walking to lunch when they discover a magic lamp. They rub it and out comes a genie, who agrees to grant each of them one wish.

The paralegal goes first and says, "I want to live in a beautiful home on the beach in the Bahamas and never have to work again." *Poof.* Done.

So the associate excitedly asks for his wish: "I want to be in Hawaii with millions of dollars and the most beautiful woman in the world and never have to work again." *Poof.* Done.

Finally it's the partner's turn. He thinks for a moment, then looks at the genie and says, "I want those two back at their desks after lunch."

When it comes to the courts, the Left is like the partner—it will always win out. No matter what political gains conservatives make at the ballot box or otherwise, unless those gains are protected and even advanced in the courts, liberals can simply use their judges to undo the Right's accomplishments. All the conservative efforts toward judicial restraint and depoliticizing judges—even if effective in the short term— will be useless in the end.

Fortunately, conservative judicial activism can help us defeat the Left.

FORCING LIBERALS TO DEFEND THEIR PREVIOUSLY WON TURF

ANOTHER ADVANTAGE OF CONSERVATIVE judicial activism is that it forces liberals to defend turf they think they've already won. If left-wingers are forced into court to deal with these cases, they will have fewer resources to devote to new causes. For instance, this strategy could apply to the death penalty. The Right could challenge the Supreme Court's 1977 ruling that said a rapist who did not kill his victim cannot under any circumstances be executed. "Rape," the Court explained, "is without doubt deserving of serious punishment; but in terms of moral depravity and of the injury to the person and to the public, it does not compare with murder, which does involve the unjustified taking of human life."[9] This decision was not unanimous then; why should it be considered sacrosanct now? Raising questions about the ruling would certainly keep the Left busy fighting on a new front. Likewise, remember the fight for congressional term limits? For the line-item veto? The Supreme Court struck down both. Haven't heard about either notion since, have we? Why is that? Because these were conservative-oriented reforms, and once we conservatives lost them in the courts, we simply walked away licking our wounds. Big mistake.

In contrast, the Left will sue the very next day after losing a case. Look at how liberals, in their war against the Boy Scouts, lost one Supreme Court case in *Boy Scouts of America v. Dale* (2000), only to immediately initiate a bunch of new lawsuits attacking the Boy Scouts on new grounds.[10] Today, despite its big win in 2000, the Boy Scouts continues to be under siege by the Left.

PRACTICING CONSERVATIVE JUDICIAL ACTIVISM *IS* FOLLOWING THE RULE OF LAW

SHOULD CONSERVATIVES DISCARD THEIR concern for the rule of law and legal precedent only because liberals have trampled all over stare decisis? What can a conservative say when accused of going to the dark side by advocating conservative judicial activism? Is this a matter of sinking to the Left's level? No.

There are quite legitimate legal and historical reasons for embracing conservative judicial activism. The Supreme Court's dismissal of stare decisis in *Lawrence v. Texas* may have been a rationalization for a favored outcome, but the Court's general point is valid: precedent is just one factor to consider in the law. The fact remains that the U.S. Supreme Court had overruled literally hundreds of its prior decisions.[11] So much for precedent!

We can talk about the evils of judicial activism in the abstract all we want, but bear in mind that courts make law all the time. And when it comes down to it, sometimes the courts *should* change the law. Who would claim, for instance, that *Plessy v. Ferguson,* which upheld racial segregation in schools in 1896, should still be the law of the land? As Duke law professors Erwin Chemerinsky and Catherine Fisk have written, the Supreme Court undoubtedly made the law by overruling *Plessy* in the landmark decision *Brown v. Board of Education* in 1954. Chemerinsky and Fisk also point out that the court was "making" the law more than sixty years ago by ruling unconstitutional "an Oklahoma law that required the sterilization of anyone convicted twice of a felony involving moral turpitude."[12]

Conservative columnist George Will put it well when he wrote, "Conservatives should be reminded to be careful what they wish for. Their often-reflexive rhetoric praises 'judicial restraint' and deference to—it sometimes seems—almost unleashable powers of the elected branches of governments." But as the *Kelo v. New London* (2005) decision eviscerating property rights showed, he said, "conservatives who dogmatically preach a populist creed of deference to majoritarianism will thereby abandon, or at least radically restrict, the judiciary's indispensable role in limiting government."[13]

As Will suggests, we do not always want courts deferring to popularly elected bodies, because the results can be harmful. Why should the Right preach judicial restraint regarding laws restricting gun, property, or economic rights? Activist courts can prevent the teaching of deviant sex to young children in public schools.[14] And they can strike down affirmative action laws elevating racial minorities and women above whites and men just because, well, they are minorities and women.

Okay, but what about conservative respect for the Founders? Does conservative judicial activism fly in the face of that? Again, the answer is no. Remember, we too often err by confusing the mechanisms of government with the rights and freedoms that the Framers designed those mechanisms to protect. In any case, the Founders designed the courts as an antimajoritarian check on popularly enacted laws that violate fundamental or "unalienable" individual rights. Conservative judicial activism will ensure that the courts fulfill this purpose. Today, U.S. courts uphold all kinds of laws that violate fundamental American rights, such as statutes permitting unduly burdensome gun control laws and economic regulations. Simultaneously they strike down laws regulating those behaviors liberals defend and even embrace; think about any "right" starting from the belt down. Modern courts create from whole cloth "rights" found nowhere in the Constitution based on politically expedient writings of twentieth-century academics who frequented the salons of Cambridge and Georgetown. Conservative judicial activism would help remedy this historical imbalance.

Courts are designed to play such an active role. While conservatives are rightly aghast that liberal judges have issued decisions changing society for the worse, we would do well to recall what could happen without a robust court system in place. If a strong judiciary is not there to help prevent the government's infringing on our rights, a constitution can be nothing more than a parchment barrier. Look at what happened in the Soviet Union. Like the United States, the Soviets actually had a written constitution that was designed to provide citizens with many rights and legal protections. In reality it provided nothing. Why? Because no institution existed in the Soviet Union that was ready, willing, and able to give teeth to their constitution.

Despite what many conservatives think, there are steps we can take to reshape the courts and the law in order to protect fundamental American rights and values. Sure, it's troubling that the system is now far removed from what the Framers envisioned. But does that mean we must throw up our hands and scream, "We give up! We can't go on without the Framers' guidance"? Certainly not. We can still support the ideals, freedoms, and values the Framers defended. Free markets, the right to realistic self-defense, the right to life—conservatives stand for all these and other principles. The Right should not only fight for these principles in the courts—it should use the Courts as allies in the fight.

THE BEST WE'VE GOT

WHILE CONSERVATIVE JUDICIAL ACTIVISM may not be the perfect judicial philosophy, it is the best conservatives, and the nation as a whole, can hope for. Winston Churchill once said, "No one pretends that democracy is perfect or all-wise. Indeed, it has been said that democracy is the worst form of Government except all those other forms that have been tried." The same holds for conservative judicial activism; it may not be "perfect or all-wise," but in today's world it's the best we've got. Let's start using it.

SIX

LEARNING TO LOVE
THE LIVING CONSTITUTION

How to Hoist Liberals on Their Own Petard

If you live in the past, you die in the present.
—BILL BELICHICK, HEAD COACH,
NEW ENGLAND PATRIOTS

Perhaps, you might say, times are changing and an aggressive conservative pushback in the courts is unnecessary. After all, haven't liberals figured out that we need judicial restraint? They're starting to defend restraint now and say we should respect precedent. Actually, they say, *We'll do you one better—we respect* super*precedents.*

But don't be fooled. When liberals talk about judicial restraint and superprecedent and such, they simply want to make certain that *their* favorite decisions remain "settled law." Over the past seventy years liberal judges have ruled on a whole group of issues, and now the Left insists, self-servingly, *Sorry, there's no going back—these are firm precedents. Tough luck.*[1] This change of heart has little to do with a newfound respect for stare decisis, the constitutional text, the rule of law, or the compelling arguments of Robert Bork or Justice Scalia. No, liberals suddenly disavow judicial activism because they realize that their left-wing buddies may no longer be the only ones wearing the black robes and dictating policy. For the Left, the phrase *judicial restraint* is code for "biding our time until we can run rampant again."

We cannot be lulled into complacency or a false sense of security that a lasting era of bilateral judicial restraint is upon us. It's not. Nor can we allow the Left to permanently frame what the courts can and cannot rule on, and what kinds of laws legislatures can pass. As long as the Left gets to determine what's settled law, the Right is in trouble—indeed, the whole country is in trouble.

Liberals claim to stand for individual rights and freedom, for eliminating homelessness and poverty, for a clean environment and good schools. Those are admirable goals. The problem is, liberal solutions do not accomplish these goals. The twentieth century was the ultimate test of the liberal deployment of government; liberalism failed the test, as one disastrous program after another—and one misguided court decision after another—showed government to be not an agent of beneficial change but a necessary evil.

Why can't the courts recognize that the factual underpinnings of so many of their precedents were fatally flawed and reverse them? Why must these precedents be sacrosanct? If twentieth-century liberal courts undid so many legal precedents to try to achieve their goals, why can't conservative courts do the same to liberal precedents from the past seventy years?

The answer is: There's no reason they can't.

Exactly how do we do it, though? Picking up the weapon of judicial activism is, as we've seen, the first step. But it's a two-step process. And at first glance, the next step—embracing another liberal tactic— might seem as repugnant to conservatives as the first, maybe even more so.

We must learn to love the living Constitution.

The living Constitution? The idea that the Constitution is a living and breathing document that must evolve over time to keep up with modern society? Isn't this the thing that sends conservatives into fits of anger or forces us to recoil in horror? Yup. But accepting it as reality is absolutely essential. In fact, it's the best way to win back the judiciary, repel the liberal assault, and turn the courts into instruments with which we advance the American way of life.

RIGHT ON, JUSTICE BRENNAN! YOU THE MAN!

LIBERALS TALK ABOUT THE living Constitution all the time. During the 2000 presidential campaign, for example, Al Gore promised to appoint judges who understand that "our Constitution is a living and breathing document, that it was intended by our Founders to be interpreted in the light of the constantly evolving experience of the American people."[2]

Judges certainly embrace the notion of a Constitution that evolves

as society does and as society's needs change. In a 2005 speech, Supreme
Court justice Antonin Scalia lamented, "We are in the era of the evolving Constitution. And the judge can simply say, 'Oh yes, the Constitution didn't used to mean that, but it does now.' We are in the age in
which not only judges, not only lawyers, but even schoolchildren have
come to learn the Constitution changes. I have grammar school students come into the Court now and then, and they recite very proudly
what they have been taught: 'The Constitution is a living document.'
You know, it morphs."[3]

Even Scalia's Supreme Court colleagues are now reciting the mantra.
In 2003, the Court stated, "Had those who drew and ratified the Due
Process Clauses of the Fifth Amendment or the Fourteenth Amendment
known the components of liberty in its manifold possibilities, they
might have been more specific. They did not presume to have this in-
sight. They knew times can blind us to certain truths and later generations can see that laws once thought necessary and proper in fact serve
only to oppress. As the Constitution endures, persons in every generation can invoke its principles in their own search for greater freedom."[4]
This from a Supreme Court the Left tells us is conservative.[5]

Justice Scalia isn't the only conservative to rail against the living
Constitution. Conservative economist Walter Williams, for instance,
has written, "Saying that the Constitution is a living document is the
same as saying we don't have a Constitution. For rules to mean anything, they must be fixed. How many people would like to play me [in]
poker and have the rules be 'living'? Depending on 'evolving standards,' maybe my two pair could beat your flush."[6] Similarly, *National
Review*'s Jonah Goldberg has argued, "A Constitution which changes
with the times will inevitably mean that the Constitution only means
whatever a handful of 'robed masters' say it means at any given time."[7]

Of course, long before the "conservative" Supreme Court came
around to the notion of changing societal standards in gay rights, affirmative action, criminal justice, the death penalty, and other cases, liberals had embraced the idea of the living Constitution. For example, in a
1977 decision, Justice Thurgood Marshall wrote that " 'traditional notions of fair play and substantial justice' can be as readily offended by
the perpetuation of ancient forms that are no longer justified as by the
adoption of new procedures that are inconsistent with the basic values
of our constitutional heritage."[8] In a tribute to Marshall, Janet Reno,

President Clinton's attorney general, praised the justice's "sense of the law as functional and evolving" and as "a living instrument in the service of a living people."[9]

The late Justice William Brennan, another liberal icon, was an outspoken defender of the living Constitution. Brennan once said, "The genius of the Constitution rests not in any static meaning it might have had in a world that is dead and gone, but in the adaptability of its great principles to cope with current problems and current needs."[10]

Justice Scalia would grimace at such a proclamation. In his 2005 speech he went so far as to say that the idea of the living Constitution "will destroy the Constitution." Maybe—but it's too late now. As much as I respect Justice Scalia, I have to say that the Right must embrace Brennan on this one. In fact, I say: Hear, hear, Justice Brennan! Conservatives should heed his advice and embrace the living Constitution.

I hasten to add that I have not become a touchy-feely liberal, booked tickets to Sundance, or begun to think we should "destroy the Constitution." Far from it. My interest, in fact, is in *preserving* the rights, freedoms, and ideals that the Constitution was written to protect and that the Founders held—and modern conservatives hold—dear. The Right should support the concept of a living Constitution not because it is intrinsically good or platonically correct but because it will work best to advance the American way of life on the modern legal battlefield. As always, we must play the hand we've been dealt.

The hand we've been dealt, of course, is this: a legal system that has been almost completely redefined by seventy years of liberal precedents. Judges have repeatedly tossed aside the "dead" Constitution to achieve policy results favored by liberal elites: inventing certain unenumerated "rights" while ignoring whole sections of the Constitution with which they don't happen to agree.

Judges must adjust their vision of a just society away from the Left's failed utopian vision and back toward what the Founders had in mind: limited government, free markets, classically defined individual rights, and so forth. We have the tools to undo the Left's work and restore the American ideal as envisioned by the Framers. Conservatives merely need to force liberals to live by the axioms and precedents they brought into the world.

That's where Justice Brennan's eloquent tribute to the living Constitution comes in. Brennan and many of his liberal judicial colleagues have passed on, but the precedents they established live with us still. Embracing the living Constitution, in addition to picking up the weapon of conservative judicial activism, is the way to turn these liberal precedents against the Left.

ROLL CALL: ALL DEAD WHITE GUYS
PRESENT AND ACCOUNTED FOR

COMPLEMENTING THE LIBERAL CAMPAIGN for the living Constitution has been the Left's forceful declarations that modern-day Americans must not follow all the dictates of a bunch of dead white men. For instance, the late Supreme Court justice Thurgood Marshall stated, "I do not believe that the meaning of the Constitution was forever 'fixed' at the Philadelphia Convention. . . . Nor do I find the wisdom, foresight, and sense of justice exhibited by the framers particularly profound."[11] The Left tells us we should not be ruled from the grave by eighteenth-century Framers such as the following:

Thomas Jefferson, *dead white male*

James Madison, *dead white male*

John Adams, *dead white male*

Alexander Hamilton, *dead white male*

George Washington, *dead white male*

Patrick Henry, *dead white male*

All right, then, we'll allow the Left to have its way. Let's agree that modern Americans have no duty to follow the lead of dead white men and the laws they left with us. So whom else does that rule out? Let's see . . . how about the following liberal Supreme Court justices?

Earl Warren, *dead white male*

Harry Blackmun, *dead white male*

William Brennan, *dead white male*

Hugo Black, *dead white male*

William Douglas, *dead white male*

Felix Frankfurter, *dead white male*

Get the picture? If, as liberals say, the dead white men who founded the greatest nation in history and wrote the Constitution aren't worthy of deference, then we shouldn't give a hoot about the views of these other dead white men who, as twentieth-century Supreme Court justices, merely *interpreted* the Constitution. And these guys are only a few of the now-dead twentieth-century liberal icons who fundamentally altered American law from their perches on the courts. Just as liberal justices of the twentieth century refused to be bound by the Constitution and laws enacted by eighteenth-century dead white men, twenty-first-century Americans, including twenty-first-century judges, shouldn't be ruled from the grave by dead white men from the twentieth century.

A CONSERVATIVE IN LIBERAL CLOTHING

ADOPTING THE LEFT'S VIEW that the Constitution is a "living" or "evolving" organism will help the Right overturn liberal legal precedents. Of course, liberals will probably change their tune about the living Constitution when they're suddenly being harmed by it. So we conservatives will need to adjust our tactics accordingly.

Although conservatives recognize that we are at war with liberals over the courts, head-on confrontation is not always the best approach. Recall left-wing radical Saul Alinsky's instruction that the best way to effect social change is to work within the system. If you want to change a Hasidic Jewish community, for example, you don't invite people over for bacon cheeseburgers; you try to blend in by serving kosher. Now, to change today's legal system, conservatives need to blend into the modern-day legal community. The best way to do that is not necessarily to spout originalist doctrine or quote the *Federalist Papers,* Thomas Jefferson, or William Blackstone's *Commentaries.* Better to appeal to the sources the Left appreciates: Brennan and those other dead white men whom liberals admire, contemporary liberal legal precedents, and "progressive" legal decisions in foreign countries.

Citing existing liberal precedents and judicial philosophies to achieve conservative results is just smart tactics. Any lawyer will tell you that his job is to put forward the most convincing case possible on behalf of his client. And legal advocates today must appeal to judges who are immersed in a modern legal culture that reflects decades of liberal precedents, not to mention almost constant liberal indoctrination. Too many of our nation's legal elites are apt to respond to a reference to Blackstone's *Commentaries* with a "Who?" or a "So?" while responding with an "Oh yeah!" to a reference to recent liberal legal scholarship. Bear in mind that no professor subscribing to an originalist legal philosophy even teaches at Harvard Law School. Wouldn't it be more effective to argue a contemporary legal case by relying on precedents established in *Roe* or *Planned Parenthood v. Casey* rather than the writings of John Locke? Of course it would.

Advocates who take a contrary approach, citing the Founders and conservative scholars such as Richard Epstein and Robert Bork, risk turning off, or being tuned out by, judges and other legal elites. This doesn't help us. Conservatives need to win in the courts, and we have a much better shot at doing so by embracing the living Constitution and other legal approaches proven to be so successful for the Left.

The reliance on foreign legal precedents as a mode of argument is something else to which conservatives should adjust. In truth, Americans should be concerned about, if not appalled by, the way foreign precedents now influence our legal system. I think the United Nations and international law have as much credibility as a James Frey memoir. But conservatives should cite foreign precedents if doing so helps them win. Attorneys appearing before any court, including the Supreme Court, should adapt to the personalities of the judges, and some judges now take foreign precedents into account. Would adapting to the courts in this manner turn a conservative advocate into a squishy Europhile ready to eat snails and pander to Jacques Chirac? Would it constitute an attempt to subvert American sovereignty to the bureaucrats of the European Union or to a bunch of bratty, fair-trade coffee-swilling NGO do-gooders? Hardly. It would just make the Right more apt to win in court. And remember, winning the war beats just winning a battle.

THE LIVING CONSTITUTION DODGES TYPICAL
LEFT-WING RHETORICAL ASSAULTS

EMBRACING THE LIVING CONSTITUTION would have the added benefit of deflecting the Left's frequent rhetorical attacks on such doctrines as originalism and strict constructionism. In modern political discourse, in which people such as Jesse Jackson and Al Sharpton seem to matter, the shortcomings attributed to the Constitution's Framers serve as a rhetorical mallet with which liberals can bash conservatives. To critics of originalism, all that matters is that the Constitution was written by white men, permitted slavery, and did not compel women's suffrage. Senator Edward Kennedy launched the most famous attack on originalism when he said that Reagan Supreme Court nominee Robert Bork would support an America "in which women would be forced into back-alley abortions, blacks would sit at segregated lunch counters, rogue police could break down citizens' doors in midnight raids, schoolchildren could not be taught about evolution, writers and artists could be censored at the whim of government, and the doors of the federal courts would be shut on the fingers of millions of citizens for whom the judiciary is—and is often the only—protector of the individual rights that are at the heart of our democracy." It didn't matter that Kennedy was completely misrepresenting Bork's originalist philosophy; the speech proved to be a powerful and successful political indictment of Bork.

That kind of rhetoric still works. So at a time when politicians always talk about moving forward and not backward, conservatives fighting legal battles should follow liberals' lead and build a bridge to the twenty-first century, not one back to the eighteenth century.

WE HAVE ROPE, TOO

TO SOME IT MIGHT seem odd that in this putatively conservative era, when Republicans have achieved so much success, I'm still talking about using the Left's tactics. Shouldn't those be consigned to the dustbin of history? After all, as Justice David Souter said at the funeral of William Brennan, "The life of the man is over; so is the liberal era when Justice Brennan's voice was the voice of the Supreme Court."[12] The liberal era is over! Let's move on! Right?

Well, except this: With all the legal precedents on the books, liberals have sown the seeds of their own destruction. This is the beauty of using their tactics against them. In the end, they can't really complain about conservatives using this new approach to force a rightward shift in the law. Why? Because the approach requires conservatives to admit that the Left was correct all along! Judicial activism *is* necessary, we concede; we *should* embrace the living Constitution. Maybe "they the unelected judges" do sometimes know more than "we the people." Let's forget those stuffy old dead white guys who didn't abolish slavery. Let's not be ruled from the grave.

Shouldn't liberals be pleased that we're finally conceding the wisdom of liberal law professors? They should be most pleased with our heeding Justice Brennan's advice to embrace the Constitution's "adaptability" for any "current problems and current needs."

Again, it's all about working inside the system. For all the conservative advances in the legislative and executive branches of government, the judiciary remains stubbornly resistant to change. Conservatives are the ones who must change and adapt to survive—in the courts and for the good of the nation. The Right will never achieve real reform merely by criticizing the courts, proposing to limit their jurisdiction, railing against judicial activism, or threatening to impeach activist judges (an essentially empty threat, given that only eleven judges have been impeached in American history). By adjusting the battle plan, conservatives can win in the courts, stop the advance of the Left's political agenda, and promote the conservative cause.

There's a story (perhaps apocryphal) from the Revolutionary War about an American soldier who was asked whether he feared that the British redcoats would hang for treason against the Crown all the American troops they caught. As the story goes, the soldier replied that he wasn't worried. Why? Because, he said, "we have rope, too."

This is why conservatives must alter their entire approach to the courts. The Left must be made to understand that the Right has the rope of judicial activism, too—and is not afraid to use it. Such a radical switch in tactics offers the best hope of thwarting liberal judicial activism. If conservatives continue to take a passive approach of calling for judicial restraint and denying the living Constitution, liberals will never have to pay the price for their activism. As soon as they can, they will reengage in liberal judicial activism.

Liberals are now fighting to make sure liberal precedents stay "settled law" because they do not want to lose any ground they gained over the past several decades. But they should not be surprised if their ideology wanes while the Right's ideology rises. As Hillary's mentor, Saul Alinsky, explained, "History is a relay of revolutions; the torch of idealism is carried by the revolutionary group until this group becomes an establishment, and then quietly the torch is put down to wait until a new revolutionary group picks it up for the next leg of the run. Thus the revolutionary cycle goes on."[13]

In this context it's conservatives who are the new revolutionaries. Since the election of Ronald Reagan in 1980, the nation has undergone a conservative renaissance. For example, the American people are finally coming to understand that the liberal revolution of expanding government has not worked—indeed, has been a disaster. The United States ran an experiment with progressivism and the experiment failed. Fortunately we didn't go as far as much of the rest of the world: Communism and socialism destroyed the Soviet Union, Africa, India (before the tech boom), and Eastern Europe, and now Western Europe is ravaged by double-digit unemployment rates and slow- or no-growth economies. But we did have the New Deal, which was enacted in response to the economic emergency of the Great Depression, at a time before we had the economic data to understand that massive government intervention only *hurts* the economy. We also had, and are still coping with, the Great Society's incredible government growth and activism.

We have an obligation not to repeat these disasters. We need to scale back all kinds of regulations and laws, many of which were imposed before we had a polio vaccine or television. And of course free markets are just one of many principles conservatives are fighting for, and on which history is on our side. Like it or not, much of the fight over these hot-button issues will be waged in the courts. So let's learn how to win—in the courts and beyond.

PART III

HERE COMES THE JUDGE!

SEVEN

DESPERATELY SEEKING JUDICIAL REAGANS

A New Model for Judging Judges

What's the most important element in the fight to reclaim the courts? That's easy: judges.

Republican presidents have had decades to put their stamp on the judiciary. Unfortunately, far too often the judges they picked morphed into liberal judicial activists. Let's go to the videotape:

Supreme Court Justice	Known For	Nominated By
Earl Warren	As chief justice, led revolution in favor of criminal rights and engaged in all sorts of loony liberal judicial activism	Dwight D. Eisenhower, Republican
William Brennan	Supported *Roe v. Wade;* thought the Constitution should evolve leftward	Dwight D. Eisenhower, Republican
Harry Blackmun	Author of *Roe v. Wade;* concluded that the death penalty was always unconstitutional	Richard M. Nixon, Republican
John Paul Stevens	Reliable liberal vote on issues such as abortion, the death penalty, and eminent domain	Gerald Ford, Republican

Supreme Court Justice	Known For	Nominated By
Sandra Day O'Connor	Upheld affirmative action and the "right" to abortion	Ronald Reagan, Republican
Anthony Kennedy	Upheld the "right" to abortion; author of *Lawrence v. Texas,* which forbids laws banning same-sex sodomy	Ronald Reagan, Republican
David Souter	Upheld affirmative action and the "right" to abortion; opposed halting the recounts in Florida in 2000 presidential election	George H. W. Bush, Republican

Get the idea? Recall the saying "with friends like these, who needs enemies"?

With this record, it's obvious that the Right needs to improve its ability to select judges. The improvement must begin immediately.

Why do Republican presidents have such a spotty record picking judges? In large part it's because conservatives have focused so much on what we *don't* want in a judge that we've forgotten to emphasize what we really *do* want.

So what exactly makes a good conservative judge?

Lots of conservatives think it's a simple answer. Usually they regurgitate the same Republican talking points we've heard for years: how we need judges who "faithfully interpret the law," who "follow the rule of law," who are "strict constructionists," who "won't legislate from the bench," even who "are in the mold of Justices Scalia and Thomas." Some might say we want "a conservative in the traditional sense of the word . . . a distinguished jurist who believes in moderation, judicial restraint, and deference to Congress."[1] But as we've seen, such breezy statements are absurdly vague and offer little real guidance to those picking judges, let alone to the judges themselves when they confront actual cases.

Think about it: What do phrases such as "strict constructionist" and "in the mold of Scalia and Thomas" mean to the millions of Americans who have never read a legal opinion or gone to law school but who are instinctively—and correctly—worried about the state of the courts? Virtually nothing. Yet these ambiguous phrases have become the terms of debate whenever conservatives talk about the courts. It's not just legal scholars and political analysts using these terms. Our favorite conservative columnists and talk-radio hosts bandy these phrases about as well. And so, sure enough, do regular Americans.

This ambiguity is a huge problem for the Right. Conservatives have encountered so much difficulty placing good right-wing judges on the bench in part because they don't ask for the right folks. Indeed, conservatives don't even know *what* to ask for.

Why on earth are we getting caught up in legal jargon—jargon that, it should be noted, doesn't even reflect the legal system as it really operates today? Do we truly expect—or want—all Americans to be able to discuss the merits of, say, a structural approach to constitutional interpretation versus a textual approach, or argue that the Supreme Court should address abortion based on the Fourteenth Amendment's privileges and immunities clause rather than the Ninth Amendment's substantive due process clause, or extensively cite Antonin Scalia's legal opinions to explain why his jurisprudence is better reasoned than Ruth Bader Ginsburg's?

No! Of course not! This is all inside baseball for law nerds.

But the court issue and the Right's concerns about the direction of American law are not issues only for law nerds. These are critical political, social, and economic issues for all Americans, including those who never attended law school and who will never set foot in a courthouse.

So how should ordinary conservatives and Americans discuss the courts? It's really quite simple. We must say what we mean, and mean what we say. The Right must stop beating around the bush about the courts. We'll never get what we want if we don't ask for it directly, so we should just come out and say what we mean. At best, phrases such as "judicial restraint," "strict constructionism," and "originalism" are, in effect, shorthand—code words for the judicial outcomes the Right favors. Conservatives want the courts to protect the values and principles described in the Declaration of Independence and the rights found in the Constitution. Why should conservatives speak in code when all we have to say is "I want a judge who will stand up for my rights to property, to bear arms, to contract; uphold the death penalty; and defend the lives of the unborn"?

As liberals learned long ago, the most important thing about a judge is not the interpretative approach he uses but rather the decisions he reaches and the real-world effects of those decisions. The Left embraced the living Constitution not because this was the perfect method of interpreting the Constitution but because doing so allowed judges to provide a legal rationale for the desired policy result. It doesn't make much difference to liberals how judges achieve those results.

Look at *Roe v. Wade,* which plenty of pro-abortion liberals acknowledge is a poorly reasoned legal decision. Jeffrey Rosen, legal affairs editor of the *New Republic,* explained that "this pro-choice magazine was correct in 1973 when it criticized *Roe* on constitutional grounds."[2] Professor Laurence Tribe of Harvard Law School observed that "behind its own verbal smokescreen, the substantive judgment on which [*Roe*] rests is nowhere to be found."[3] Edward Lazarus, noted author and former law clerk to Justice Harry Blackmun, the author of *Roe,* argued, "As a matter of constitutional interpretation and judicial method, *Roe* borders on the indefensible. I say this as someone utterly committed to the right to choose, as someone who believes such a right has grounding elsewhere in the Constitution instead of where *Roe* placed it, and as someone who loved *Roe*'s author like a grandfather."[4] And before she became a Supreme Court justice, Ruth Bader Ginsburg argued that *Roe* "halted a political process that was moving in a reform direction and thereby, I believe, prolonged divisiveness and deferred stable settlement of the issue."[5] Yet is there any doubt that Ginsburg—or any other liberal critic of *Roe*—would reaffirm the right to abortion if given the chance? Exactly which abortion advocates are urging the Supreme Court to revisit *Roe* because of the decision's flawed legal reasoning? All the Left cares about is that abortion remain legal. The legal rationale upon which *Roe* rests matters little.

To be honest, we can't really fault the Left for this mind-set. Let's look in the mirror. It's hard to imagine that pro-lifers go to bed praying that above all else the text of the Constitution be honored; it's much more likely that they are praying for abortion to be outlawed to spare the unborn from an unjust death. Similarly, members of the National Rifle Association want courts to vigorously defend their right to buy, own, and carry guns; whether judges do so on the basis of the Second

Amendment or an unenumerated right to self-defense is mostly immaterial. It is certainly immaterial to the woman who thwarts a rapist because she carries a gun legally, thanks to a court's pro-gun ruling. Neither the woman nor the rapist cares about the legal rationale articulated in some judge's opinion; they just care that she has the right to carry a gun. The real-world result matters far more than the interpretative method a judge used to reach the result. The Left gets this.

Consequently, members of the vast right-wing conspiracy need to take a radically different approach to picking judges. We need to learn a whole new vocabulary for talking about the kinds of people we want on the bench. This goes for individuals at all levels of the conservative movement: for the president of the United States, who must decide which people to nominate to the federal bench; for U.S. senators, who must to decide whether to vote for or against confirming judges; and, yes, for ordinary citizens, who not only must make their priorities known to politicians but who also can vote their priorities when casting ballots for judges in state and local elections.

We need to demystify the entire process of picking good judges, to disentangle it from outmoded, ambiguous legal jargon. Fortunately, it's easy to do so.

Conservatives need a bold new model. We need "Judicial Reagans."

WHAT IS A JUDICIAL REAGAN?

RONALD REAGAN, A HERO to conservatives and a president whose significant achievements even liberal observers are coming to acknowledge, excelled as a leader in large measure because he made crystal clear what he stood for: limited government, individual freedom, low taxes, free markets, a strong national defense, the right to life, and traditional families. Agree or disagree with Reagan, he at least made it clear where he stood.

The values Reagan fought for from the Oval Office are precisely the things we need judges to defend from the bench. In sharp contrast to inscrutable phrases such as "judicial restraint" and "strict constructionism," the values Reagan stood for represent clear goals that ordinary Americans can understand and support.

A Judicial Reagan, then, will defend and honor an entire set of conservative beliefs about the roles of free markets, family, and government in American life. Such a judge will, in short, be a proud and committed conservative above all else. This might seem like a puzzling qualification for someone who occupies a supposedly apolitical position. But don't forget that a judgeship is anything but apolitical. Indeed, we must think of judges as politicians in black robes. They have become the terminal legislative body and must be treated as such.

Thus we need judges who have the right values and beliefs, just as we want legislators and presidents who champion our values and beliefs. And we should learn about prospective judges' values and beliefs *before* they don black robes and are given almost unlimited power to direct the law. Our priority cannot be confirming judges who buy into mostly meaningless platitudes about "respecting the rule of law" and "abiding by the Constitution"; it should be confirming judges who recognize the importance of advancing the conservative cause, which naturally encompasses the nation's fundamental ideals and freedoms, and the American way of life. When we select legislators and presidents, we demand to know where they stand on major issues; we should expect nothing less of judges, who also profoundly affect virtually every major policy dispute in contemporary America.

A strong-willed Judicial Reagan would defend core principles rather than the elite opinion of the *Washington Post* and the *New York Times*. He would not only love America but also recognize that this nation is the greatest nation ever to exist; understand that evil exists and must be fought domestically and internationally; appreciate the importance of a strong military and thriving free markets; be skeptical of government interference in the economy; and accept that the best way to resolve many moral and social issues is on a community-by-community basis rather than by nationwide judicial fiat. If a town in Tennessee puts up a crèche in a public park at Christmas while New Yorkers subsidize a dung-covered Madonna or Robert Mapplethorpe's homoerotic art, then (if I may quote the Left) "live and let live." A Judicial Reagan would recognize that government is a necessary evil—not an agent for positive social good, as the Left thinks.

Following the Reagan model, conservative judges must aim to *win*. Just as President Reagan challenged the status quo and reversed the country's path toward socialism, recession, and failed foreign policies, we need judges with the backbone to aggressively challenge the status quo and attack many of the current assumptions that characterize our legal system. A Judicial Reagan would not be content merely to thwart ongoing liberal legal machinations but would also work to undo "well-established" liberal precedents, pushing the law back to the right. His goal would be to make the law more consistent with the Founders' vision of limited government—to paraphrase Cato Institute scholar Roger Pilon, a nation of individual liberty with islands of government power and not a sea of government power with small islands of liberty.[6] A Judicial Reagan would never forget that the presumption in the law is (or should be) toward individual freedom and not toward more government.

Is the notion of a Judicial Reagan a radical one? Maybe, but so what? In the 1970s most political commentators considered Ronald Reagan too radical to get elected president. What they missed was that Reagan's adherence to principles drew more and more Americans to the conservative movement. By standing firm on principle and emphasizing results over good intentions, the president won the hearts and minds of the American people. Judicial Reagans would likewise attract admirers by boldly articulating and defending core principles.

Seeking to appoint Judicial Reagans who will attempt to revolutionize the law to the right is consistent with how famous, respected judges become famous and respected in the first place. As federal trial judge James Zagel and attorney Adam Winkler explain, "The famous jurists of American history . . . tended to challenge the accepted standards of the law—and ultimately reinvent those standards and establish new ones."[7] So too would a Judicial Reagan "challenge the accepted standards of the law" and work to "reinvent those standards and establish new ones."

And why not challenge the existing standards of law? As Judicial Reagans would recognize, deciding cases correctly is far more important than respecting the "time-honored traditions of the Court" and the like. Conservatives need judges who are clearly critical of the status quo, not go-along-to-get-along milquetoasts (think Reagan over Ford, George W. Bush over George H. W. Bush, Winston Churchill over Neville Chamberlain). As Professor Paul Gewirtz of Yale Law School told the *New York Times,* candidates for the Supreme Court who "self-identify as critics of the court" probably won't be changed by the experience of serving as justices—that is, they won't "evolve" to the left.[8] On the other hand, "those who feel themselves connected to the basic trajectory of American law remain open to observing changes in society." With the current leftward trajectory of American law, conservatives can't afford judges who remain so "open." We need outspoken critics such as Robert Bork, who has condemned the Supreme Court for its "lethal" combination of "absolute power, disdain for the historic Constitution, and philosophical incompetence."[9]

If the Supreme Court makes a wrong decision, it's silly to suggest that fixing the decision would make the court appear illegitimate in the eyes of the public. Would it make sense to uphold *Dred Scott* or *Plessy v. Ferguson* in order to protect the "good name" of the court? Besides, as noted, the Supreme Court changes its mind quite often. To take a notable example, in the same-sex sodomy case *Lawrence v. Texas* the Court had no qualms about shifting course from its 1986 decision in *Bowers v. Hardwick*. What are we worried about, embarrassing the judges who issued decisions? If so, *Roe v. Wade* is now fair game, since none of the nine judges who ruled on that case is alive today to be embarrassed (though some rolling over in their grave is distinctly possible).

With so much liberal precedent fair game and with conservatism on the ascendancy in America, conservative judges need not apologize for their values or their judicial rulings. President Reagan made clear, declaratory statements that were unapologetically conservative, and he stood firmly by his beliefs. Judicial Reagans would do the same. They should be savvy, principled individuals unafraid to be seen as card-carrying members of the conservative movement. I am not talking about inside-the-Beltway, "moderate Republican," establishment types; we need judges who, as Reagan did, understand and connect with Red State America. Judge Bork is right that judges write into law the values they have absorbed; that's why future judges should be movement conservatives rather than establishment Republicans. They should be able to tell you about the last book they bought from the Conservative Book Club, their favorite Fox News Channel show, and the last *Rush Limbaugh Show* they heard (and quoting from *South Park* or *The Family Guy*'s Stewie would also be a plus). If they start gushing about Nina Totenberg or *All Things Considered,* then, as Tony Soprano might say, "forget about it."

This is more than a question of political ideology—although conservative ideology is essential in any judge chosen. A Judicial Reagan would understand the experience of *ordinary Americans*. We don't want someone who thinks that the average American rows crew on the Charles River in Boston. If you put black robes on John Kerry, would that give him any new familiarity with ordinary Americans? Absolutely not. A few trips to Wendy's on the campaign trail—before scampering away to munch on quail eggs at a French bistro—just doesn't cut it.

The need to avoid picking liberals and squishy moderates should remind conservatives that we need not feel constrained to select only conservatives with Ivy League credentials; as we will see in Chapter 14, the elite law schools are liberal breeding grounds. William F. Buckley Jr. was absolutely right to suggest we'd be better off governed by the first two thousand people listed in the Boston phone book than by the Harvard faculty. Reagan was no Ivy Leaguer, and look what he did for the conservative movement and for the whole country. Of course, this is not to preclude the nomination of individuals well schooled at the Ivies. After all, Buckley, Clarence Thomas, Samuel Alito, and George W. Bush hold Yale degrees. (Heck, if you can spend so many years among the future liberal elites at these institutions and leave a staunch conservative, then you may be the right person for the job!)

OUR TEAM VS. THEIR TEAM

CLEARLY, THE JUDICIAL REAGAN model is a radical departure from the common conservative conception of a judge. But conservatives must disabuse themselves of the notion that selecting judges comes down to finding people who subscribe to the "right" mode of judicial interpretation. The real distinction is not right versus wrong; it's a matter of right versus *left*. In fact, thinking about good versus bad judges is almost a worthless framework if conservatives want to defeat the Left's legal assault. The big issue is picking judges on our team. Why? Because that's how the liberals do it, and they've been steamrolling us in the courts for decades.

Surprised to hear it put so bluntly? If so, that's a shame. It means too many conservatives have been fooled. For years liberals have used coded language to describe their judicial agenda, which is really a *political agenda*. They've been engaged in judicial activism all along and have been desperate to get "their guys" on the court. Look at how they smear any remotely conservative judge as an extremist but portray even the biggest lefty as "moderate" and part of the "mainstream." When President Bush picked John Roberts and Samuel Alito to be on the Supreme Court, Democrats predictably labeled them "extremists," "divisive," and "outside the mainstream." They even made Mrs. Alito cry. But at the same time liberals—and the mainstream media—call Ruth Bader Ginsburg a "moderate." For example, Yale's Paul Gerwitz suggested that "the spectrum of views on the court today represents a particular range, from ardent conservative to central or moderate liberal."[10]

Moderate? Should Ruth Bader Ginsburg be considered a moderate? How about "I report, you decide"? Before sitting on the Supreme Court, Ginsburg served for years as a top legal eagle for the ACLU. Is the ACLU a "moderate" organization well within the American mainstream? Was Ginsburg showing her true colors as a "moderate" when she penned the book *Sex Bias in the U.S. Code,* published by the U.S. Commission on Civil Rights, to help support the proposed Equal Rights Amendment? In that volume she

- Supported passage of the Equal Rights Amendment

- Called for the elimination of single-sex prisons

- Demanded the sexual integration of the Boy Scouts and Girl Scouts

- Questioned the propriety of Mother's Day and Father's Day as separate holidays

- Asserted that laws against bigamists are probably unconstitutional

- Called for permitting women to be drafted into the military for combat duty

- Objected to laws against prostitution, which she called "a consensual act between adults"[11]

Are these notions shared by most Americans? If Ginsburg can subscribe to these views and still be considered a mainstream moderate, then the definitional game being played here is out of whack. Or think about this: Justice William Douglas, who wrote the decision in *Griswold v. Connecticut* inventing the "right to privacy," is termed a "New

Dealer." The phrase "New Dealer" designates a political viewpoint and affiliation, not a judicial philosophy. Calling a liberal judge a "New Dealer" is akin to calling a conservative judge a "Reagan Republican" or a "free marketer." So why it is acceptable for liberals to label justices they admire as New Dealers and liberals, but not for conservative judges to be, well . . . conservatives?

We must get past the Left's misdirection and remember an elemental fact: All judges, without exception, will explain why their decision in a particular case is the result of an honest application of the law. Even when judges change the law they will assert that the alteration is completely consistent with the rule of law because the law evolves over time. And (this is important) they will honestly and earnestly believe what they are saying. For example, despite voting to uphold affirmative action and *Roe v. Wade* and to outlaw same-sex buggery, Justice Ginsburg has written, "Judges, however, are not political actors. They do not sit as representatives of particular persons, communities, or parties; they serve no faction or constituency. . . . They must strive to do what is legally right, all the more so when the result is not the one 'the home crowd' wants."[12] Sounds like a conservative, doesn't she? And that's the point: judicial activism, like art and beauty, is all too often in the eye of the beholder.

I do not share the view of many conservatives that liberal judges act disingenuously, nefariously, or dishonestly. The problem is more basic: They are liberals, and donning a black robe doesn't change that. Any guess as to whether Hillary Rodham Clinton or Jesse Jackson would change political views if confirmed to the Supreme Court? Sure, conservatives might be aghast at the tortured logic liberal judges employ to justify their decisions, and those decisions can be the subject of legitimate debate. But it's a debate that can rarely, if ever, be resolved definitively. In most cases liberal judges can construct a justification for their belief that they are following the law—after all, what are judicial opinions but the justification for judges' views? Clarence Thomas and William Brennan couldn't be more different in their outlook on the Constitution and justice, but they both took the same oath of office to uphold the Constitution. Really, it's no different from Ronald Reagan and Jimmy Carter taking the same oath of office; each man earnestly tried to make the world a better place and protect the nation, but they had different views on how to fulfill that duty.

Conservative judges can certainly make rulings with an eye toward protecting and even encouraging fundamental American values. To do so would be taking a cue from the Left. Liberal commentators, remember, have long given hosannas to their favorite judges by focusing on the effects or results of their decisions, not on how they reached those decisions. We've already seen how they heap praise on Justice Harry Blackmun for defending women's rights by authoring *Roe v. Wade,* and on Justice Thurgood Marshall for empathizing with the plight of every imaginable victim class. Justice William Brennan usually gets shout-outs for advancing free-speech rights. For instance, Jeffrey Rosen of the *New Republic* asserts that Justice Brennan "surely ranks among the most important defenders of free speech in the history of the Court."[13]

To the Left, the name of the game is *results.*

Wouldn't it be nice to see a Supreme Court justice praised as "one of the most important defenders of property rights, the freedom to engage in commercial transactions, the right to life, and the Second Amendment"? But no, conservatives talk about how a judge respects the Constitution, the Framers, the rule of law, and judicial restraint. This is all a bunch of legalese.

WE MUST STOP SPEAKING IN CODE

THE RIGHT MUST STOP speaking in code. We don't have that luxury if we hope to fundamentally alter American law. Liberals can content themselves with small, incremental changes to the law because of how far they have already moved American law to the left. Conservatives, in contrast, must reject timidity and seek judges who will advocate for very specific and bold legal outcomes. We want to get law back to the point where the courts actively work to ensure that the individual is in charge of his own life and where the government cannot insert itself into every crevice of our lives.

The thing is, conservatives don't *need* to speak in code. The conservative majority in this country favors the values and policies conservatives prioritize—even though the *New York Times* editorial page loves to portray conservative priorities as "extreme." Conservatives really are the mainstream in this country, which is why Republicans continue to control the White House, both houses of Congress, and the majority of the nation's governorships and state legislatures.

Liberals, however, need to speak in code if they are to have any hope of winning over the public. For instance, they must talk about "social justice" when they really mean socialism and Communism. They must defend "affirmative action" when they really mean racial discrimination. They must call themselves "pro-choice" activists when they really mean they approve of the murder of the unborn. They must suggest (as John Kerry's campaign did in 2004) that the United States is experiencing its "worst economy since the Great Depression" when in reality the economy isn't even in a recession.[14] And on and on it goes.

Conservatives do not need to speak in code. It's the Reagan model once again: Don't apologize for your principles. We need "our guys" issuing conservative judicial decisions, and we can't be afraid to say it.

HOW WOULD A JUDICIAL REAGAN ACT?

EVEN IF WE KNOW that we want judges who are committed conservatives and who aren't afraid to challenge the liberal legal establishment, the question remains how Judicial Reagans should act once they are on the bench. A Judicial Reagan would, first and foremost, be a pragmatic conservative. I'm not, I hasten to add, using the term *pragmatic* the way liberal admirers often described Justice Sandra Day O'Connor, who lacked a strong guiding conservative ideology. Instead, I mean a strong conservative holding strong conservative views, yet with a practical sense of how to undertake a conservative revolution in the courts one case, one decision, and one precedent at a time. This type of incrementalism is important. Time is needed to accomplish a judicial revolution. After all, liberals did not legalize abortion or gay marriage overnight; they slowly established precedents—from *Griswold v. Connecticut* (privacy) to *Roe v. Wade* (abortion) to *Romer v. Colorado* (laws granting gays special protection) to *Lawrence v. Texas* (same-sex sodomy a consensual right) to *Goodrich v. Massachusetts* (gay marriage)—to fundamentally change American law.

Chipping away pragmatically at liberal precedents requires an appreciation of the political and legal implications of any decision and consideration of public sentiment and the political climate. There is nothing wrong with a pragmatically minded judge provided that his ideology is solidly conservative. Pragmatism would lead to good decisions that appeal to common sense. As Reagan himself demonstrated, political shrewdness and ideological commitment need not be mutually exclusive.

Let conservative judges take one case at a time and slowly move the court and the country rightward. Rather than strike down the New Deal overnight, a Judicial Reagan would seek to revolutionize the courts case by case, precedent by precedent. Perhaps he would strike down new restrictive laws such as smoking bans in bars, which prevent free and voluntary exchange between consenting adults (sound like same-sex sodomy?), and then use those as precedents for greater change. In the long run, of course, the objective would be clear: protecting fundamental American rights and deconstructing the existing pro-big-government, pro-lawyer legal regime, which is so favorable to the liberal order but so inconsistent with the Constitution, the Declaration of Independence, and the American way of life. Judicial Reagans would advance core conservative principles in a number of areas: economic liberties, gun rights, crime and punishment, taxes, and more.

Let's take a quick look at some examples of how Judicial Reagans might act. (We'll explore some of these subjects in more detail in Part IV.)

Property Rights

A JUDICIAL REAGAN WOULD understand that property rights are fundamental rights, and thus would be wary of any government encroachment on them, much as liberal judges fret over any regulations touching on abortion. Though a conservative judge would respect the government's need in certain cases to preserve resources, he would make certain that this need would not come at the expense of the individual property owner.

The Supreme Court's ruling in *Kelo v. New London* would therefore be a prime target for a Judicial Reagan. The judge would vigorously enforce the Fifth Amendment's takings clause ("nor shall private property be taken for public use, without just compensation"), compelling government to compensate property owners enough to cover both the property taken and the inconvenience of the taking. Since the government payment would come from the taxpayers' wallet, the government would be under extra pressure not to take property, because if you subsidize something, you get more of it, but if you tax something, you get less of it. Vigorously enforcing the takings clause would increase the cost of expanding government via the power of eminent domain and, thus, would help reduce governmental intrusion into property owners' lives.

A Judicial Reagan could even rely on existing *liberal* precedents to produce the desired ruling. He might use the *Lawrence v. Texas* case, in which the Supreme Court explained why the government cannot outlaw buggery between two consenting adults. If two consenting adults can agree to engage in sexual conduct with each other without benefit of a government-issued license or permit, and without government altering the terms of their exchange, those same consenting adults should be able to agree to an economic transaction between themselves with the same level of court-protected individual freedom. After all, doesn't the Left tell us to get "your laws off our bodies"?

A Judicial Reagan would also see through the myth the Left tries to perpetuate that social conservatives share a fundamentally different approach to life and politics from economic conservatives. In fact, the values and ideals held dear by social conservatives are essentially the same as those held by economic conservatives—the views and agendas of the two groups are not mutually exclusive, despite what the mainstream media often report. After all, a healthy social environment contributes to a thriving economy, because a moral society with strong families and strong communities minimizes social disorders and makes for a more productive, law-abiding workforce and happier consumers. Likewise, a stronger economy leads to greater personal and private wealth, which gives ordinary Americans the ability to do more things and enjoy a happier life. (Keep in mind that products, inventions, opportunities, travel, and so forth that used to be accessible only to the wealthiest among us are now available to the poorest.) A better economy also leads to stronger families, as many of the stresses in families arise from financial issues. Social and economic conservatives value many of the same things: individual freedom, a strong national defense, and love of country, to name a few.

The Right to Contract

A JUDICIAL REAGAN COULD strike down anti-free-market laws by nibbling around the edges of the modern nanny state. For example, he might invalidate local laws prohibiting smoking or dancing in bars and restaurants or invalidate certain zoning laws hindering economic development. A great target may be certain labor laws that build into the system economic distortions. Today, under state and federal labor laws, employees who receive hourly wages (i.e., nonsalaried employees) must be paid time-and-a-half compensation for every hour worked beyond forty hours in any given workweek. In other words, someone who earns $10 per hour for the first forty hours of work a week will get $15 for each additional hour. This government mandate can actually hurt workers. Say an employee wants to work more hours to earn extra money but the employer resists because it cannot pay the time-and-a-half rate. The employee won't get any extra money at all, thanks to the government. Why shouldn't the employee be able to work at his normal hourly rate if he so desires? Why should government be allowed to intercede in a voluntary arrangement between employers and employees (at least those employees capable of earning far above minimum wage)?

A Judicial Reagan would recognize that government lacks a substantial interest in interceding in the voluntary contracts between employers and employees. Thus the judge could strike down mandatory overtime laws that applied to middle-class workers (say, those earning $60,000 a year or more) while keeping them in place for those earning closer to minimum wage. Such a decision would open up a debate that conservatives should welcome, and it would give pause to politicians contemplating further interventions in the American economy.

Gun Rights

A JUDICIAL REAGAN WOULD also protect gun rights. Why? First, the right to bear arms is a clear constitutional right that government cannot take away. Second, Americans have a right to defend themselves against criminals; indeed, absent a realistic right to self-defense, many people would lose the fundamental right to life, as they would be vulnerable to violent predators. Third, gun control punishes law-abiding citizens in the same way government regulations on business punish business owners with compliance costs. A Judicial Reagan would understand that, ultimately, the government's primary responsibility is to ensure that the people are protected from foreign and domestic predators—and that the people need to have the ability to defend themselves and their family. Bear in mind that it was not government employees who downed the hijacked plane over Pennsylvania on 9/11—it was ordinary American citizens.

Crime and the Death Penalty

ALTHOUGH AN OVERWHELMING MAJORITY of Americans (64 percent) support the death penalty, the justice system moves painfully slowly. Indeed, over half a million people have been murdered in the United States since 1977, and yet only about one thousand murderers have been executed in the three decades since 1977.[15] A Judicial Reagan would recognize this wholly unjustified discrepancy and would strongly push back against the Left's ongoing efforts to ban the death penalty. Of late liberals have fought at the fringes, carefully working until they have five Supreme Court votes to abolish the death penalty altogether. First they targeted the death penalty against the mentally retarded (and won) and then they targeted the death penalty against minors (and won). The Left will move on to the next battle and will not be satisfied until the death penalty is abolished.

A key left-wing strategy is to tie up death-penalty cases in the courts for years, so a Judicial Reagan could help thwart this effort by creating a bright-line rule for death-penalty cases, much like Earl Warren's *Miranda* decision, which created a bright-line rule for when criminal confessions are deemed voluntary. For example, a conservative judge could streamline death-row appeals for those cases where there exists DNA proof connecting the criminal defendant to the murder or clear videotape of the same (think Jack Ruby shooting Lee Harvey Oswald). This pragmatic solution would eliminate years of wasteful foot-dragging by the capital defense bar, because it would allow the Right to use once again liberals' arguments against them. Specifically, the Left has gone hog-wild using DNA evidence or a lack thereof as proof of insufficient evidence to execute someone for murder. Well, if the Left thinks that DNA evidence is so powerful, then so be it! That means the DNA evidence can also prove a criminal defendant did it. Likewise, if we can catch you on a surveillance camera tape killing someone, then go ahead and try to persuade us that our eyes are lying to us.

And in presiding over criminal cases generally, a Judicial Reagan would also refuse to sign on to the culture of victimhood that inspired liberal decisions. To the Left, everyone is a victim—minorities, women, Muslims, people from the Congo, people with two mommies, sex offenders without a therapist, and members of just about every other group with the word *coalition* in its name. Conservative judges cannot let American taxpayers continue to foot the bill for lavish special privileges the courts afford to these "victims."

Tax Cuts

LIBERAL JUDGES HAVE USED the courts to try to rectify many "social injustices." For example, in response to a desegregation lawsuit in Kansas City, Missouri, a federal judge ordered the state to develop an elaborate system of "magnet schools" to eradicate any vestiges of discrimination. The judge even ordered an increase in income and property taxes to pay for the magnet school system, which was so elaborate that Missouri taxpayers ended up forking over more than $1 *billion* to implement it. Why so much? Well, first of all, the judge ruled that the salaries of the schools' staff be increased. But beyond that, the court-ordered schools were absurdly lavish. The Kansas City schools, according to Supreme Court justice Anthony Kennedy, had "air conditioning, an alarm system, and 15 microcomputers [in every classroom]; a 2,000-square-foot planetarium; greenhouses and vivariums; a 25-acre farm with an air-conditioned meeting room for 104 people; a model United Nations wired for language translation; broadcast-capable radio and television studios with an editing and animation lab; a temperature-controlled art gallery; movie editing and screening rooms; a 3,500-square-foot dust-free diesel mechanics room; 1,875-square-foot elementary school animal rooms for use in a zoo project; swimming pools; and numerous other facilities."[16]

But if a judge can force a state or city to *raise* taxes, why can't a judge order a state or city to *cut* them, too? Or why can't a judge find that the appropriate judicial remedy for an unconstitutional school system is to void the teacher union contracts and implement a school voucher system? Why is it that every time a judge issues an order forcing the government to act, it almost always cherry-picks from the usual liberal wish list of more government, higher taxes, more teacher pay, smaller classrooms, and the like? You know why—but it doesn't have to be this way.

WHY ASK FOR JUDICIAL REAGANS AND NOT SCALIAS AND THOMASES?

WHEN PRESIDENT BUSH had to appoint two justices to the Supreme Court in 2005, again and again we heard leading conservatives calling for justices "in the mold of Scalia and Thomas." That sounds okay, since conservatives should love these justices. But the very description—"in the mold"—is so vague that it can get Republicans in trouble when the time comes to pick new judges. (If you don't believe me, ask President Bush and Harriet Miers.)

What does it even mean to be a judge "in the mold" of Scalia and Thomas? What is it that conservatives, including the vast majority who have never read a legal opinion, are supposed to love about Scalia and Thomas? The phrase may be code, but code for what? Most conservatives seem to refer to Scalia and Thomas to emphasize the significance of a certain formal judicial philosophy (that is, they are "originalists," are "strict constructionists," or "believe in judicial restraint"), but this, again, boils down to legalese that doesn't tell us much about how judges behave in specific hot-button cases.

Asking for judges in the mold of Scalia and Thomas suffers from a bigger problem than just imprecision: If conservatives truly intend to push U.S. law back to the right, conservatives want judges who will do more than Thomas and Scalia do for conservatism and the country.

To compare future judges to Scalia and Thomas is to risk overemphasizing their judicial philosophies and underemphasizing the results we desire. In today's legal system, where most constitutional lawmaking is indeed performed by the courts, a process-oriented jurisprudence will come up short. We need *results-oriented* judges devoted to advancing fundamental American principles, the same way the Left has focused on results to get what it wants through the courts.

This is a *political* fight, remember. It is also a fight for public perception, which matters a great deal. And the American people perceive judicial decisions based on their results, not on the process used to arrive at the decisions. That's key. Ordinary Americans quite rightly prefer to let law geeks debate the legal niceties (the process, the analogies, the arguments, the rationale of the decision, and so on); what counts are the broader issues and how decisions affect the real world. How many Americans who hold a strong view, either pro or con, on *Roe v. Wade* have actually read the lengthy opinion? Probably not that many outside of lawyers and politicos (if even them). For example, does it really matter, in the end, what the Supreme Court said to justify its ruling in *Kelo v. New London*? No, all we need to know is that the court cut into fundamental property rights by allowing an unwarranted government power grab. In today's world of activist courts, to appoint a judge who is interested only in the process by which you decide constitutional questions is to miss the broader political ramifications.

If we continue to use the vague criterion of judges "in the mold of Scalia and Thomas" rather than the much more explicit qualifications of a results-oriented, yet principled, Judicial Reagan, we will almost certainly miss the mark on future judicial picks, just as Republican presidents have misjudged jurists repeatedly over the past few decades.

Conservatives who cling to Scalia and Thomas as the model for good judges would do well to remember that the two justices themselves often differ in their modes of constitutional interpretation. In point of fact, there is no precise "mold." Justice Scalia and Justice Thomas disagree about the relevance to constitutional law of foundational documents such as the Declaration of Independence: Scalia downplays the Declaration's significance while Thomas believes that it should be considered as part of American law.[17] Professor Tom Krannawitter of Hillsdale College and the Claremont Institute notes the difference between the two justices when he writes, "Savvy liberals . . . are right to be more concerned with Thomas than Scalia because Thomas' natural-law jurisprudence represents the greatest threat to the liberal desire to replace limited, constitutional government with a regulatory-welfare state of unlimited powers."[18] Conservative confusion on the Scalia-Thomas issue only underscores the fact that there is no one proper judicial doctrine, no magic formula that will always lead judges to the correct interpretation of the Constitution. (It should be noted that liberals, too, with their focus on political gain above all else, pay little attention to where the two justices diverge; many crudely and inaccurately portray Thomas as a puppet of Scalia.)

And then there's this problem with Justices Scalia and Thomas: *They're really moderates.* That's right, the same justices whom the Left paints as right-wing extremists are actually moderates.

MAKING THE LEFT DESIRE SCALIA

SENATOR CHARLES SCHUMER, New York Democrat, regularly explains that he seeks "moderation" in Supreme Court justices. "I do not want too far Left or too far Right," he insists.[19] But let's look at the abortion issue to see how "moderate" Schumer's favorite judges are. What is the Left's position on abortion? Not too hard to discern—abortion, including the gruesome partial-birth abortion procedure, should be permitted, with virtually no government regulations. Liberal lions such as the late William Brennan and Harry Blackmun positioned the right to abortion as so fundamental that it must remain above the political fray and thus cannot be subject to legislation or regulation.

And now let's look at the so-called conservative position that Scalia and Thomas defend. It says nothing about whether abortion should be legal or outlawed; it merely holds that the question about abortion should be left to the American people and the democratic process. According to this view, California could choose to subsidize abortion while Mississippi outlawed abortion.

How conservative is this Scalia-Thomas position, really? Not very conservative at all, in fact. This approach does not represent a true counterweight to the liberal approach. A truly conservative judge might actually read the U.S. Constitution to be imbued with a fundamental right to life. In *Roe,* the Supreme Court's majority acknowledged that if the fetus were to be considered a human, then all the rights of a human—including the right to life—would attach. It would follow that the courts should outlaw any federal or state statute that *permitted* the abortion of unborn persons, or the killing of the elderly or anyone else who became a burden on society. A truly conservative Supreme Court would invalidate as unconstitutional laws permitting abortion on the grounds that these laws infringe the most fundamental right to be protected by government—the right to life. (Or perhaps the correct constitutional approach would be to permit a state to allow women to have an abortion but only after fetuses were provided years of appeals, as if they were death-row inmates.)

Justice Scalia, though correct in much of his jurisprudence, is not the type of judge we should seek today. Believing that the Constitution has a fixed meaning, he rejects attempts by both liberals and conservatives to use the "living Constitution" to advance policy preferences. "Conservatives are willing to grow the Constitution to cover their favorite causes just as liberals are," he said in a speech. To illustrate the point, he cited his dissenting opinions in two cases that happened to be decided on the same day in 1996; one decision liberals cheered, the other ruling conservatives celebrated. Scalia would have none of it. He argued that in each case, the majority ruled a statute unconstitutional only because that was the policy preference it favored. In his speech he declared, "I say, 'A pox on both their houses.' It has nothing to do with what your policy preferences are; it has to do with what you think the Constitution is."[20]

A goal of the conservative judicial activism movement should be to push the courts far enough to the right that Scalia and Thomas seem like moderates in the same way Justice Ruth Bader Ginsburg and Stephen Breyer (both liberal votes in virtually all key cases) are viewed as moderates now. Here again, conservatives will only be doing what liberals have done to great effect. The reason justices such as Ginsburg and Breyer can be considered moderates is that they are not as far to the left as such liberal heroes as Harry Blackmun (author of the *Roe v. Wade* decision) and William Brennan (the pro-*Roe*, anti-death-penalty justice). That's just another example of how skewed to the left the courts are today, and how conservatives have been fighting a losing fight for decades.

Until we approach the courts from a new perspective and prevent liberals from setting the terms of debate, we will always lose, no matter how many Republican appointees make it to the federal bench.

Until Justices Scalia and Thomas are viewed as mainstream moderates, more work will need to be done.

NOW LET'S GO OUT AND FIND THEM

IN THE NEXT COUPLE of chapters we'll see exactly how to choose specific judges and help get them confirmed (or elected). But it's important to note here what we *don't* need to concern ourselves with in the search for results-oriented Judicial Reagans.

Conservatives need not find candidates with a comprehensive legal philosophy. That departs from the conventional understanding of how to find good judges. But remember, process is overrated.

With so many perfectly legitimate ways of interpreting the law available to judges, conservatives must concern themselves with what we are seeking to preserve and protect through the courts, not with modes of interpretation. This is particularly true because, despite the naive belief that there is something close to a perfect way of interpreting the Constitution and the body of American law, judges are free to use one methodology or mental process for one case and an entirely different one for another type of case. In this regard judges are not all that dissimilar to the lawyers who argue before them; from my career as an advocate I can tell you that lawyers are hired to use every interpretative means possible to persuade the court to rule in their clients' favor. In any given case, a Judicial Reagan should take the approach that will best serve the conservative cause and the defense of fundamental American rights.

Once more, this is a lesson liberals learned long ago. For example, the Left views it as completely consistent to argue for a fundamental right to engage in buggery but for limited personal liberty in the economic realm. Likewise, the Left sees no inconsistency in opposing the death penalty for convicted, proven murders under all circumstances while showing little interest in the lives of the unborn, who haven't been given the chance to commit a crime. Nor do they see a problem with opposing a simple nativity scene in a public park at Christmas while the Supreme Court opens its sessions with the public declaration "God save this honorable court!" How are these inconsistencies explained? It's because the mode of reasoning the liberal judge brings to the gay rights case is completely different from the mode he brings to a case involving economics rights; his thinking on the death penalty stands apart from his reasoning on abortion. The deciding factor is the judge's ideology. That's why we need judges who will prioritize conservative values.

The only way to determine whether prospective judges share those priorities is to demand a long and clear paper trail establishing a solid conservative bent. Future judicial nominations cannot be based and defended on rumors—true or not. Conservatives should not have to reach out and call all their friends or Washington insiders to receive reassurances that they knew someone who worked with someone who knew the nominee and said that the nominee was a right-winger. The nominee's record should be clear and undisputable.

A good example is Bush's second Supreme Court nominee, Samuel Alito, who in his 1985 job application to the White House proudly boasted, "I am and always have been a conservative and an adherent to the same philosophical views that I believe are central to this Administration. . . . I believe very strongly in limited government, federalism, free enterprise, the supremacy of the elected branches of government, the need for a strong defense and effective law enforcement, and the legitimacy of a government role in protecting traditional values."[21] Alito also wrote of being a member of the Federalist Society and of submitting articles for publication in the *National Review* and the *American Spectator.* Sounds like a conservative to me.

Some conservatives will undoubtedly object to picking judges who so eagerly state their bona fides as conservative activists and ideologues. Many on the Right believe they are making a practical argument—namely, if Republicans pick too bold a conservative, that judge will never get through the Senate confirmation process. But by conceding the fight before it even begins, conservatives are once again letting liberals dictate the issue. The reality is that regardless of whom a Republican president nominates, the Left will portray him as a right-wing extremist. This happened with John Roberts and Samuel Alito, of course, but also with David Souter—not exactly the model of a modern Judicial Reagan.

When Souter was nominated in 1990, for instance, Molly Yard, then president of the National Organization for Women, called him "almost Neanderthal" and said his "constitutional views are based on the 'original intent' of the Framers 200 years ago, when blacks were slaves and women were property of their husbands." Eleanor Smeal of the Fund for the Feminist Majority declared, "We find him a devastating threat" because Souter "would be the fifth vote" for outlawing abortion. Ralph Neas, now president of People For the American Way, questioned Souter's "commitment to constitutional guarantees of individual rights and liberties." The NAACP said it was "troubled" by the nomination. William H. Freivogel of the *St. Louis Post-Dispatch* argued that Souter would "provide the decisive fifth vote for a broad counterrevolution in constitutional law overturning decisions on abortion, affirmative action, and criminal procedure."[22]

If liberals mounted such a furious attack on *David Souter,* it's foolish to try to defuse left-wing attacks by putting forward a "mainstream" or "moderate" candidate. Doing so only plays into the Left's hands, which is a weak and ridiculous strategy at a time when Republicans control the White House, the Senate, and the House of Representatives.

In any case, to those who maintain that a strong conservative judge cannot win confirmation by the Senate, I say, "So what?" There is no benefit to conservatives or Republicans to win confirmation of a Souter or a John Paul Stevens. Conservatives should not be interested in meaningless victories inside the Beltway if those wins do not help achieve victory in the war against liberalism. The Right can never win that war if it continues to let the Left control the fight. Conservatives must go on the offensive and capitalize on our significant political advantage. Rest assured, if Republicans repeatedly nominate strong conservative judges, liberals will have to adjust their views as to what is "extreme" and what is palatable to them. Again, conservatives must teach liberals that Antonin Scalia is not at the far right end of the spectrum but toward the middle of the conservative spectrum. If liberals understand that the choice they face is not between a Souter and a Scalia but between a Scalia and a Mark Levin or an Ann Coulter, they'll think twice about going all out to thwart the Scalia nominee.

Finally, picking a Judicial Reagan will make conservatives more confident that the judge will not "evolve" to the left once on the bench, as so many Republican picks have. (And even if far-right nominees do move left, they will hopefully remain to the right of center.) Any judge, or politician, who has to stick his finger into the wind to figure out what he thinks about a topic will never be able to withstand the pro-government gravitational pull of Washington, D.C. Ronald Reagan never had to stick his finger in the air or consult with pollsters to figure out what he believed—though he may have had to ask folks what he could realistically accomplish or what he had to settle for. Unless a judge has an ideology and belief system that can provide an equal and opposite force to resist the natural left-wing gravity of D.C., then the risks of his evolving leftward will be high.

AN END TO IDIOCY

CONSERVATIVES SIMPLY CAN'T IGNORE the Right's abysmal record of picking judges. We've been burned over and over, and so the Right must adopt a new approach.

True, we have some great judges already on the bench, including Supreme Court Justices Thomas and Scalia and, in all likelihood, Alito and Roberts. But many more judges are needed, and we will need to draft the best ones. To do so, Republicans must use the best available criteria to select future judges. Let us not forget that for every Republican appointment of a Clarence Thomas, there have been multiple David Souters, John Paul Stevenses, Sandra Day O'Connors, and Anthony Kennedys. A new strategy is needed to ensure better and more consistent results.

We've had a Reagan in the White House. Now we need many Reagans on the bench.

NO MORE SOUTERS

The Case for Litmus Tests

Trust, but verify.
— PRESIDENT RONALD REAGAN

When in doubt, keep them out.
— SUGGESTED CREDO FOR CONSERVATIVES
PICKING JUDGES

If Dr. Phil heard conservatives explain the strategy Republican presidents have used to select judges, he'd deploy his signature sarcasm and ask, "So how's that been working for you?"

Year after year, on issue after issue, conservatives appear dumbfounded when the Supreme Court sides with liberals despite the fact that seven of the nine justices are Republican appointees. But there's nothing puzzling about the situation.

Historically, liberals have been far more aware of the president's power to shape the law and the government by selecting the appropriate judges. Harvard law professor Laurence Tribe, who represented Al Gore in *Bush v. Gore,* explained that presidents can "reshape the Court to reflect their visions of the Constitution and of the nation's future." He added, "When the opportunity to make appointments to the Court does arise, the prospect for constitutional changes of far-ranging impact should never be underestimated. . . . [A] President with any skill and a little luck can usually avoid [rude surprises]—and can, with fair success, build the Court of his dreams." And of course, as Tribe pointed out, "Justices help govern the nation, and lay down the ground rules for the rest of government, long after the Presidents who appointed them have left the White House."[1] And when did Tribe make these comments? In 1985—less than two years before President Ronald Reagan nominated Robert Bork to the Supreme Court.

Republican presidents have made the same mistakes over and over. Conservatives must learn from these failings.

We know the pattern by now: A Republican president appoints a judge to the Supreme Court. The president's supporters assure conservatives that the appointee has strong conservative credentials. The "conservative" judge gets confirmed and quickly turns liberal on the bench. Republican Dwight D. Eisenhower placed Chief Justice Earl Warren and Justice William Brennan on the high court; when asked if he made any mistakes as president, Eisenhower replied, "Yes, two, and they are both sitting on the Supreme Court." President Richard Nixon appointed Harry Blackmun, who subsequently wrote the majority opinion in *Roe v. Wade*. President Gerald Ford picked John Paul Stevens, who votes overwhelmingly with the Court's liberals. President George H. W. Bush thought David Souter would advance the conservative cause. And let's not forget President Reagan's appointees, Sandra Day O'Connor and Anthony Kennedy, who have only inconsistently supported the conservative agenda in their rulings.

The big problem, of course, is that Republican presidents haven't even been looking for the right kind of judges. Where we need Judicial Reagans, they've been looking for judges who fit vague categories such as "will interpret the law rather than make it." As we've seen, it's virtually inevitable that judges will legislate from the bench, if for no other reason than that on complicated legal issues, they are essentially *required* to "make the law."

But now that we know the kinds of judges we need to look for— principled conservatives who want to protect traditional American rights and values and who will focus on results rather than merely process—how we do find our Judicial Reagans? As any of my ex-girlfriends can tell you (and certainly as any of Bill Clinton's can), a woman knowing what she wants in a man is a far cry from her actually finding one who meets those criteria. It's the same with conservatives who are selecting judges: There's no guarantee we'll appoint Judicial Reagans just because we have certain qualities in mind. The real problem is the way conservatives have approached judicial appointments.

Currently, the president and his staff are discouraged from asking any pointed policy or legal questions of people whom the president might select for lifetime, democratically unaccountable positions on the federal bench. Republican politicians—including President Bush—talk about the evils of such "litmus tests."

This is absolutely ridiculous!

We demand that elected officials tell us where they stand on issues from foreign policy to gun control, from the Middle East to abortion, from the Family Leave Act to Social Security. Yet we can't ask unelected judges who will likely preside over cases involving these very same issues what they think? Why in the world shouldn't the president know where judges stand on the day's most important issues before giving them extraordinary power to shape the nation's laws? It is simply silly *not* to apply litmus tests. From now on, conservatives must embrace litmus tests. Certainly liberal politicians and special-interest groups do. (Or do you think Howard Dean and the People For the American Way would applaud a pro-life appointee for merely following the rule of law or voting for his convictions?)

Exactly what is a litmus test? It is nothing more than a set of criteria against which prospective job applicants are evaluated. Every business in America applies a litmus test when it evaluates job applicants, to be certain they hire only those individuals who are on board with the company's mission statement. No well-run business or organization would hire someone in an influential position who did not agree with its organizational goals. Would Greenpeace hire someone who did not support environmental conservation? Would a fashion business hire a designer with no fashion sense? Would the Democratic National Committee choose a pro-life activist as its chairman? Of course not. So if ordinary businesses and organizations apply litmus tests in hiring employees, shouldn't the leader of the free world use a litmus test for lifetime appointments to the most powerful court in the world?

And yet the term *litmus test* has become a bugaboo among the conservative set. Many on the Right flatly reject the notion of using a litmus test in the selection of judges. President Bush has repeatedly stated that he opposes the use of a litmus test. During the 2004 presidential debates, the president said point-blank, "Will I have a litmus test for my judges? And the answer is no, I will not have a litmus test."[2]

But why not? Just like companies and organizations around the country, the president has a "mission statement"; his is a clearly articulated position on the most important issues of the day. It's absurd to think he and his advisers should not apply a well-designed litmus test to ensure that a judge's views on a wide variety of issues comport with the president's.

And it's not just the president who needs to embrace litmus tests; all conservatives should. Don't forget, thirty-nine states hold some form of judicial elections. That's right, ordinary nonlawyers get a direct say in the election of state court judges all across the nation.[3]

We can't wait any longer to adopt a tactic the Left has been employing for years.

GETTING IT WRONG

EVER SINCE REAGAN'S ELECTION in 1980, as the nation has moved steadily rightward, liberal politicians and advocacy groups have terrified the Birkenstock Nation into believing that the country will fall into the hands of "right-wing ideologues" who seek to undo the liberal social revolution. Thousands of candlelight vigils, "Vote or Die" concerts, and MoveOn.org commercials later, even Linda Greenhouse, the *New York Times* Supreme Court reporter, acknowledges that during the eleven-year period in which the composition of the Supreme Court went unaltered—a period, remember, when seven of the justices were Republican appointees—there was no "revolutionary change." She explains, "To the extent that there was basic change, it was to the left rather than the right: a firmer foundation for affirmative action, a constitutional framework for gay rights."[4]

Unfortunately, Greenhouse is correct. Despite the conservative ascendancy, the revolutions concerning free markets, foreign policy, and gun rights, the rise of the new media, and everything else, the one institution that has not undergone a transformation rightward is the judiciary.

While the media sometimes describe the U.S. Supreme Court as "conservative," the Court's rulings belie this myth. Four of the seven justices who voted to strike down laws against gay sex were nominated by Republican presidents. Likewise, three Republican-appointed justices voted to uphold racial discrimination by the University of Michigan Law School. In contrast, the two justices nominated by Democrat Bill Clinton virtually never vote with the conservative bloc on any case of political significance. Stephen Breyer and Ruth Bader Ginsburg voted with the Court's liberal wing in favor of abortion in *Planned Parent-hood v. Casey,* against the death penalty in *Roper v. Simmons* (minors) and *Atkins v. Virginia* (mentally retarded), against guns in *United States v. Lopez,* against reining in the size of the federal government in *United States v. Morrison* and in *Lopez,* and in favor of affirmative action in *Grutter v. Bollinger.* This consistency reflects the fact that liberal presidents get the court issue right.

There's a famous (albeit apocryphal) line from Soviet leader Joseph Stalin: "It doesn't matter who votes, but who counts the votes." The American Left (which of course sympathized with the Communists) might have taken a cue from this line, realizing that having control over who interprets American law is just as important as controlling who makes the law in the first place. The Left worked diligently to ensure that "their people" sat on the courts in a position "to interpret the law." This became abundantly clear in the 1930s when President Franklin D. Roosevelt tried to pack the Supreme Court with sympathetic justices who would rubber-stamp New Deal programs even though the programs violated the Constitution's many express references to economic liberties. That particular scheme failed, as we've seen, but Roosevelt and his liberal successors didn't abandon their results-oriented approach to picking judges. It's no coincidence that conservatives haven't won a major Supreme Court victory since 1936 (and remember, merely thwarting liberal attempts to win policy issues by judicial fiat is not the same as winning for the Right—it just means we didn't lose).

Democrats embraced litmus tests back in FDR's time, and they continue to embrace them today. Every time a Democrat running for president promises to appoint only justices who will vote to uphold a "woman's right to choose," he is promising a litmus test. Every time John Kerry stated, "I will not appoint a judge who will overturn *Roe v. Wade,*" he was promising to use a litmus test—that is, he was guaranteeing his nominees' votes on certain cases before the cases even began.

And if Republicans refuse to employ litmus tests, it's not as though Senate Democrats will refrain from assessing judicial nominees purely on ideological grounds. It is the "simple truth," Laurence Tribe has written, "that the [Senate] has been scrutinizing Supreme Court nominees and rejecting them on the basis of their political, judicial, and economic philosophies ever since George Washington was President." The

Senate, he said, "has long judged" Supreme Court nominees "on the basis of what they believe."[5] What Tribe doesn't say is that the Left has taken such judgments to new heights.

To say that the Left has applied its own litmus tests to judicial appointments would be an understatement. Manuel Miranda, former counsel to Senator Bill First, points out that "every rejected nominee since [Abe] Fortas, and almost every controversial nominee, has been appointed by a Republican president at a time when the Democrats controlled the Senate. . . . By contrast, not since Fortas have Republicans attempted to block a Democratic high court nominee."[6] Sure enough, in the 1970s a Democratic Senate rejected Nixon Supreme Court nominee Clement F. Haynsworth after the AFL-CIO adamantly opposed him because it considered several of his prior judicial rulings to be "antiunion."[7]

And ever since George W. Bush became president in 2001, Democrats have done almost nothing to hide their efforts to impose ideological litmus tests on judicial nominees. As the *New York Times* reported, in April 2001 Senate Democrats attended a retreat "to hear from experts and discuss ways they could fight a Bush effort to remake the judiciary." According to the *Times,* the panel of liberal legal experts told the Democratic senators that they "could oppose *even nominees with strong credentials* on the grounds that the White House was trying to push the courts in a conservative direction" (emphasis added).[8] Thus we've seen the Democrats' strategy of labeling one Bush nominee after another as too "conservative" or as an ideological "extremist" regardless of the nominee's competence. Instead, liberal senators would probe and probe and probe to try to determine how Bush nominees would vote on the Left's pet issues. New York Democrat Charles Schumer explained the strategy in the summer of 2005, saying, "With a flick of a pen, [Supreme Court justices] can change people's lives. To just say, 'OK, tell us where you went to law school and what your career was, and have you ever broken the law? You're on the Supreme Court'— no way."[9]

Conservatives can't be lulled into believing that left-wing litmus tests don't matter anymore just because John Roberts and Samuel Alito got through the Senate confirmation process. Democrats have successfully blocked, or at least held up for years, the appointment of well-credentialed Bush appellate-court nominees on ideological grounds. The Left won't even give the nominees a fair hearing.

A notable example is the way liberals opposed, assaulted, and defamed Judge Janice Rogers Brown, whom Bush nominated to the federal court of appeals in Washington, D.C. Judge Brown is *a black woman,* and despite the fact that liberals claim to be the defenders of minorities, they view Brown as the enemy because she defends values that are not aligned with the Left's. Judge Brown has publicly criticized the New Deal and the accompanying liberal judicial revolution. In opposing her nomination, powerful left-wing interest groups such as the NAACP and the People For the American Way alleged that Brown had a "record of ideological extremism," citing a *Los Angeles Times* report that Brown was "prone to inserting conservative political views into her appellate opinions."[10] By making such arguments, the Left held up Brown's appointment to the federal bench for nearly two years; only the extraordinary Senate compromise orchestrated by the so-called Gang of Fourteen in 2005 got her over the hump.

Conservatives must learn from their prior mistakes in appointing judges as well as from the Left's success in employing results-oriented litmus tests. It's time to change the policies and habits (or lack thereof) that helped to bring about a Supreme Court with seven Republican justices that nonetheless upholds affirmative action, legalizes same-sex sodomy, upholds *Roe v. Wade,* fails to protect property rights, and strikes down multiple death-penalty laws as unconstitutional. The failure to revolutionize the Right's approach to the legal system puts at risk any policy successes conservatives may achieve legislatively and otherwise.

Absent a fundamental rethinking of the courts, virtually any conservative gain in the other branches can be undone by unelected judges. Every state referendum, act of Congress, and executive order will be in danger of being nullified by liberal judges. Unless conservatives appoint unabashedly right-wing judges, the conservative agenda is endangered regardless of its success at the polls.

And having a litmus test is the best way to ensure we get unabashedly right-wing judges.

TWENTY QUESTIONS: THE CONSERVATIVE LITMUS TEST

So what should a conservative litmus test look like? How do we make sure conservatives pick the right judges?

We can do it by playing Twenty Questions—the judicial version.

Before a Republican president appoints anyone to the Supreme Court or another federal court, he should know the prospective nominee's views on each and every one of the following twenty questions. Likewise, conservatives going to the polls to select judges in state elections should know how the candidates would respond to these questions:

1. Is the recitation of the Pledge of Allegiance in public schools unconstitutional if it includes the words "under God"?

2. Does the Second Amendment, which the Framers included in the Bill of Rights, reflect a fundamental individual constitutional right for law-abiding Americans to own and carry guns?

3. Who should decide whether the death penalty is warranted in a particular case—the judge and jurors evaluating the credibility of witnesses at trial or by appellate judges who never met the defendant?

4. Do you believe the "unalienable rights" mentioned in the Declaration of Independence exist, and if so, how does that influence your understanding of the Constitution?

5. Should judges consider European trends or foreign precedents in interpreting the U.S. Constitution?

6. Do you trust free markets to best allocate societal resources?

7. Do individuals have the fundamental right to be free from an overactive, overreaching, and powerful government?

8. Does the Fourteenth Amendment's equal protection clause prohibit the government from providing preferential treatment to whites over blacks or vice versa?

9. Does the Fourteenth Amendment's equal protection clause permit public universities to discriminate against impoverished white children from West Virginia's Appalachian Mountains in favor of the children of Jesse Jackson and Colin Powell?

10. Should questions about the rights to gay marriage and abortion be decided by "we the people" or by nine unelected judges in Washington, D.C.?

11. Is it unconstitutional to have a Santa Claus or a nativity scene in a public park in December given that the Supreme Court still opens its court sessions with a marshal stating, "God save this honorable court"?

12. What level of constitutional protection should the individual right to own and use property receive in comparison to the right of a female stripper to dance topless—more protection, less, or the same amount?

13. Can Congress constitutionally enact a law outlawing flag burning?

14. Should courts ever oversee the operation of prisons, public school systems, or homeless shelters?

15. Is pornography protected by the First Amendment?

16. Is it appropriate to subjugate part of our population based on age, health, development, or state of mind?

17. Is a private letter from Thomas Jefferson to the Danbury Baptist Church in 1802 sufficient constitutional basis to recognize an absolute separation of church and state?

18. Does the Constitution protect the unalienable right to life?

19. Should it be illegal for organizations such as the Boy Scouts and Girl Scouts to meet in public schools?

20. Should our schools be barred from presenting students with alternative views on theories such as evolution?

WHAT ARE WE WAITING FOR?

SO THERE IT IS—a twenty-question litmus test that will get us our Judicial Reagans and help us avoid the pitfalls Republican presidents have fallen into over and over. There's absolutely nothing stopping us from employing such tests. It is, after all, undeniable that *all* judges have biases and leanings that affect their views about what is "fair" or "just" and, thus, their rulings. So it is utterly foolish not to determine what those leanings are before conservatives pick judges.

Refusing to employ litmus tests in selecting judges does not serve conservatives or the nation; it serves the left-wing assault on America. Warren, Brennan, Blackmun, Stevens, O'Connor, Kennedy, and Souter: How many times do we have to get it wrong before we fix the problem? Ann Coulter had it right when she wrote, "Fool me eight times, shame on me."[11]

With a clear litmus test, we won't get fooled again.

NINE

JUDICIAL DARWINISM

Getting Judges to Evolve Rightward

One of the things that laymen, even lawyers, do not always
understand is indicated by the question you hear so often:
"Does a man become any different when he puts on a gown?"
I say, "If he is any good, he does."
—SUPREME COURT JUSTICE FELIX FRANKFURTER

I ain't evolving.
—SUPREME COURT JUSTICE CLARENCE THOMAS

Ever since Charles Darwin formulated the theory of evolution in the
mid-nineteenth century, biologists have debated how organisms survive in and adapt to their environments. Conservatives, however, hardly
need a biology lesson to understand that judges, especially Supreme
Court justices, often evolve—to the left.

The leftward evolution of judges—the process of surviving in and
adapting to the liberal legal environment—is so well established as to
be a cliché. In the liberal online magazine *Slate,* Dahlia Lithwick wrote
that "the tendency of justices to 'defect,' or 'evolve' (circle the word
you prefer) to the left during their careers on the high court is leg-
endary."[1] Larry Sabato, director of the University of Virginia's Center
for Politics, studied the matter and concluded that fully a quarter of
confirmed Supreme Court nominees in the past half century clearly
evolved "from conservative to moderate or liberal."[2]

Unfortunately for conservatives, the evolution always goes in the
wrong direction. In fact, as Stuart Taylor explained in *National Journal,* the very term *evolved* was first used by liberal law professors and
journalists to describe, approvingly, Supreme Court justice Harry Black-

mun's journey to the far left after President Nixon appointed him in the hopes that he would be a solid conservative vote (as indeed he seemed to be for a couple of years).³ But Republican appointees were "evolving" even before the phenomenon had a name: Believe it or not, ultra-liberal justice William Brennan was generally viewed as a moderate when President Eisenhower appointed him. And Republican judges have evolved ever since, too: Lewis Powell, another Nixon pick, saved affirmative action by claiming it advanced a "compelling state interest."⁴ Sandra Day O'Connor, Reagan's choice, defended abortion and racial preferences.⁵ John Paul Stevens, Anthony Kennedy, David Souter—all these and others have "evolved," or "grown," to use another euphemism favored by the liberal elite. (The *New York Times* editorial page, for instance, insists that "any judge or justice should" demonstrate the "capacity to grow on the bench.")⁶ We're still waiting for the judicial equivalent of David Horowitz—a liberal who moves squarely into the conservative camp.*

Some chalk up these leftward evolutions to poor judicial appointments by Republican presidents. And there's a lot to that claim. As we've seen, Republicans have never had an effective game plan for scouting, choosing, and confirming judges who hold a firm and clear conservative philosophy—the kinds of conservatives who, to use Clarence Thomas's words, "ain't evolving" no matter what. So it shouldn't surprise us that judges without clear conservative convictions—without a north star to guide them—would be swayed by the contemporary legal culture, which stands far to the left of mainstream America.

But picking great new judges is merely a start in the fight to recapture the courts—a good start, but a start nonetheless. Really, our work is only beginning when our judges get confirmed or elected. Sure, once we employ our litmus test to select Judicial Reagans, we should feel confident in the judges' ability to defend conservative values and traditional American rights. But why take a chance that these people will end up sabotaging the conservative cause?

More important, consider the literally thousands of judges who are *already* on the bench, in both state and federal courts. There's nothing

---

* Note to law nerds: Some claim President John F. Kennedy nominee Justice Byron "Whizzer" White moved rightward, but even if he did, his marginal shift was nowhere near as pronounced as the leftward evolutions of many of his Supreme Court colleagues.

our litmus test can do about them. Indeed, no single president can completely refashion the judiciary, considering how many judges have lifetime appointments; no president has ever had more than 382 judicial nominees confirmed during his tenure.[7] We must always remember that winning in the courts is a long-term challenge. And one of our most pressing long-term objectives is to ensure that sitting judges do not fall under the influence of the liberal legal establishment.

In today's legal environment, judges are surrounded by liberals. More disturbing, most professional incentives come from the Left, whether it is career advancement; praise and recognition from colleagues, journalists, and professional associations; bar association awards; or anything else. It is foolish and dangerous to deny that these incentives make a difference. They matter immensely, actually. Judges are like the rest of us: They strive for higher rank, more authority, public recognition for their work, and more money. These incentives help account for the leftward evolution we've seen over and over again.

Should conservatives merely sit and watch as judges continue to evolve to the left? Absolutely not. We can keep that from happening. There's a solution at hand, and we need to grasp it immediately. Here again, we can learn from liberals, adapting the Left's simple "evolutionary" tools for the conservative cause.

Now, conservatives usually get upset at talk of a judge's "evolving," just as we get angry at the mention of the term "judicial activism." We've been burned so many times by Republicans who evolved to the left that we consider the notion of evolution to be a terrible thing. In reality, though, evolution is, like judicial activism, neither good nor bad in and of itself. Judges' evolving *to the left* is bad. But what about judges' evolving to the right? That trend would be welcome.

And it's a trend we can encourage. Not only can we discourage judges from shifting leftward, but we can actually guide jurists to the right end of the spectrum. To do that, we need to create a social and political environment that encourages judges to evolve to the right. We have the tools to do just that. Indeed, with conservatism on the ascendancy, with Republicans in power, with the growth of the new media and conservative organizations, we have a glorious opportunity to guide judges rightward.

If we get this right, we may see our judicial David Horowitzes after all.

PLAYING THE POLITICAL GAME

WHILE CONSERVATIVES GENERALLY LOATHE the idea that judges evolve on the bench, it's only natural that some jurists' views will change over time. Remember the essential truth that judges do not, simply by virtue of carrying gavels, become magically insulated from politics or society. Nor do they become immune to the blandishments of their profession. Some people might be bothered that social and political incentives influence judges' thinking, but how could they not affect jurists? As Thomas Jefferson observed, judges have "the same passions for party, for power, and the privilege of their corps" as any other high-ranking officials.

For starters, there's the simple fact that to become a judge, especially a federal judge, requires connections and political savvy. This shouldn't shock anyone. Even the website eHow.com, which boasts that it provides "clear instructions on how to do (just about) everything," has this to say about becoming a judge: "Remember that this is a very competitive field and that you will need political support to be appointed or elected."[8]

Federal appeals judge Alex Kozinski, who himself would make an excellent Supreme Court justice, has aptly summarized the political realities that weigh on all judges' minds. "How does a judge reconcile his career ambitions with principled application of the law and sensitivity to individual justice?" Kozinski wrote. "Let's say you're a district judge hoping for promotion. In criminal cases, do you consider that the attorney general, who has considerable say in the appointment and elevation of federal judges, has adopted a policy of keeping track of district judges who sentence defendants below the range suggested by the sentencing guidelines? How do you keep it out of your mind? Every magistrate judge is a district judge in waiting, every district judge is a circuit judge in waiting, every circuit judge is an associate justice in waiting, and every associate justice is a chief justice in waiting. Every state judge wants to be re-elected and promoted."[9]

Kozinski added that high-profile cases become especially fraught with complications. In such instances, "judges are well aware that certain outcomes are far more likely than others to gain them personal fame and prestige." We wouldn't remember John Sirica today if he had ruled that President Nixon didn't need to turn over his White House tapes, for example. Before Watergate, Judge Sirica "led an undistinguished judicial career and was known around the D.C. district courthouse as Maximum John for his harsh sentencing practices," Kozinski observed.

Because of the Nixon case, the judge "became *Time*'s Man of the Year in 1973."[10]

This is not to say that Sirica or other judges improperly decided cases solely for fame. But the prospect of winning hosannas can certainly be a powerful inducement to some judges, just as it can be for other political figures. Wasn't Bill Clinton's push to bring peace to the Middle East motivated at least in part by a yearning for a Nobel Peace Prize—an award he reportedly lobbied for?[11]

Heck, some Supreme Court justices have actually been known to read fan mail.[12] And others, rather than remaining above the fray, as the image of the disinterested judge portrays it, have been known to get into public spats to defend their rulings and their authority. For example, in 2005 Justice O'Connor delivered what the *Legal Times* called "a rip-snorting defense of judicial independence" in response to criticisms of the courts by Republicans in Congress. Around the same time, Justice Stevens felt the need to publicly rationalize (almost apologize for) the Supreme Court's decisions in *Kelo v. New London* and *Gonzales v. Raich,* the medical marijuana case.[13]

Don't tell me judges are completely uninterested in how others view them.

THE GREENHOUSE EFFECT

THE DESIRE FOR PRAISE, or to avoid public criticism, can have a powerful effect. In a 1992 speech, federal appellate judge Laurence Silberman revealed how judges' vanity sometimes comes into play in connection with glowing tributes penned by liberal reporters to judges who "grow in office." Judge Silberman criticized many liberal reporters for their "unbalanced" and "tendentious" advocacy journalism, but he singled out Linda Greenhouse, the *New York Times*'s legal affairs reporter (the term *reporter* is used loosely with Greenhouse). She was so adept at co-opting judges, Silberman said, that her influence was known as the "Greenhouse effect."[14] Well over a decade later, Greenhouse is still in place at the *Times,* and the Greenhouse effect remains an unfortunate reality.*

---

* Greenhouse's praise for liberal judges has won her privileges of her own. Greenhouse, who had lauded Justice Harry Blackmun's shift to the left (and would do so later in the 2005 book *Becoming Justice Blackmun: Harry Blackmun's Supreme Court Journey*), was one of two journalists given special priority to review and discuss the 1,576 boxes of

As Silberman suggested, Linda Greenhouse is not the only member of the mainstream media who has heaped praise on judges who toe the liberal line. To take just one example out of many, the *Washington Post* editorial page offered this paean to Justice William Brennan upon his death: "[Brennan] play[ed] a historic role in shaping much of the country's legal and social agenda . . . in his relentless pursuit of what he thought right and good for the country. . . . Over the years we agreed with much of what he did: for civil rights, equal representation, prisoners' rights and a free press—and against the death penalty."[15] Note the focus on liberal policy goals, which is all too typical of the liberal media's treatment of judges.

Brennan, of course, was not around to hear that particular tribute, but the mainstream press had long saluted him for his "growth" and "compassion" and hailed him as a towering figure in judicial history. This is heady stuff for at least some judges. Who wouldn't want to be called an intellectual or constitutional giant? Does anyone think that if Bill Clinton became a Supreme Court justice, as some have wished, his yearning for fawning press coverage and to create a glowing legacy for himself would suddenly diminish? I doubt it.

There's something else to consider about the Greenhouse effect and other liberal media tributes to judges who "grow in office." The mainstream media held a virtual monopoly until little more than a decade ago, meaning that such tributes went unchallenged for years and years. When you realize this, you start to understand why judges to this point have evolved in one direction only—to the left.

THE LURE OF THE ELITE

THOUGH LIBERALS TYPICALLY ASSERT that judges who evolve to the left are making the law reflect "progress" in society's attitudes on certain issues, in many cases judges reshape their views not to reflect the popular will but to conform with *elite* opinion. As reporter Stuart Taylor explained, the Supreme Court has defended the liberal position on abortion rights, racial preferences, and school prayer at a time when

---

personal papers Blackmun donated to the Library of Congress. The other journalist wasn't anyone from the *Wall Street Journal,* the *Washington Times,* or the Fox News Channel. It was Nina Totenberg of National Public Radio. Apparently, Walter Duranty was unavailable for the assignment.

"the public has not become perceptibly more liberal" on these issues. In other words, the Court evolved to the left on these issues even though society had not.

Why would justices follow the elite opinion? It's "only human," said Taylor. Consider their environment: "The justices' closest professional collaborators are their extremely bright young law clerks, recent graduates of elite law schools where liberalism reigns supreme and the views of ordinary Americans are widely scorned. And the justices' reputations are shaped by predominantly liberal news media, law professors, lawyers' groups such as the American Bar Association, women's groups (which often honor first-woman-Justice O'Connor), and other civil rights groups. New justices soon learn that siding with conservatives gets them caricatured as intolerant zealots, and siding with liberals wins them praise for 'evolving.' "[16]

Richard Posner, a federal appeals judge and a prominent legal scholar, backs up Taylor's contention. He argues that judges are motivated by, among other things, a desire to maintain a good reputation among "other judges" and "with the legal profession at large."[17] Similarly, Northwestern University law professor John McGinnis suggests that Supreme Court justices in particular are keenly aware of "their judicial reputations," which are widely discussed in legal circles, and therefore they are "likely to alter their jurisprudence, at least at the margins, toward what they would expect members of the legal academy to prefer."[18]

That some judges are cognizant of how their work is perceived by their professional peers should surprise no one. All professionals want their peers to view them favorably. Who wants to be known as the dumb or incompetent plumber in the union? Nor are these professional pressures new. In the nineteenth century, Charles Darwin kept his theory of evolution secret for more than a decade, fearing that its disclosure might destroy his professional reputation. It would be strange to think that judges were somehow above such concerns. True, judges with lifetime appointments do not need to worry about job security, but many of them still hope to climb higher up the professional ladder. And even those who don't have such aspirations might naturally look for some outward recognition of how they are performing on the bench.

The Left takes advantage of this instinct. Liberals have built an elaborate reward system to encourage judges to evolve to their side. Consider: In November 2003, the Massachusetts Supreme Court ruled in *Goodrich v. Massachusetts* that the Commonwealth's 223-year-old Constitution recognized gay marriage. Four months later, the judge who wrote that opinion received a prestigious honor: She delivered the Tenth Annual Brennan Lecture on State Courts and Social Justice at the New York University School of Law, one of the nation's elite law schools. And which judge gave the Brennan Lecture the previous year? The former Vermont Supreme Court judge who had authored the opinion ordering the state legislature to enact gay marriage or civil union laws. Of the thousands of state court judges in the United States, why did NYU Law School pick these judges to speak? And what messages does this send to other judges across the country? I'll leave that to you to decide.

And think about the mainstream legal culture more broadly. Many attorneys, bar associations, lawyer organizations, legal publications, and law schools encourage big government, more laws, and more lawyers. That culture as a whole leans distinctly to the left. Take the American Bar Association and the Association of Trial Lawyers of America, arguably the two most important legal organizations in America. Their members contribute millions of dollars to Democratic political efforts and also encourage the creation of ever more laws and victim classes ready to sue anyone with deep pockets. The ABA has even ordered law schools to violate the law, according to the *Wall Street Journal,* in order to achieve a liberal policy goal: racial preferences in hiring and admissions. The *Journal* reported, "Under [the ABA's] standards, any law school that seeks to maintain or acquire ABA accreditation will be required to engage in racial preferences in hiring and admissions, regardless of any federal, state or local laws that prohibit of such policies."[19] Such groups make up the legal elite in this country—the peer group many judges turn to for recognition and approbation.

Of course, not all judges evolve into liberals and not all judges seek kudos from the mainstream media and the modern legal culture. But left-wing judges have achieved such prominence over the past several decades that their rulings affect even nonliberal judges, especially lower court judges. These other judges may feel obliged (or at least incentivized) to follow the legal precedents already in the law books, and as noted, those precedents usually tilt left. That's why, as a midlevel appellate judge, Samuel Alito followed precedents such as *Roe v. Wade* and *Planned Parenthood v. Casey*—because they were the law of the land.

PUSHBACK

WITH SO MANY FORCES out there luring judges to the liberal side, it might seem as if conservatives are fighting a losing battle. Fortunately, though, there is no natural law requiring judges to evolve to the left. Conservatives just need to be smart about how we fight back against leftward evolution.

The first step to guiding judges to the right is to remember the Alcoholics Anonymous credo: "Grant us the serenity to accept the things we cannot change, courage to change the things we can, and the wisdom to know the difference." That is to say, some judges can be encouraged to evolve rightward and some can't. To begin, there are judges who are already solid right-wingers and who rule accordingly, and thus we cannot expect them to move further right; Supreme Court justices Scalia and Thomas, and (we hope) Roberts and Alito, fall into this category. At the other end of the spectrum are left-wingers whose rulings adhere to liberal tenets; Justices Brennan, Blackmun, and Thurgood Marshall were in this camp, for example. There's not much we can really do about getting these judges to evolve, either.

The good news is that many other judges fall somewhere in the middle. Judges from this third group often lack a clear guiding political or judicial philosophy. They want to perform their job of applying the rule of law, and they want to be respected professionally. These are the judges who can be guided to the right. They should be the focus of a comprehensive conservative strategy to fix the courts. Through education, adulation, proper motivation, and massaging, we might gently and subtly influence the environment in which these judges practice. By doing so, we might convince more judges that the conservative view of the law is *the* rule of law.

A PLAN OF ACTION

SO HOW DO CONSERVATIVES get more judges to evolve to our side? There are many different tactics we can employ, but no magic bullets. Some approaches will work better than others, but we should try them all, for even the most subtle changes can bring real benefits over time. The law is not something that can be revolutionized in an instant. Many if not most changes occur at the margins. But over time those incremental changes add up and can have a profound influence on

American law. Many of the Left's "well-settled" precedents, remember, had almost no basis in the law at one point, but liberals fought long enough and diligently enough to force their desired changes on the American people.

When it comes to moving the courts out of the Left's corner, virtually all ideas should be on the table. But here are three steps conservatives should take to help sitting judges evolve to the right.

1. *Keep winning elections.* This sage advice hardly justifies the price of the book or even a can of soda. Still, we can never overestimate the importance of GOP political success. Right before Judge Alito won confirmation to the Supreme Court, Representative Rahm Emanuel, an Illinois Democrat, explained why his party could not complain about the president's Supreme Court nominees: "George Bush won the election," he said. "If you don't like it, you better win elections."[20] While riding an elevator down the U.S. Senate Dirksen Office Building to attend the confirmation vote of John Roberts, a prominent Senate Democrat turned to a despondent staffer and remarked, "If we won an election once in a while, this wouldn't be happening."[21] Dead on. Court appointments are the spoils of political warfare.

The GOP's success at the polls in the past decade has produced a new incentive for judges, especially on the lower courts, to shift rightward, as evolving in that direction could be a good way to be promoted to a higher court. Lots of judges are careerists who want to do what will advance them in their profession. That's not necessarily an awful thing. Keep in mind that a fair number of elected politicians switch political parties, usually because they sense the direction of the prevailing political winds. Bob Dole joined the Republican Party in the first place simply so he could get elected. Dole recalls that when as a young man he decided to enter politics, a mentor advised him to become a Republican because Kansas only elected Republicans.[22] And ever wonder why all those former Democratic politicians have switched to the Republican Party, people such as Alabama senator Richard Shelby, Colorado senator Ben Nighthorse Campbell, and even the late South Carolina senator Strom Thurmond? The desire to get elected, remain in office, or serve in the majority can motivate politicians to switch parties. Even Vermont senator Jim Jeffords's decision to leave the Republican Party and award control of the U.S. Senate to the Democrats, which now looks boneheaded, occurred *before* 9/11, at a time when the Republicans looked vulnerable; in the short term, the move allowed the obscure small-state senator to become national news—"A One-Man Earthquake," according to a *Time* magazine headline.[23]

Like elected politicians, some judges pay attention to the way the political winds are blowing. After all, if a judge wants to keep advancing, his side of the political aisle had better keep winning elections. And certainly if a young lawyer has aspirations to become a judge one day, he would do well to keep his eye on how the political scene is developing. (Note: Given my prior comments about American Indians, feminists, and all New York sports teams, I obviously lack such aspirations.) There are plenty of talented, largely apolitical legal careerists who enjoy toiling away in the legal profession and who view judgeships as light indoor work with no heavy lifting. It's also nice to be called "judge" or "Your Honor" all the time. These individuals view becoming a judge the same way a young athlete views playing professional sports: They are more interested in obtaining the job—any judicial job—than in which team they play on. Aspiring judges just want to play major league baseball; they are less concerned with whether it's for the Red Sox or the Yankees.

2. *Use the new media.* Winning elections is important, but it's not enough to keep some judges from moving to the left. Conservatives need to generate other incentives to remake the judiciary. Fortunately we now have a fabulous tool with which to entice judges to our side and keep them from moving to the other side: the new media.

As we've seen, liberals have proved remarkably adept at using the mainstream media to lure judges to their view of the law and justice. Judges who vote the Left's line receive lavish praise from the *New York Times,* the *Washington Post,* and the rest of the media elite. But with the rise of the new media, conservatives finally have a means to counter the Left's maneuvers. We must use the new media to provide positive coverage of decisions with which we agree and, perhaps more important, to praise critical swing judges. Supreme Court justice Sandra Day O'Connor received many pats on the back from the mainstream media for being a swing vote—that is, for being the decisive vote for the liberal side. For example, the *New York Times Magazine* massaged

O'Connor's ego by describing her as "the most powerful woman in America" because of her votes to uphold the right to abortion. The article, by Jeffrey Rosen, explained, "We are all living now in Sandra Day O'Connor's America. Take almost any of the most divisive questions of American life, and Justice O'Connor either has decided it or is about to decide it on our behalf."[24] One assumes Rosen wrote these lines bent over with his lips puckered.

The new media can and must create a reverse "Greenhouse effect"—with the praise bestowed not by Linda Greenhouse and the *New York Times* but by Fox News and Rush Limbaugh. Perhaps the evolution of judges rightward will become known as the "Rush Effect," or the "Legal Hannitization Tour," or the "New O'Reilly Factor."

Actually, we've already seen how the "New O'Reilly Factor" could work. For much of 2005, Bill O'Reilly, host of the Fox News Channel's *O'Reilly Factor,* railed against judges whose decisions he considered "soft" on child molesters. O'Reilly vigorously supported Jessica's Law, which would mandate long prison sentences for sex offenses against children. Then, in January 2006, O'Reilly stirred a tremendous controversy when he called out Vermont state judge Edward Cashman for sentencing a convicted child rapist to a mere sixty days in jail (Cashman said he thought punishment "accomplishes nothing of value" and that the rapist needed treatment more than punishment). O'Reilly showed his viewers a picture of Judge Cashman and said, "You may be looking at the worst judge in the USA." The national media storm O'Reilly created prompted calls to boycott Vermont and to impeach the judge or have him resign. Following this hue and cry, the Vermont Department of Corrections changed its policy to allow low-risk sex offenders to receive treatment in prison. The judge then increased the sixty-day jail sentence to a minimum of three years in prison.[25]

O'Reilly's crusade against the Vermont judge highlights another important role the new media can play: not just praising judges for making the right decisions but also publicly criticizing those who issue outrageous rulings. By holding those jurists up to public scorn, we can make other, less politically committed judges think twice about issuing rulings that would subject them to such public criticism. Does anyone doubt that at least a few judges in the future will think about Judge Cashman and Bill O'Reilly before sentencing a sex offender? In today's world, being viewed as soft on crime cannot be a good label for judges to bear. (For example, in 2004 a sitting West Virginia Supreme Court justice lost his race for reelection after television ads portrayed him as being soft on crime.) As longtime Republican strategist Grover Norquist has put it in another context, sometimes a person's role is to teach us what *not* to do.

Bloggers can contribute to this effort as well. Upon learning of good or bad decisions, bloggers can forward this information to a national clearinghouse that tracks the rulings of all the country's judges. Several groups track the decision of those judges who frequently appear on "short lists" for U.S. Supreme Court appointments, but of course those lists cover a tiny percentage of the thousands of judges in this country. Conservatives can use technology to track judges at all levels; with more attention focused on bad rulings, liberal judges—at least those in Red States—don't stand a great chance of advancement.

As another defense against leftward evolution, conservatives can use the new media to gauge prospective judges and other leaders of the Right's legal efforts. After all, we want individuals who are in tune with Red State conservatives, not with the mainstream media elites or the inside-the-Beltway crowd. Think about it: Would you prefer a judge who longs to be praised in the *New York Times Magazine* or one who asks himself, "How will this play on talk radio?" Actually, we've already seen a judge who indicated that he was in tune with the conservative movement in this way: Samuel Alito. In his job application to the Reagan Justice Department, the young Alito boasted about submitting articles to *National Review* and the *American Spectator*— not the *New York Times*. Bingo! This is the exact attitude the new media can and should foster. If we're confident that judges have this perspective, we can be more confident that they will not slide to the left on the bench.

We can even use the new media to defend our judicial nominees, whether for appointed or elected positions. If conservatives make sure the Left can't block strong conservatives, we won't need to settle for weaker judges who will be more susceptible to evolving to the left. Imagine if the new media had existed in 1987, allowing conservatives to counter the Left's vicious and unfounded attacks on Reagan Supreme Court nominee Robert Bork. Reagan might never have needed to settle for Anthony Kennedy, an unreliable conservative.

Today, Democrats and far-left groups such as People For the American

Way still try to portray virtually all Republican judicial nominees as extremists, even racists. Senator Ted Kennedy's repeated charges that Samuel Alito was racist never quite stuck, but we must remember that Supreme Court nominees draw far more media attention than do nominees for lower courts. For those lower court positions in particular, conservatives need to become much more aggressive about using the new media to counter the liberal spin. For example, Bush federal court nominees Priscilla Owen and Charles Pickering were both labeled racists. Without a concerted campaign to refute these charges, the Left's attacks worked: The Senate rejected Pickering, and Democrats held up Owen's confirmation for more than four years.

If using the new media more aggressively means letting the nominees defend themselves publicly, I say so be it. Sure, tradition holds that judicial nominees do not campaign for their positions, which means they do not give media interviews. But it is important to remember that this is a tradition, *not* a law. It harks back to a time when judges were viewed as apolitical; to campaign for an apolitical position would be unseemly, it was thought. As we know, however, judges are not apolitical. By clinging to that false and anachronistic notion, conservatives make poor strategy decisions. Just think about how powerful it would have been to have Charles Pickering—an extremely well-qualified judge with a strong record on civil rights issues—tell his own story to Bill O'Reilly or Rush Limbaugh. Yet Pickering remained mum, and the smear campaign against him worked. (After the Senate rejected Pickering, President Bush used a recess appointment to put him on the bench.)

The new media, in short, can be both carrot and stick to bring judges along to the right. We can also use alternative media outlets to ensure that the Left can't keep out of the judiciary strong conservatives who "ain't evolving." We have a powerful tool now. Let's use it.

3. *Ban ivory-tower law clerks.* In order to get judges to move to the right rather than to the left, conservatives must eat away at the liberal orthodoxy in the legal culture. One way to do that is to help law schools hire more conservative faculty, for as we will see in Chapter 14, law school faculties are overwhelmingly liberal. But that process will take a lot of time. If we're looking for a quick and effective move to diminish the influence of liberal legal academics over the law, we can pass a law: Congress should enact legislation that precludes a federal judge from hiring a law clerk unless the clerk has been out of law school for at least five years.

Some of you are probably thinking, *Law clerks? Who cares? What in the world would that do?* After all, the term *clerk* calls to mind a cipher, a Bob Cratchit type who simply does the bidding of his Ebenezer Scrooge boss. Unfortunately, few law clerks shiver behind green eyeshades in drafty offices. In fact, clerks can have considerable influence on their bosses—the judges—and ultimately on the outcomes of cases. For example, virtually all law clerks draft opinions. In fact, as Supreme Court historian David J. Garrow acknowledges, "Some of the best-known opinions of such renowned former justices as Felix Frankfurter and John M. Harlan II were written almost entirely by their clerks." Often, too, a clerk can influence how the judge rules in a particular case. Garrow, after reviewing Justice Harry Blackmun's private papers, concluded that this hero of the American Left "ceded far too much of his judicial authority to his clerks." For example, Blackmun's clerks "were almost wholly responsible for his famous denunciation of capital punishment in his dissent in *Callins v. Collins*"—the 1994 opinion in which Blackmun declared, "I no longer shall tinker with the machinery of death."[26] This is what reporter Stuart Taylor had in mind when he said clerks fresh out of law school are "the justices' closest professional collaborators."

So what would we accomplish by requiring federal law clerks to be at least five years removed from law school? To answer that, you must first realize that America's elite law schools—which produce most federal judicial clerks in this country—are hothouses of liberalism. And then you must remember the statement often attributed to Winston Churchill: "Any man who is under thirty and is not a liberal has no heart; and any man who is over thirty and is not a conservative has no brains."

Conservatives want judges to be aided by law clerks with brains but certainly not with bleeding hearts. Let law students spend five years working for lawyers and realizing that criminals are not always framed by "the man" and businesses are more often the good guys than crybaby employees or "do-gooder" government bureaucrats. Let them pay taxes and twiddle their thumbs waiting in line at the Department of

Motor Vehicles. As Nathaniel Persily, a University of Pennsylvania law professor, has explained, "Insofar as an elite law school might push students to the left, corporate law firms might bring them back to the center."[27] Let young lawyers gain this real-world experience and *then* advise judges.

Simply put, if law clerks were not so young and inexperienced as they are today, many of them would not buy into the Left's agenda as readily. The five-year rule would give young legal eagles the chance to see and understand the world as it really exists and not as seen through the eyes of some dewy-eyed liberal law professor wailing about the loss of the good old days when he served as a young staff lawyer on the Watergate committee. The myths perpetuated by ivory-tower law professors don't hold up in the real world.

Justice Samuel Alito seems to understand this point. After his confirmation he hired as a law clerk a thirty-seven-year-old senior vice president at Time Warner who had previously served as counsel to Attorney General John Ashcroft. The *Washington Post* commented that the appointment was "unusual" given the clerk's age and experience level, since "the vast majority of clerks are recent law school graduates."[28]

The five-year rule could help solve a little-noticed but significant cause of judges' leftward "evolution."

JUDICIAL WATCH

HAVING READ THAT three-step plan, some of you might be wondering, *Hey, what about impeachment?*

Some commentators suggest that impeaching judges who deviate from the Constitution would be incentive enough to keep judges in line. But throughout this book, I've tried to deal with realistic options, and impeachment just isn't a realistic deterrent to leftward evolution. Barring criminal conduct, sitting judges will not be impeached and probably should not be. Thomas Jefferson recognized the futility in the suggestion of impeachment when he noted, "Experience has already shown that the impeachment [the Constitution] has provided is not even a scarecrow."[29]

Suggesting impeachment for judges to check their activist tendencies makes no more sense than referring an offending jurist to an international tribunal of space aliens for trial and judgment—it's a fantasy.

Some other suggestions for fixing the courts are likewise unrealistic. For example, some critics of the courts have suggested that federal judges serve limited terms rather than receive lifetime appointments. But it is exceedingly unlikely that we could make this change happen, because to do so would require ratification of a constitutional amendment—something that is extremely difficult to achieve (think Equal Rights Amendment or anti-gay-marriage amendment). In any case, conservatives would do well to remember that while term limits might send a Justice Brennan packing after a certain number of years, they would also send home a Justice Thomas.

Much the same could be said for the idea that all judges, including Supreme Court justices, be elected. This too would require a constitutional amendment. It's simply unrealistic to think we could make that happen, not least because powerful liberal legal organizations, including the American Bar Association, have long opposed the election of judges.[30] Besides, the idea of George Soros and MoveOn.org funding elections for Supreme Court justices should not sit well with conservatives—remember, there might not even be any electoral college check in judicial elections.

So I've tried to put forward ideas that take advantage of tools that are already available to us. Even the five-year rule on law clerks could be effected rather quickly; after all, adding a short rider to an omnibus transportation bill is much simpler than ratifying a constitutional amendment. But the key point is, conservatives should use all the tools available to us to make sure fewer judges evolve to the left and more judges start leaning to the right. At the very least there is no harm in trying to create a sympathetic, nurturing, and even protective social, political, and media environment for conservative judges.

If conservatives institute this plan of attack—creating effective deterrents to judges who would engage in liberal activism while also encouraging conservative rulings—we can start pushing the courts and the law back to the right. By influencing the legal culture and creating the same sorts of incentives, privileges, and rewards the Left has long dangled in front of judges, we too can influence the courts. Taking action will certainly be much more effective than simply arguing that judges should "apply the law."

The fight is on.

PART IV

BETTER LIVING THROUGH LITIGATION

UNLEASHING THE RAPACIOUS VELOCI-LAWYERS ON THE LEFT

Time to Start Suing

They're lethal. . . . [They have] cheetah speed. . . . They show extreme intelligence. . . . They never attack the same place twice. They were testing the fences for weaknesses. Systematically.
—DESCRIPTION OF THE VELOCIRAPTORS
IN THE FILM *JURASSIC PARK*

Up until this point I've used the term *judicial activism* as it is commonly employed: to describe what judges do. But in reality, judges can't be activists in isolation. They need help. Judges are by necessity more *reactive* than active; they can only *respond* to the lawsuits brought before them. And who is responsible for bringing those lawsuits? Lawyers and their inspired clients—ordinary Americans like you and me. Conservatives must remember this as we set out to dismantle the liberal legal monopoly.

The lesson is simple: We're *all* judicial activists now.

How do conservatives outside the small contingent of judges join the fight to reclaim the courts? By this point in the book you should know the answer to that one: *Why, copy the Left, of course!*

THE LIBERAL LITIGATION MACHINE

LIBERALS DOMINATE CONSERVATIVES in the legal arena because early on they recognized the power of the lawsuit, even one merely threatened. When it comes to the courts, left-wing lawyers and "public interest" groups such as the ACLU operate like the vicious velociraptors in the dinosaur movie *Jurassic Park,* based on Michael Crichton's novel: They're lethal, they move quickly, they show extreme intelligence, and they systematically "test the fence for weaknesses"—for a chance to break through and advance liberalism (while building the résumés of liberal legal elites).

Let's give credit where it's due: Left-wing "veloci-lawyers" have made extraordinary gains for the Left's political agenda—though it's usually at society's expense. By wielding politically motivated lawsuits as a weapon, liberals have made abortion legal nationwide, allowed gays to get married, won taxpayer money to pay for criminals' attorneys and for the education of kids of illegal immigrants, enabled large developers to take your property if your local politicians want more tax revenue, given Taliban fighters imprisoned at Guantánamo Bay access to American courts, won billions of dollars from businesses for all sorts of imagined wrongdoing, and even won the release from prison of a woman who (whoops) set fire to her home, killing her three kids.

Activist liberals use lawsuits in all kinds of ways:

- To undo laws they oppose—notable examples include antiabortion laws and laws forbidding homosexual sodomy

- To circumvent the normal political process to achieve their goals—usually because liberals know that they could never secure approval for their objectives in the normal process (think gay marriage)

- To gather inside information about their legal and political adversaries, which they can use later even if not in that particular case

- To bring public attention to their cause and frame the issue— the ACLU, for example, has built virtually its entire agenda around the concept of suing

- To win the public relations battle regardless of the outcomes of the lawsuits, and to draw attention to supposed social problems that aren't even obvious legal matters ("If it offends your sense of justice," says Indiana University law professor Florence Roisman, "there's a cause of action")[1]

- To intimidate their opponents into complying with their wishes—settling a case is often cheaper than paying lawyers to defend it

Of course, left-wing public interest groups have powerful allies in the legal establishment—the trial bar, academia, even private law firms willing to donate free attorney services to help advance trendy liberal causes. Liberals heap praise on legal "do-gooders" who advance liberalism. Take the example of the "idealistic" Yale law students who sued President George H. W. Bush and took the case all the way to the Supreme Court. The students, whose story is recounted worshipfully in the 2005 book *Storming the Court,* received the support of a sympathetic dean of a prestigious Ivy League law school, influential law professors, and a powerful national law firm donating free legal help. And what exactly was the public interest that needed vindicating by this fearless band of law students (willing to withstand the imminent danger of paper cuts)? Forcing the U.S. government to move hundreds of HIV-infected Haitians from Guantánamo Bay to America. Oh, joy. Let's chalk up another win for justice and the American way!

So far, the Right doesn't have the same friends in high places in the legal establishment. Nevertheless, conservatives can—indeed, must—deploy lawsuits to advance the conservative agenda and protect the American way of life.

The new rallying cry for the Right should be: *Let's start suing!*

LAWSUITS HELP THE RIGHT, TOO

AH, BUT THERE'S A problem: The mere mention of lawsuits often sends conservatives into conniption fits. (In the 1992 presidential election, the Bush-Quayle ticket attacked "tasseled-loafered lawyers.") And for good reason. There are, in fact, far too many unnecessary lawsuits in this country, which tie up the legal system and create a massive drag on the economy and on innovation. Conservatives who cry out for tort reform and rail against trial lawyers—a major source of contributions to Democrats—do not naturally think of lawsuits as potentially powerful political tools for the Right.

Indeed, many conservatives act as if the way to fix the courts is simply to close our eyes, click our heels, and repeat, "Nothing beats voting! Nothing beats voting!" But any referendum or piece of legislation can be struck down or ignored by the terminal legislature—the courts. So no matter how hard the Right may work through democratic means, a court can always come along and undo the effort. For example, California residents enacted Proposition 187, restricting government welfare payments to illegal immigrants. Then, within a day, a court enjoined the law, and Proposition 187 was never fully implemented. In 1992, Colorado residents enacted Proposition 2, which precluded localities from enacting laws defining gays as a legally "protected class" in the same way racial minorities are a "protected class." The U.S. Supreme Court struck down that law as unconstitutional. In 2000, the Supreme Court struck down as unconstitutional a federal statute specifically designed to eliminate the necessity of police giving *Miranda* warnings to accused criminals.

Even when laws have been intended to counter judicial rulings, the courts have responded by striking down the attempts to curtail their authority. For instance, in 1993 Congress passed the Religious Freedom Restoration Act (RFRA), making it harder for states to regulate certain religious activities, after the Supreme Court had upheld an Oregon law restricting religious expression. But in the 1997 case *City of Boerne v. Flores,* the court struck down RFRA as unconstitutional.

With the courts able to void just about anything the Right accomplishes legislatively or by referendum, conservatives cannot refuse any longer to use lawsuits offensively. We've been playing defense too long; it's time to put the Left on defense for a change.

Still, some conservatives might oppose a conscious strategy of suing more, saying that instead we should try to stop the onslaught of liberal lawsuits and should use lawsuits ourselves only as a defensive shield, or a weapon of last resort. But as always, we must not close our eyes to the reality of the political scene. And the facts are clear: Whether we like it or not, lawsuits are now ubiquitous. They are standard weapons of modern political warfare. And the Left has won victory after victory exploiting that as a political weapon. We can do all we want to try to ban politically motivated lawsuits, but that's a quixotic effort. It will be about as effective as Lady Diana's efforts to ban land mines. A fine idea, but it will never work.

Like land mines—and like judicial activism—lawsuits are not inherently evil; they can be good or bad depending on who is using them and why. Lawsuits per se don't hurt conservatives; *liberal* lawsuits do. Suing, like playing PacMan or watching *March of the Penguins,* can be fun for the whole family; it need not be left exclusively to liberals.

Lest we forget, legal actions occasionally benefit the Right at the expense of the tie-dyed T-shirt gang. It was a lawsuit—Paula Jones's—that led independent counsel Kenneth Starr to discover that the purported champion of women's rights, President Bill Clinton, perjured himself to deny a working woman her day in court. This legal imbroglio arose thanks to a civil lawsuit costing a few hundred bucks to start. And what did the Right win with this cheap lottery ticket? Only the end of the Clinton agenda and victory by George W. Bush over Vice President Al Gore in 2000. As they say about the lottery, you have to be in it to win it. The Right bought a ticket to the lawsuit lottery and won big.

Even better news for the conservative cause, and for the country as a whole, is that all of us can contribute. We don't always need to count on lawyers and conservative legal organizations to protect our core freedoms. In fact, many of the best suits aren't even politically motivated; they can result from an individual's desire to protect what is his.

Take the case of Arizona rancher Jim Chilton, who in 2005 turned the tables on a litigious environmental group, suing the Center for Biological Diversity for defamation. (With the phrase "biological diversity" stenciled on the door, you know the group's angle.) For years, Chilton said, the center had complained about alleged environmental degradation on lands he leased from the federal government. The center had tried to show the alleged destruction by posting misleading photos of Chilton's land on the Internet. When the rancher showed his own photos in court, the jury concluded that the center had exaggerated its claims, and awarded Chilton $600,000.

Ironically, the cofounder of the center—which derived fully a third of its $3 million budget from court awards and settlements in 2003—complained that Chilton was "litigious." He claimed that paying the award could financially devastate the center.[2]

Well, turnabout is fair play. Groups such as the Center for Biological Diversity just aren't accustomed to being on the receiving end of lawsuits. We must put pressure on the Left. They've been bullying us in the courts for decades. And despite what you might hear from New Age educators who support scoreless soccer games as a way of building self-esteem, the best way to stop a bully is to punch him in the nose. Rather than sit helplessly as liberal bullies place more restrictions on guns, secure more rights for criminals, ensure fewer obstacles to abortion, and so much more, we can fight back with our own lawsuits.

Conservatives need to seize opportunities to give the Left an ultimatum of sorts: either risk losing a lawsuit or settle and move rightward. Even the threat of lawsuits may suffice to achieve conservative policy gains. Groups that don't want to risk paying monetary damages, being tied up in court, disclosing confidential information and incurring costly attorney's fees will want to avoid litigation—and will adjust their behavior to do so.

LITIGATION AS POLICY MAKING

"THERE IS A LONG tradition in the United States of policymaking by litigation. Like lobbying, campaign contributions, and media campaigns, litigation is another weapon in a public policy battle."[3] So explains Professor Barbara Hinkson Craig, author of *Courting Change: The Story of the Public Citizen Litigation Group.*

Craig is exactly right. Organizations such as the ACLU and the NAACP were among the first to show that public interest litigation can profoundly influence policy. Much later, some conservative and libertarian legal groups formed as well, such as the Landmark Legal Foundation, the Pacific Legal Foundation, the Institute for Justice, the Atlantic Legal Foundation Center for Individual Rights, the Washington Legal Foundation, and the Alliance Defense Fund. The efforts of these and other conservative public interest groups are admirable, but such organizations are mere ankle biters compared with the Left's legal behemoths. In large part because so many on the Right view lawsuits with disdain, it's the Left that has achieved the most in the courts.

In just about every area of policy, left-wing interest groups are waging war in the courts. The Massachusetts Supreme Court (known formally as the Supreme Judicial Court of Massachusetts) shocked many Americans in 2003 by striking down the state's ban on gay marriage. This decision arose not out of thin air but only after decades of legal strategizing by the Left. As far back as 1979, the *New York University Review of Law and Social Change* published papers from a conference titled "The Fight for Gay Rights"; the papers included "Securing Gay Rights Through Constitutional Litigation," "Homosexuality and the Constitutional Right to Privacy," and "Procedure and Strategy in Gay Rights Litigation."[4] The Left understands that a long-term legal strategy should be part of any overall political game plan.

The NAACP realized this a long time ago. During the civil rights movement, NAACP lawyers figured out that although they'd lose a lot of individual court cases, they were employing a long-term winning strategy. As Professor Genna Rae McNeil explained, the NAACP recognized that even with a "high probability of losing," it would be able to use "the case to achieve beneficial by-products, such as calling attention to the evil, using the court as a forum, building public sentiment around the case, and creating a sufficiently strong threat for some temporary ameliorative action to be taken."[5]

The ACLU also figured out that losing one particular court case doesn't mean the end of the fight. University of Texas law professor Lino Graglia explains that the ACLU "never loses in the Supreme Court, even though it does not always win." How can that be? Well, Graglia says, the ACLU "either obtains from the Court a policy decision, such as the prohibition of state-sponsored prayer in public schools, that it could obtain in no other way because [the policy is] opposed by majority of the American people, or it is simply left where it was to try again on another day. The opponents of Connecticut's anticontraception law, for example, finally got the Supreme Court to invalidate it in *Griswold* only on their third try."[6]

More recently we have seen the Left's relentlessness in the legal crusade against school choice, the movement to provide school vouchers, tuition tax credits, and other measures to provide greater educational opportunities for children who desperately need them. Left-wing legal activists swung into action, heading into court with their tasseled loafers and I SMOKE DOPE AND I VOTE buttons to try to strike down school choice laws. In 2002 the Supreme Court dismissed the Left's claim that school choice violated the First Amendment's prohibition of the establishment of religion since it gives parents the option to send their children to parochial schools. So anti-school-choice activists simply started a new legal challenge, this time in state courts. Dropping the First Amendment argument, the Left said that school choice violated, among other things, the state-enacted Blaine Amendments, which prohibit the transfer of state monies to religious sectarian schools. Never mind that the Blaine Amendments were enacted in the nineteenth century as a result of anti-Catholic bigotry.[7] In January 2006, the Left's relentless legal effort paid off when the Florida Supreme Court found Florida's limited school choice program to be illegal. The ruling would toss poor, inner-city minority kids back into failing public schools.

Ralph Nader is another who understood how much the courts can effect change. In the 1960s and '70s, Nader and other "public interest" lawyers worked within the system to achieve exactly what they wanted. One of "Nader's Raiders" explained how this legal strategy was much more effective than the hippie protests of the era. "We were the conservatives of the radical movements of the sixties," the Naderite told Barbara Hinkson Craig.[8] "We did not see civil disobedience as an effective means to reach a more just system. We embraced the promise of the law, as it was supposed to be, as the best route to justice."

Naderites and other liberals love to point to the "promise of the law" and the beauty of the American justice system, which is that even a poor man can pay a small filing fee and sue the largest corporation. True, this shows that nobody is above the law, but in practical terms the ease of suing means that anyone with a political agenda or personal grudge can often concoct a reason to sue, harass, annoy, or embarrass someone else.

And all this policy making occurs outside the democratic process, of course. Brian Wolfman, director and general counsel of the Nader-founded Public Citizen Litigation Group, has said the beauty of the courts is that if he files a lawsuit against a private company or a government department, "they have to answer." Anywhere else, "in Congress, the executive, or the board room, they can completely ignore you, swat you like a pesky fly, or pay you symbolic momentary attention. But in court they ignore you at their own peril, to put it mildly. And that in itself is something that makes the courts a powerful playing field. Moreover, because of the legal culture they not only have to answer, but they have to answer in a certain way and in a certain time frame. They have to answer the question you ask, deal with the specific arguments you make and the specific facts you allege."[9]

The left-wing legal campaigns continue apace today. For instance, liberal groups are devoted to fighting for "voting rights"—which many conservatives would say is a euphemism for lining up as many Democratic voters as possible, even if they're felons, illegal aliens, or dead.* In 2005, after the Democratic governor of Iowa, Tom Vilsack, announced that he was giving ex-felons the right to vote, the *New York*

---

* Former Louisiana governor Huey Long once said that when he died he wanted to be buried in Louisiana so he could remain active in politics.

Times explained matter-of-factly, "Across the country, advocates have filed lawsuits to expand voting rights."[10]

Many left-wing groups succeed because their opponents can't match their firepower. The ACLU often sues local towns over the display of nativity scenes at Christmas. Small towns lack the resources to fend off well-coordinated legal assaults by the ACLU, with its deep-pocketed donors from Hollywood and Manhattan, and the free legal assistance it receives from wealthy private law firms.

Fortunately, conservatives can prevent the Left from overwhelming us if we fight back with our own lawsuits.

THE BENEFITS OF SUING

WHY ARE LAWSUITS such an effective political weapon? Some of the benefits aren't so obvious, though left-wing legal strategists shrewdly recognized the power of lawsuits decades ago.

For starters, there's the benefit that groups such as the NAACP and gay rights organizations count on: You can win with a lawsuit even if you lose the case in court or withdraw the suit.

Public interest law is a lot like streaking, it has been said: "No one knows how or whence it comes but when it does it sure gets public attention."[11] Lawsuits serve as message creators. By suing—and announcing the suit with a press release and a press conference—you generate news. When the media report on the lawsuit, they give full voice to the allegations in the complaint. The plaintiff's allegations—*unproven* allegations—become the story before the defendant even knows what hit him. By the time the defendant has drafted and filed an answer to the complaint, weeks or even months after the plaintiff filed the lawsuit, the response is no longer newsworthy. As Mark Twain supposedly said, a lie can travel halfway around the world before the truth puts its boots on.

In the 1970s, the news media loved reporting on Ralph Nader's lawsuits, and Nader exploited this advantage to set the terms of the debate. "Nader provided great copy—a juicy story right away and promises of a continuing saga to report as the crusader fought on," Barbara Hinkson Craig wrote. "Nader's *modus operandi* was to call a press conference to detail harm being done and to furnish exhaustive statistical and technological evidence of abuses knowingly perpetrated by an industry. To follow up on the diagnosis, he would lay out a specific remedial plan."[12]

In playing this game, liberals have traditionally exploited a natural advantage they had: the echo chamber of the liberal media. Walter Cronkite, *60 Minutes,* and the rest of the mainstream media lapped up the unproven allegations about evil corporations or governmental abuse shouted by liberal public interest groups and law firms. For years the Right was almost completely shut out by the mainstream media, as former CBS reporter Bernie Goldberg exposed in his book *Bias.* Of course, the rise of the new media has ended the Left's monopoly of the news. In the age of websites, blogs, Fox News, and talk radio, conservatives can get out their story and challenge the Left's misstatements. The Drudge Report's revelation of Bill Clinton's tryst with Monica Lewinsky and the blogosphere's destruction of Dan Rather highlight the point.

Sometimes lawsuits are filed almost solely for the purposes of generating publicity. Think about the lawsuits against McDonald's and other fast-food chains alleging that these restaurants should be held responsible for obesity in America. The publicity value of those suits was fantastic, although the cases themselves petered out.

Another example? In 2005, the Shinnecock Indians sued New York State, seeking, as the *New York Post* reported, the "return of 3,600 acres of prime real estate 'stolen' by the state a century and a half ago." The 1,300-member tribe also sought $1.7 billion in monetary damages and 150 years of back rent and interest.[13] The "prime real estate" the Shinnecock wanted just happened to be in the Hamptons, the wealthy enclave on the end of Long Island where countless celebrities, including Steven Spielberg, Billy Joel, and Howard Stern, have homes. Though the mere thought of a judge awarding Steven Spielberg's house to a downtrodden Indian tribe is delicious, the fact remains that by commencing this lawsuit—silly or not—the tribe drew huge media attention to its effort to receive federal recognition in order to open a casino in the Hamptons. And as the old adage goes, all publicity is good publicity.

Or how about the Left's lawsuits against President George W. Bush? The suits, many of them meritless, draw public attention to the Left's criticisms of the president. In December 2005, for example, eight advocacy groups filed a lawsuit against the federal government challenging aspects of the new prescription drug benefit. A federal trial judge tossed out the case in December, but the advocacy groups still succeeded in drawing attention to their criticism of the Bush-endorsed prescription drug plan.[14] The Left also trots out lawsuits to make Bush look bad on the environment. Hardly a day passes without some so-called environmental advocacy group commencing yet another lawsuit about global climate change, greenhouse gases, snowmobiling in national parks, Smokey the Bear—you name it. Each lawsuit, and each press release that inevitably accompanies it, hammers home the same message: The Bush administration doesn't like the environment. This message is conveyed even if a judge later dismisses the lawsuit as meritless.

SUING TO CAPTURE THE LANGUAGE AND CHANGE THE TERMS OF DEBATE

AN ADDED BENEFIT of suing is that it often helps political groups capture the language of a political issue. Liberals have long displayed the skill to frame public policy issues to serve their political ends, whether it's calling a reduction in the rate of increase for a public benefit a "cut," calling race discrimination by state universities "affirmative action," or calling lying under oath in a federal lawsuit an issue "just about sex."

Consider how liberals label opponents of gay marriage. Anyone who opposes civil unions or gay marriage is, according to the Left, "homophobic." A phobia is a psychological diagnosis of an irrational fear of something. So the Left wants to paint all those people who oppose gay marriage as being terrified of hairdressers and Judy Garland impersonators. In reality, the case against gay marriage is driven by concern about the deterioration in traditional values and morals in society. Once gay marriage is permitted, there is no rational reason to deny Americans the right to marry multiple spouses. Consider this "slippery slope" argument far-fetched? It's not. In September 2005, a husband and wife in Belgium married another woman, thereby creating a threesome. A judge in Utah is fighting to retain his job despite having three wives. Legalized group marriage here we come! If Paris and Nicky Hilton are reading this (or someone is reading this to them), call me ASAP. Heck, some people even harbor a fancy for horses, such as the unfortunate soul killed by copulating with an equine in Washington State, where bestiality is legal (and you thought legalizing prostitution in Las Vegas was problematic).[15]

Since liberals factor the courts heavily into their overall political strategy, they naturally use lawsuits to play this language game. Longtime conservative activist Paul Weyrich, who established the Heritage Foundation, described when he first realized how the Left used lawsuits to help frame political issues. In 1969 he attended a meeting with "every liberal group imaginable" at which they discussed their strategy to thwart a Nixon administration initiative. At the meeting, Weyrich recounted, "the ACLU said they would file a lawsuit not because of any aggrieved party, but in order to control the polemics of the issue."[16] This eye-opening experience taught Weyrich that the Right had to do a much better job of capturing the language of the debate. Think tanks, talk radio, cable TV, and the Internet all help the Right frame political messages—now let's deploy lawsuits, too.

There's no reason the Left should have a monopoly over using lawsuits to frame critical political messages. By filing well-timed and well-publicized lawsuits, the Right can set the terms of the political debate and call attention to real problems—and to conservative solutions.

SUING AND LOSING—BETTER THAN NOT SUING AT ALL

GIVEN THE CURRENT STATE of the judiciary, conservatives might understandably think that our chances of winning suits are uncertain at best. But that should not convince the Right to lay down the weapon of the lawsuit. As noted, you don't need to win every suit to advance a political cause. Remember what Obi-Wan Kenobi told the evil Darth Vader during their light-saber duel in Star Wars: "If you strike me down, I shall become more powerful than you can possibly imagine." Sure enough, Obi-Wan returned in a transcendental state to guide Luke Skywalker.

Or if you're not a Star Wars fan, you should listen to the left-wingers who have made an art form of this strategy. Alan Morrison, cofounder of Ralph Nader's Public Citizen Litigation Group, has said, "We always try to remember the perfect is the enemy of the good." In other words, as author Craig explained, "A loss in court may be a strategically acceptable tactic for securing a win elsewhere; an unpopular ruling, for example, might stir Congress to act."[17]

Both the Left and the Right have benefited politically after failing legally. Liberals lost their legal push to steal the 2000 election for Al Gore. But politically, they gained. In most mythological tellings, the legal battle was not about Gore trying to overturn the results of an election but about a "Republican Supreme Court" that "awarded the election" to Bush. In reality, the Supreme Court did not award the election to Bush, for Bush never trailed in Florida. True, the U.S. Supreme Court's decision prevented Gore from using the Florida Supreme Court to undo the election results in Florida, but the U.S. Supreme Court needed to intervene only after Gore and his supporters created the chaos by suing. In any case, the outcry from the Left created the false impression that Bush did not really win the election, and undermined his administration.

The Right, meanwhile, suffered a major legal loss in the case of *Kelo v. New London* in 2005, but that decision drew so much publicity to eminent domain abuses that it sparked a conservative campaign against burdensome government regulations. The U.S. Supreme Court prompted an uproar when it eviscerated much of the remaining protections afforded to private property by the Constitution's Fifth Amendment. Not only were conservatives incensed; even liberals such as Bill Clinton criticized the decision. In response, many states acted to change their laws to prohibit the kind of taking at issue in the *Kelo* case.[18] And the media drew additional attention to eminent domain abuses. Fox News's *Hannity & Colmes* began covering eminent domain stories in prime time and even encouraged viewers to share their personal experiences with eminent domain. In essence, the legal loss in *Kelo* was a short-term setback, but it could well inspire many more long-term gains for the property rights movement.

The Terri Schiavo case could also become a landmark in that it led many Americans to realize the importance of the courts. After all, the courts had the power to stop Schiavo's own family, and the U.S. Congress, from saving her life. Though Congress enacted legislation granting Schiavo's parents standing to argue that their daughter should not be starved to death, federal judges denied their request for immediate relief. In short, a court ruled that a human being could be starved to death—something that it would be illegal to do to a dog. Conservatives lost the case and Terri Schiavo lost her life. But by highlighting the legal problems concerning critical right-to-life issues, the case could produce benefits for the nation in the long run. Certainly the sweet yet powerful "chick flick" *Almost Heaven,* which tells the story of how a woman recovers from a supposedly irreversible coma, helps place the Schiavo matter in a whole new light with mainstream America.

And of course, conservatives lost badly when the U.S. Supreme Court struck down laws banning homosexual sodomy and then the Massachusetts Supreme Court created gay marriage. But the outcry the rulings prompted among many Americans helped George W. Bush retain the White House in 2004, as a gay marriage referendum in the swing state of Ohio helped deliver the state to Bush.

Why sit on the sidelines when even losing lawsuits can help us in the end?

COLLATERAL CONSEQUENCES

ONE OF THE LEFT'S tried-and-true tactics is to use lawsuits to uncover data about adversaries that otherwise would be unavailable. In fact, in many cases, the flow of information is only one-way—that is, the defendant government agency or business must reveal all kinds of information to the liberal group, but the liberal organization need not divulge much, if anything, about its inner workings. For example, Charles Houston, one of the most prominent attorneys for the NAACP during the years leading up to the Supreme Court's decision in *Brown v. Board of Education* (1954), explained, "We have very little money, very few trained investigators. But all we need is about $10.00. Then we can file a case in court. Five dollars more and we can bring the whole state education department into court with all its records, put each official on the stand under oath and wring him dry of information."[19]

Just as Republican operatives broke into the Democratic National Committee's headquarters at the Watergate Hotel to get inside information about the Democratic election strategy against Richard Nixon in 1972 ("back when Democrats had ideas worth stealing," to quote Jay Leno), the Left sues corporate America, Republican politicians, and the Bush administration to gain information that can be used against those groups later—in the courts, in Congress, or even in the court of public opinion.

Do you think those on the Left wholeheartedly supported the lawsuit seeking to acquire information about Vice President Dick Cheney's National Energy Task Force because they were concerned that some silly administrative regulation might have been ignored? Hardly. The real goal was to uncover embarrassing information about the task force or, if that failed, to create the public perception that the Bush White House could not be trusted. The lawsuit became an effective propaganda tool against the Bush White House. A Democratic National Committee website focused on the task force's "corruption and abuse of power" and tried to tie the group to Enron.[20] Even when the Dems lost in the Supreme Court, they didn't treat it as a loss; instead, the DNC stated, "Although the conservative-dominated Supreme Court found in favor of Cheney, questions remain about Cheney's activities on the Energy Task Force. Cheney refused to reveal who he met with while he was formulating the national energy policy . . . [but] it was clear from the small number of documents that had already been released that he granted energy industry insiders their greatest wishes when crafting the national energy policy."[21]

The Left understands the value of uncovering politically embarrassing disclosures from legal proceedings. That's why we see a whole host of liberals working diligently to sue under the federal Freedom of Information Act and other laws to gather information about the events at Abu Ghraib prison or at Guantánamo Bay. For example, in 2004 the ACLU sued the Bush administration and issued a press release stating that the prisoner abuses at Abu Ghraib were a "predictable result" of U.S. detention policies and that the administration had "deliberately skirted the rule of law and American values." The press release highlighted the ACLU's demand that the government immediately turn over "information on the reported torture of detainees held in the war on terrorism."[22]

And keep in mind that sometimes the true benefits of lawsuits are not felt for years after the suit begins. A good example is the Left's lengthy crusade to destroy the Boy Scouts—or, perhaps more insidious, to "reform" them. Back in the 1970s, Ruth Bader Ginsburg, now a "moderate" Supreme Court justice, advocated merging the Boy Scouts with the Girl Scouts—in effect eliminating the Boy Scouts. Then the Left sued to allow a gay scoutmaster to take young Boy Scouts into the woods on overnight camping trips. A New Jersey court sided with the gay scoutmaster. The Boy Scouts finally won the case in the Supreme Court, but only after declaring that religion was critical to their mission. With that victory the Boy Scouts ensured defeat down the road: Acknowledging the importance of religion inspired the ACLU to threaten still other lawsuits, this time against public schools and other taxpayer-funded government agencies that supported the Boy Scouts of America. And guess what? To avoid the costly lawsuits, the Boy Scouts pulled the charters of thousands of Scouting units from public schools.[23]

So much for the open-minded liberals who purportedly love poor and underprivileged children—the exact kids harmed most by the Left's anti–Boy Scout agenda.

EXPANDING THE CONSERVATIVE BASE

By WIELDING LAWSUITS as a weapon, the Right could expand the ranks of conservative supporters and at the same time weaken support for the Democrats. Today, powerful and wealthy trial lawyers overwhelmingly support the Democrats, and the Democratic Party relies on the plaintiff's bar for money and as a voting bloc. But the reality is that, given the proper financial incentives, trial lawyers can also be effective mercenaries for the conservative cause. Trial lawyers are in a profit-driven industry like any other, in which new markets are always desired.

Remember that for every politically motivated lawyer, you have many more who are motivated by the incentives Adam Smith described in *The Wealth of Nations*. As Smith explained, "It is not from the benevolence of the butcher, the brewer, or the baker, that we expect our dinner, but from their regard to their own interest. We address ourselves, not to their humanity but to their self-love." In many other public policy areas conservatives realize that economic incentives trump irrational biases against races, genders, and, yes, political groups, as conservative economist Thomas Sowell has documented in his work on affirmative action.[24] Why wouldn't it be the same with trial attorneys? The truth is, lawyers will have powerful incentives to help the conservative cause even if they don't necessarily agree with the politics; they can make money for themselves and their firms, and generate publicity, which brings in more business.

The monetary incentives are undeniable. As members of the vast right-wing conspiracy well know, if you subsidize something, you get more of it, and if you tax something, you get less of it. These economic realities apply equally to lawyers and the lawsuits they file. Creating economic incentives for lawyers to sue for the Right will generate such suits.

Attorneys often work on a contingency basis or collect statutory attorney's fees—either way, they will have an economic incentive to advance the conservative cause regardless of their personal political orientations. And under many statutes, especially civil rights statutes and others by which ordinary individuals and their lawyers are empowered to advance the "public interest" in the courts, the lawyers in effect become private, unelected attorneys general. Fortunes can be won if conservatives unleash successful lawsuits against local, state, and federal government. Like other conservatives, I am disturbed that taxpayers must foot the bill for outsized court settlements, and I firmly support tort reform. But again, we must work within the system as it actually exists now. And no victory comes without its costs. The achievements that conservatives can make by using lawsuits as a weapon outweigh the costs.

And those conservatives who fret (rightly) over the proliferation of lawsuits should never forget that the best hope for significant tort reform could come from using lawsuits to inflict real damage to liberal causes and institutions. If liberals no longer reap all the benefits of lawsuits, and come to see that their ox can be gored by lawsuits, too, they might finally come to the table to bargain on tort reform. Inflicting political and financial pain on liberals might be the *only* way to get liberals even to think about reducing the number of lawsuits. Peace through strength, baby!

An aggressive use of lawsuits will also eat into Democratic support among trial lawyers. The plaintiff's bar supports the Democratic Party mainly because Democrats want to pass more laws, create more victim classes, and create more opportunities to make money for attorneys. If conservatives create economic incentives for attorneys to attack liberal institutions, the GOP may split a Democratic-leaning voting bloc just as Ronald Reagan attracted "Reagan Democrats."

Think I'm being too idealistic? I'm not. Politics makes for strange bedfellows and sometimes so do lawsuits. Remember how the ACLU and the NRA teamed up to sue over federal campaign finance laws? Current trends reflect more businesses reaching out to contingency-fee lawyers, and many doctors are hiring trial lawyers to sue HMOs and insurance companies. And trial lawyers certainly can see how Republicans dominate the American political scene, controlling the White House, both houses of Congress, and a majority of statehouses and governorships. For trial lawyers, whose livelihoods depend on laws, currying favor with the politically powerful ain't a bad strategy.

Conservatives might not like the idea of working with trial lawyers, but we need to, because, like it or not, they play an essential role in all our most important political debates. No less a liberal icon than Justice William Brennan pointed out that attorneys have been central figures in our "legalistic society from the beginning." Writing in the *American Bar Association Journal,* Justice Brennan declared that since revolutionary times, our society has framed "urgent social, economic and political questions in legal terms." America places "great problems of social order in the hands of lawyers for their definition, and in the hands of judges for their ultimate resolution," Brennan wrote. "It seems to me unquestionable that the lawyer in America is uniquely situated to play a creative role in American social progress."[25]

Brennan wrote that nearly forty years ago. It's about time conservatives sought to deploy attorneys and exploit the legal system for political gain.

HOW TO ACHIEVE CONSERVATIVE GOALS

RIGHT NOW CONSERVATIVES are in a particularly strong position to employ an aggressive legal strategy because we can wield our political power in the other branches to pave the way for conservative lawsuits that the trial bar would be incentivized to join.

Democrats have never been shy about using the legislature to stack the deck in favor of their lawsuits. Democratic-controlled legislatures have enacted statutes that make it easier for plaintiffs to sue for all sorts of wrongdoings, perceived or real, and have created countless causes of action permitting individuals and organizations to sue. Among the alleged victims legislatures have passed laws to help sue are those affected by telemarketers, predatory loans, and discrimination on the basis of race, gender, or sexual orientation. Legislatures have also loosened the standards of proof necessary for plaintiffs to satisfy in products liability cases. They have even outlawed discrimination against lawyers in rental housing decisions.

Republicans could enact legislative proposals helpful to defending the nation's core values and freedoms. For example, we would want laws that

- Permit landowners to recover from reductions in the economic value of their property due to new government regulations, and ensure that successful suits produce attorneys' fees for the property owners' attorneys—a boon to the property owners and the trial bar while helping check rapacious local governments

- Provide an Academic Bill of Rights ensuring ideological diversity among faculty at state colleges and, where the required diversity is lacking, permitting applicants for faculty positions to sue for relief[26]

- Permit lawsuits seeking monetary damages by unborn children who are injured or killed by drunk drivers or others who assault them and their mother

- Ensure that women who seek abortions and abortion advice are covered by the same consumer protection laws that apply to all other businesses and service providers

- Force cities that prevent the law-abiding from carrying guns for self-defense to pay monetary damages to crime victims whom the police failed to protect.

These and other bills would help advance the conservative cause and create desirable incentives to sue for the same.

REFUSING TO SUE IS A SELF-DEFEATING GAME PLAN

CONSERVATIVES MUST LEARN THIS lesson about politically motivated lawsuits: *Meekness fails.*

To wit: The incumbent Republican John Ashcroft lost the 2000 U.S. Senate election in Missouri to Democrat Mel Carnahan, a dead man. Ashcroft probably would have won a legal case if he had argued that the deceased Carnahan was ineligible to be on the ballot. But Ashcroft did not sue, and instead Carnahan's wife, Jean, was appointed to the Senate seat. The result was a 50–50 split in the U.S. Senate, and soon thereafter, Senator Jim Jeffords of Vermont left the Republican Party, giving the Democrats operational control of the Senate.

Of course, Ashcroft was only following in the footsteps of other Republican politicians. Richard Nixon, also an attorney, refused to challenge the 1960 presidential election despite evidence of voter fraud in Chicago and in Texas. Nixon decided to place the best interests of the country ahead of his presidential ambitions. The result? Lyndon B. Johnson got us stuck in Vietnam and launched the Great Society. And what do Democrats do in the same situation? Just ask Al Gore and the Democrats. They sue and then lie that "not every vote was counted in Florida" and now assert that George W. Bush is an illegitimate president.

While conservatives were winning elections and legislative battles, liberals marshaled their resources and used lawsuits to effect social change. All this litigation has proved to be as important and influential as any law enacted by Congress. Conservatives need to change our entire outlook on the lawsuit issue. Remember the story of the Revolutionary War soldier who said the British wouldn't hang American troops because "we have rope, too"? Lawsuits give conservatives another length of rope. Liberals should be as fearful of conservative lawsuits as the British were of American rope. The threat of conservative suits may force left-wing groups to think twice about going to court. It may also cause liberal politicians to pause. Never forget, we conservatives have rope, too.

WHAT A DIFFERENCE A GUN MAKES

Suing for Gun Rights

In January 2001, a husband and wife, both professors at Dartmouth College, were brutally murdered by two teenage boys wielding knives. The stabbings stunned their quiet New Hampshire community and became a national news story. But the shock over the Ivy League saga mostly obscured the true object lesson of the story: Before the teenagers killed the beloved (and unarmed) Dartmouth professors, they had planned to murder another local family, but turned away when they got to the house. What made them call off the plan? The man who answered the door, a husband and father, appeared with a loaded 9-millimeter handgun.

The gentleman later told police the simple truth: "If it wasn't for that God damn Glock, I'd be dead today."[1]

You'd never hear that kind of straight talk from the Left. Liberals have an irrational fear of guns, and they've never hesitated to deploy the coercive power of the legal system to force Americans to give up their right to self-defense. The right to bear arms, enshrined in the Second Amendment ("the right of the people to keep and bear arms, shall not be infringed"), is a clear constitutional right that government cannot take away. You might choose not to own a firearm, but there is no denying that each of us has a fundamental, unalienable right to self-defense. It should, in fact, be one of the most preciously guarded in the panoply of American rights. After all, if we don't have a realistic right to self-defense, that threatens the most fundamental right—the right to life. Remember, you can't enjoy protesting WTO meetings, hugging trees, paying taxes, or viewing homoerotic art if you're dead. (Just ask Dutch filmmaker Theo van Gogh, killed in 2004 by Islamo-fascists.) If we can't protect ourselves, we are left vulnerable to predators like the teenagers who stabbed the unarmed Dartmouth professors.

It's laughable to speak about the right to self-defense in theory but then deny an individual the realistic ability to effectuate that right—the ability to own and carry a gun. Without a handgun, most Americans are defenseless at the hands of a violent thug. How many of us, after all, have the physical strength or the martial arts training to repel an aggressive predator, especially someone who is armed with a deadly weapon? Yet the courts, by engaging in the "judicial restraint" the Right encourages, have aided and abetted anti-gun politicians to make it far too difficult for many Americans to protect themselves. Usually they buy into the gun-control crowd's spin that having guns around is too dangerous. But those claims are patently false. In fact, even beyond the moral case for self-defense, there is a strong practical case: Clear empirical evidence shows that guns *save* lives and reduce crime, and that the anti-gun lobby's dire warnings about the dangers of guns don't hold up to scrutiny.

The time has come for conservatives to turn the tables on liberals and use the courts to protect fundamental gun rights. We can actually do liberals a service here and help them overcome their gun phobia. Judicial Reagans would certainly recognize that gun-control laws deprive ordinary Americans of their fundamental right to defend themselves and their families. But judges alone can't fight this battle against the Left. We rank-and-file conservatives must contribute as well, ensuring that law-abiding citizens have the ability to defend themselves. Once again, the lawsuit can be a weapon for the Right. We should seek court orders striking down unconstitutional and immoral gun-control laws, thus preserving gun rights.

PROTECTING OUR RIGHTS—AND OUR LIVES

THE UNITED STATES IS a gun culture. In April 1775, when the British dispatched armed troops from Boston to the towns of Lexington and Concord, their objective was not to rape and pillage the countryside, but to seize the guns the colonists had collected. After winning their independence from Britain, the Framers of the Constitution made certain to protect the right to bear arms in the Second Amendment. Today, somewhere between 75 million and 86 million Americans own over 200 million guns, including about 65 million handguns.[2] Thus, if any individual activity is deeply rooted in the nation's past, it is the right to own a gun for self-defense.

So how did so many Americans in so many parts of the country lose their fundamental right to protect ourselves in a realistic fashion? It probably won't surprise you to learn that one of the first big changes came during the 1930s, when the federal government passed the National Firearms Act, requiring automatic weapons and certain other firearms to be registered with the Treasury Department. In the case of *United States v. Miller* (1939), the Supreme Court focused on the amendment's opening clause: "A well-regulated militia being necessary to the security of a free state . . ." The court said that the Second Amendment did not guarantee the right to keep and bear the weapon in question in this case (a short-barreled shotgun), since the defendants failed to supply evidence showing that the gun "has some reasonable relationship to the preservation or efficiency of a well regulated militia."[3] Anti-gun judges and attorneys would disingenuously seize on the *Miller* decision to uphold countless future gun-control laws.

Bigger changes came in the 1960s, when gun control became a hot-button issue after the assassinations of John F. Kennedy, Robert F. Kennedy, and Martin Luther King Jr. Congress passed the first comprehensive law restricting gun rights with the Gun Control Act of 1968. Thereafter, court after court interpreted the Second Amendment to mean that it did not protect the individual right to bear arms, instead maintaining that the amendment guaranteed only the "collective right" of a state to have a formal state militia (often referring to the state's National Guard).

The liberal courts got their way, at the expense of our safety and fundamental rights.

TIME TO DEFEND THE RIGHTS OF LAW-ABIDING AMERICANS, NOT CRIMINALS

As LIBERAL JUDGES BEGAN curtailing Americans' gun rights, they took extraordinary steps to defend criminals. The Left advocates the same strategy in the fight against criminals as in the Iraq war: preemptive surrender. Many liberal judges pride themselves on understanding the plight of the criminal ("if he only had a puppy and better after-school programs growing up") and bend over backward to help criminal defendants. Sure, criminals have constitutional protections against rogue prosecutions (think of political grandstanders such as Tom DeLay's friend Ronnie Earle). But judges often give criminals the benefit of every doubt, not just reasonable doubt. The courts invented rights, procedural protections, and countless other technicalities that allow savvy defense attorneys to get criminals off the hook.

The courts insist that all these protections are mandated by the Constitution. But I'm not sure how anyone can say that phrases such as "due process of law" and "unreasonable searches and seizures" could produce the layers upon layers of judge-invented procedures and rules that make it so difficult for police to serve and protect ordinary citizens. The bulk of these "rights," in fact, went undiscovered until the latter half of the twentieth century. For example, the "right" to free attorneys paid for by taxpayers in all state criminal cases didn't exist until the Supreme Court said it did in 1963 in *Gideon v. Wainwright*.

Liberal judges usually say that they must interpret the Constitution broadly to give constitutional rights practical application, to make them "real" somehow. For instance, to effectuate the right not to self-incriminate, judges insist that police read criminal suspects their rights when they are arrested—these are the so-called *Miranda* rights. This is a little odd, isn't it? If I am arrested and they ask if I did it and I am stupid enough to say yes, then so be it. That's a far cry from coercing criminal confessions through torture. The so-called exclusionary rule is similarly questionable. This rule holds that evidence law enforcement gathers through unconstitutional methods cannot be used in a trial against a criminal defendant. It is supposed to protect the constitutional rights of the accused, but what about the rights of the law-abiding public? If a police officer makes a procedural mistake with evidence, he isn't the one punished when a judge throws out that evidence. No, the real victim is the public, put at risk when a person guilty of a violent crime is set free on a mere technicality.

Why didn't judges go to the same lengths to defend the rights of law-abiding citizens? There is nothing in the Constitution that compelled such criminal-coddling remedies; the courts took it upon themselves to regulate the police and stand up for criminals' rights using broad and expansive interpretations of the Constitution. Yet no such broad and expansive interpretations of the Constitution have been forthcoming in favor of providing law-abiding Americans with a realistic right to defend themselves against those same criminals.

Fortunately, we can make sure the courts protect guns and rework the criminal justice system in favor of the law-abiding public, not criminals. But how? By embracing the tactics and judicial philosophies of the Left!

IT'S UP TO US, NOT THE POLICE

DESCRIBING POSSIBLE FUTURE RESTRICTIONS on the right to abortion, Harvard Law professor Laurence Tribe explained that "the court will cut back on *Roe v. Wade,* step by step. Not just to the point where, as the moderate American center has it, abortion is cautiously restricted but to the point where the fundamental underlying right to liberty becomes a hollow shell."[4]

A hollow shell? That's exactly what the right to self-defense has become in so many parts of the United States today. Liberals always tell us they want to give rights meaning in the real world, so let's do that for the right to self-defense so that Americans can truly benefit from it. The only way to make the right to self-defense realistic—the same way liberals made criminals' rights realistic—is to allow a citizen to buy, own, and carry a firearm. A firearm is the great equalizer—just ask a 5'3", 100-pound woman who is attacked by a 220-pound man. Only if she is armed can she avoid becoming the victim of a violent crime such as rape or murder.

The Left likes to argue that when we are confronted with a dangerous situation, our recourse should be to call the cops. Get real. It's strange enough that the same liberals who generally consider cops to be untrustworthy, incompetent, racist, sexist oppressors of the underprivileged (the ACLU's website proclaims, "Police abuse continues to be a major civil liberties problem in the U.S., particularly in poor communities and communities of color") would be so deferential to the police in the gun-control area. Stranger still is the absence of logic behind their argument. We'd all like to think the police can protect us. And, unlike liberals, we conservatives respect American law enforcement. But the reality is that preventing crime is a small part of what the police do. Their primary job is to investigate and solve crimes *after* they're committed. To put it bluntly, by the time the police get to the scene, someone is usually a chalk outline on the ground already. And no candlelight vigil or "We shall overcome" chant will bring that person back to life.

Take the most infamous acts of violence in recent American memory—

the Columbine High School shootings and the 9/11 terrorist attacks. In Columbine, law enforcement arrived on the scene quickly but delayed entering the school despite the fact that they knew gunmen were shooting their way through the building and victims were bleeding to death. (Obviously, entry into the building would have been too dangerous—for the cops.)[5] And of course, on 9/11 the federal government failed to defend Americans against terrorists. Luckily, at least some people on a plane over Pennsylvania—civilians—took action.

As it happens, the police have no legal duty to protect Americans from rapists, robbers, murderers, and other predators. In the summer of 2005 the Supreme Court pronounced in *Town of Castle Rock v. Gonzales* that even an individual who has received a restraining order against another person has no right to expect protection from the police. At the same time, though, the law holds that prisoners in police custody are entitled to police protection. So there you have it: According to our legal system, police have a greater duty to protect the lives of prison inmates than the lives of law-abiding citizens whose taxes pay for the police and the prisons.

You and I will never have a police officer on our doorstep 24/7, so we need to take responsibility for defending our own lives. The courts must now help us assume that vital responsibility in a realistic way.

EMBRACING THE "LIVING CONSTITUTION" TO SAVE GUNS—AND LIVES

WITH GUNS AS WITH other issues, the "living Constitution" can be the Right's great ally. If the Constitution and the law should evolve to keep up with the times and the new needs of society, then the law needs to do a lot of catching up to reflect what we've learned about the value of guns.

Of course, when not teasing Dick Cheney about hunting accidents, liberals insist that guns don't deter crime. Really? Then why do liberal anti-gun politicians and activists surround themselves with guys carrying guns? Whether it is Hillary Clinton surrounded by the Secret Service, Kofi Annan surrounded by United Nations security officers, or Rosie O'Donnell protected by an armed private detective, the very same liberals who rail against civilian gun ownership don't deny themselves the life-preserving benefits of guns. Next time a liberal politician wants to outlaw guns, ask whether he is willing to give up his *armed* bodyguards.

And if the presence of guns doesn't deter crimes and violent predators, then why do we issue guns to police and soldiers at all? Couldn't we just give them lighters and MP3 downloads of John Lennon's song "Imagine"? Think about it: How often have you heard of uniformed police officers being robbed? Criminals stay away from cops. They do so not because police officers dress in blue or wear cool hats, but because they know cops carry guns—guns that can kill criminals.

Even liberals concede that guns help law enforcement officers serve and protect us. Nobody would dispute the importance of issuing a firearm to a physically fit 200-pound male police officer who is charged with apprehending an armed rapist. So why would we deny a gun to a 100-pound woman who is at risk of being victimized by that same rapist? To deny her the realistic ability to protect her unalienable right to life is immoral and unconstitutional.

If you have any doubt about the defensive value of guns, ask your liberal friends if they would rather have a gun or a peace symbol if a violent criminal picked them as his next victim.

We don't have to rely on common sense alone to defend the importance of guns. Liberals argue naively that everything would be perfect if we could just ban guns. Would that solve the problem of violent crime? Well, no. Look at Washington, D.C., which has a virtual ban on firearms—you can't even keep a loaded gun in your home in D.C. And yet every year Washington has extremely high rates of violent crime.[6] In contrast, Vermont has virtually no gun-control laws—you can carry a handgun concealed on your body virtually everywhere. The state vies every year for the lowest violent crime rate in the nation.

Scientific study after scientific study proves that guns save lives. To take just one example, researchers James Wright and Peter Rossi interviewed 1,874 imprisoned felons in 1982 and 1983 and found that 81 percent agreed that smart criminals try to learn whether someone has a gun before deciding to attack, 74 percent agreed that criminals avoid occupied homes if arms are in there, and 57 percent feared being shot by citizens more than being shot by police.

Another example: In the 1990s University of Chicago economists John Lott Jr. and David B. Mustard conducted a comprehensive study on the effect of gun-control laws, examining crime data for every

county in the United States over a period of sixteen years. Lott and
Mustard found that those counties with many restrictions on gun ownership had much higher violent crime rates than those counties with
fewer restrictions on gun ownership. The report concluded that "allowing citizens to carry concealed weapons deters violent crimes and it
appears to produce no increase in accidental deaths. If those states
which did not have right-to-carry concealed gun provisions had adopted
them in 1992, approximately 1,570 murders; 4,177 rapes; and over
60,000 aggravated assaults would have been avoided yearly." Lott and
Mustard added, "When state concealed handgun laws went into effect
in a county, murders fell by 8.5 percent, and rapes and aggravated assaults fell by 5 and 7 percent." They also pointed out that Americans
use guns in self-defense as many as 2.5 million times a year, and that
400,000 of the people who use firearms defensively believe that using a
gun "almost certainly" saved a life.[7]

In 1987, Florida implemented a law permitting law-abiding citizens to carry concealed handguns in public. The result? During the first
five years after the law went into effect, Florida's homicide rate fell by
23 percent. During that same period, the overall U.S. homicide rate
rose 9 percent. Little wonder, then, that in a 2001 survey of the nation's
23,113 police chiefs and sheriffs, 62 percent said they believed that a
"national concealed handgun permit would reduce rates of violent
crime."[8]

Why in the world does the Left continue to ignore this evidence
that guns protect people? Liberals cast themselves as the defenders of
minorities, women, gays, and other "oppressed" classes. But what better way to defend them than to give them the ability to defend *themselves,* literally? In June 2005, a man in Brooklyn, New York, was
brutally beaten by three men yelling antigay slurs.[9] The truly compas-
sionate response to this unfortunate crime would be, "Too bad the victim didn't have a gun." The Pink Pistols, a group encouraging gun
ownership among gays, have this motto: "We no longer believe it is the
right of those who hate and fear gay, lesbian, bi, trans, or polyamorous
persons to use us as targets for their rage. Self-defense is our right."
They're correct.

The same goes for women, too. Every year college campuses fea-
ture "Take Back the Night" rallies, in which students (mostly women)
hold a candlelight vigil and then march to raise awareness of violence

against women. The march organizers' goal is admirable, but perhaps there is a better way to take back the night than to wave banners and light candles. A woman takes back the night all by herself by carrying a real handgun loaded with real bullets.

Simply put, guns can stop evil people from doing evil things. Liberals fail to acknowledge this essential fact when they rail against the supposed dangers of guns. True, criminals use guns to commit all manner of crimes. But of course, police also use guns when they track down criminals, and millions of Americans use guns to protect their families. Perhaps more to the point, criminals also use knives, bricks, rope, automobiles, airplanes, and many other objects to commit heinous crimes. Nobody came out after 9/11 to pass another "airplane law" outlawing the hijacking of airplanes with the intent to fly them into buildings, did they? Nobody seeks to enact laws against "box cutter violence," "knife violence," or "brick violence," just "gun violence." The gun is, like those other things, a tool—dangerous in the wrong hands, but extremely valuable and protective in the proper hands. By ignoring the well-documented benefits arising from civilian gun ownership, as many courts and politicians do, we prevent enough guns from getting into the right hands.

Not only do liberals ignore the benefits of gun ownership, they overstate the dangers as well. Let's look at the statistics bandied about by the gun haters. For example, while testifying before the U.S. Senate in 2001, Michael Barnes, then president of the anti-gun organization Handgun Control Inc., claimed that nearly eleven children die from gun-related violence every day in this country. Really? No, of course not. Barnes counted as "children" anyone age nineteen or younger, even though that group includes one of the most active criminal groups in the country—teenagers. Violent crime is largely a young man's game, conducted by gang members and drug dealers, so Barnes's effort to portray all these "children" as innocent victims was completely misleading. According to crime statistics compiled by the National Center for Health Studies, of the 3,012 gun-related deaths for "children" nineteen and younger in the year 2000, only 433 deaths affected children fourteen or younger. That's a daily average death rate of 1.2—a far cry from what the anti-gun crowd wants us to believe.

Though any death of an innocent child is tragic, we must put the 1.2 deaths per day in perspective. As John Lott, now of the American Enterprise Institute, has noted, "The dangers of children getting into guns pale in comparison to many other risks." For example, in 1999, 1,260 children under age ten died in motor vehicle accidents; 484 died from residential fires; 93 children drowned in bathtubs; 36 under age five drowned in five-gallon plastic buckets. Lott concluded, "More children under five drown in this one type of water bucket than children under ten die from any type of accidental gunshot."[10]

Similar evidence came from an unlikely source: the best-selling book *Freakonomics* by economist Steven D. Levitt and journalist Stephen J. Dubner—a work the liberal media fawned over. Levitt and Dubner showed that children are in more danger if you have a swimming pool in your backyard than if you have a gun in your home. Perhaps the liberals who gushed over *Freakonomics* didn't realize it had shot a huge hole in the argument that guns must be regulated because they are too dangerous in citizens' hands.[11]

Besides, if a criminal predator is bearing down on you, tossing out a few Canadian crime statistics won't protect you. Nor will singing "Give Peace a Chance." Blowing a hole through him will.

HOW TO WIN

CLEARLY THERE IS a very strong moral and practical case to be made for preserving the right to bear arms. But this means nothing to the millions of Americans forced to live in the bluest cities in the bluest states—such as those living in New York City, San Francisco, and Washington, D.C. When loony liberalism reigns supreme, rational policy arguments about guns fall on deaf ears, just as arguments opposing racial segregation fell on deaf ears in the South for decades. So what can be done? A little Red State judicial activism at the expense of Blue State laws is warranted. Conservatives need to make a push in the courts to reverse the restrictions the Left has imposed on the American people.

The Right's eagerness to encourage courts to engage in judicial restraint in favor of democratic outcomes returns to bite conservatives on the butt in the gun context. It's unacceptable to put up with onerous gun restrictions in one jurisdiction because federalism contemplates that each state can enact its own laws favored by the local populace. Each state should not be allowed to set its own gun laws when doing so infringes on the fundamental individual right to self-defense. Conservatives must appear in court ready to win and not to compromise politically. After all, the Left refused to be satisfied with abortion being legal in California but not in Alabama. The Left wanted it all in the political war over abortion and managed to win; the Right should fight for the same objective with guns.

As with so many other battles we're waging in the courts, we can turn left-wingers' arguments against them. Liberals love to talk about the "real world" application of constitutional rights. So, for example, courts protect abortion providers because without them, the Left says, women cannot exercise the "right" to an abortion; the right becomes meaningless in practice if abortionists necessary to effectuate that right aren't readily available to women. Well, courts should protect the right to own and carry guns in order to ensure that law-abiding citizens can exercise their realistic right to self-defense. All the current restrictions on owning, carrying, and using firearms impinge on our fundamental rights.

The notion of the "living Constitution" can be our friend in another way, too. If the Supreme Court can conclude that homosexual sodomy should be constitutionally protected in part because more and more states are eliminating laws forbidding such conduct, then it should take notice of how both the states and the federal government are recognizing the importance of guns. More and more states are adopting concealed-carry laws like Florida's; as of 2006, thirty-eight states had adopted laws permitting individuals to carry guns for self-defense. Moreover, in the fall of 2005 Congress passed and President George W. Bush signed into law the Protection of Lawful Commerce in Arms Act, which immunizes gun manufacturers against liability actions for crimes committed with their guns. The clear national trend is toward more guns and fewer gun controllers. Even foreign precedents point in the pro-gun direction. In late 2005, Brazilian voters rejected overwhelmingly a referendum seeking to outlaw the sale of firearms and ammunition. Who says all foreign precedents are bad?

Of course, these new tactics do not preclude the Right from also using the courts to debunk the Left's ridiculously narrow interpretation of the Second Amendment, and properly applying that provision to federal, state, and local gun laws. The full text of the Second Amendment reads: "A well-regulated militia, being necessary to the security of a free state, the right of the people to keep and bear arms, shall not be infringed." The liberal argument, in essence, is: *The Second Amendment confers no individual right to own guns but merely allows states to keep a militia, now known as the National Guard.* Such careful parsing is bizarre for the Left because, as we know, liberal judges interpret their favorite constitutional clauses broadly, and when the text fails to give them a basis to support the desired result, they discover "penumbral" rights. (Or maybe in all my readings of the Constitution I've just missed the clear and unambiguous language supporting the right to engage in anal sex and to receive a free attorney paid for by the taxpayers.) The good news for conservatives is that we don't need to rely on such sleight of hand in protecting the fundamental right to bear arms.

First, the Second Amendment provides that "the people" shall have the right to keep and bear arms. In interpreting the term "the people" as used in the Second, Fourth, Ninth, and Tenth Amendments, the Supreme Court has made clear that it refers to individuals.[12] The first ten amendments to the U.S. Constitution were concerned with identifying individual rights, not conferring power on government, so it would seem strange that the second item on that list would say nothing about an individual right and instead would provide state governments with the power to create a national guard. These amendments, after all, were called the Bill of *Rights,* not the Bill of Government Powers.

Beyond that, despite the Left's claims, the term "well-regulated militia" does not refer to the National Guard. The Guard, as formally constituted today, didn't come into existence until 1903. In fact, the Framers understood the term "well-regulated militia" to apply to all able-bodied adult men. Consider, for instance, that the federal Militia Act of May 8, 1792, required every "free able bodied white male citizen" to provide himself with a "good musket or firelock."[13]

Furthermore, the Founders made abundantly clear the importance of keeping the citizens armed. Remember, their war with the British had begun when the king's soldiers marched toward Lexington and Concord not to rape and pillage the Massachusetts countryside but to capture guns. When the time came to write the Bill of Rights, and specifically the Second Amendment, the Framers made certain that their new government would never infringe on the individual's fundamental right to bear arms.

Even better news for conservatives is that a few courts have recently endorsed the view that the Second Amendment guarantees the *individual* right to bear arms, rather than a collective right. Two federal courts reached this conclusion in reviewing the case of *United States v. Emerson* ("We have found no historical evidence that the Second Amendment was intended to convey militia power to the states . . . or applies only to members of a select militia. . . . We reject the collective rights and sophisticated collective rights models for interpreting the Second Amendment").[14] Here the judiciary has followed the lead of legal and historical scholars: there has emerged a consensus—among both liberal and conservative scholars—that the Second Amendment protects an individual right. More encouraging news has come from the Bush Justice Department. In 2001, then–Attorney General John Ashcroft issued a policy statement saying that the Second Amendment guaranteed an individual right to bear arms, and in 2004 the Justice Department issued a formal memorandum opinion making this point ("The Second Amendment secures a right of individuals generally, not a right of States or a right restricted to persons serving in militias").[15]

We need to push courts further on this point, but the trend is encouraging. We have a golden opportunity, relying on evolving national and international trends, reams of scholarly data, and the Left's beloved living Constitution, to defeat the gun haters and firmly establish our fundamental right to self-defense. Let's not blow it.

TWELVE

KEEP YOUR ECONOMIC LAWS OFF MY BODY!

Suing to Protect Free Markets

Conservatives rightly celebrate the free-market-driven economic re-forms and trends ushered in during Ronald Reagan's presidency, which continue to this day. Finally the U.S. government turned away from what had seemed like an irreversible trend toward bigger govern-ment, higher taxes, and more restraints on free markets. Reagan turned the tide, fighting for tax cuts that spurred an annual economic growth rate of 3.9 percent and ultimately created 20 million new jobs. Repub-licans kept pressing the effort into the 1990s—forcing even liberal Bill Clinton to acknowledge that "the era of big government is over." (It wasn't really, unfortunately, but given where we were not many years earlier with the Great Society, we can't complain too much.) And today we have a conservative president who has pushed multiple tax cuts that have sent the economy surging. Not too shabby.

The conservative economic revolution is all the more impressive when you consider that left-wing judges and existing legal precedents offer little legal protection to free markets and economic liberties. Our economy has flourished *in spite of* the courts and the law, not because of them. (The United States, "the land of the free," ranked only ninth in the Heritage Foundation/*Wall Street Journal* 2006 Index of Eco-nomic Freedom, which demonstrates that "the countries with the most economic freedom also have higher rates of long-term economic growth and are more prosperous than are those with less economic freedom.")[1]

We've already seen how the first casualties of the left-wing judicial revolution starting in the 1930s were property rights and other eco-nomic liberties the Founders considered unalienable. It's absolutely galling that liberal judges have sat idly by while politicians interfere with the economy and attack our economic rights, ignoring numerous protections provided in the Constitution, the clear intentions of the Founders, and nearly a century and a half of unequivocal Supreme Court rulings (or maybe I'm just missing the nuance in the Supreme Court's 1923 declaration that the freedom to contract "is settled by the decisions of this Court and is no longer open to question"). Remember, the right to property doesn't cover only the right to buy stuff; it is (or at least was for most of this nation's history) one of the most important of all the individual rights. As John Adams put it in 1787, "Property is surely a right of mankind as [real] as liberty. . . . The moment the idea is admitted into society, that property is not as sacred as the laws of God, and that there is not a force of law and public justice to protect it, anarchy and tyranny commence."[2]

Before anybody accuses me of being too nostalgic for the eighteenth century, I'll give you some more recent reminders of why fundamental economic rights are essential to preserving a just and flourishing society. Go ahead and ask the leaders of the Soviet Union. . . . Oops, I forgot—the Soviet Union exists only as a figment of the imaginations of those hippie professors who fill the minds of young students with pipe dreams of "from each according to his ability, to each according to his need." The history of the twentieth century shows us clearly that, to put it mildly, capitalism and free markets beat socialism and government-controlled economies.

So why do so many legal precedents still on the books allow the government to interfere with free markets and curtail our essential economic liberties? And how can the courts keep getting away with these shocking decisions? Why hasn't the American judiciary caught up with the rest of the country—and the world? The Supreme Court's infamous *Kelo v. New London* ruling—which permits your local selectmen to take your property and give it to a land developer or corporation—came in 2005. God only knows what other intrusions into the economy by politicians we can expect the courts to condone.

What do we do? We fight back. Starting now. Using our "secret weapon," conservative judicial activism, we can use the courts to help lead the nation through an economic revolution in favor of free markets, smaller government, lower taxes, and—most important of all—our unalienable property and contract rights and our other fundamental economic liberties.

How do we do it? It's tempting to base our case on the text of the

Constitution, the writings of the Founders, and the long history of court rulings that declare in no uncertain terms that the economic rights of American citizens should be vigorously protected against government encroachment. After all, we could make a devastating case along these lines. (I've given just a few examples, here and in Chapter 2, of how strongly the Founders believed in economic liberties and how ardently the courts protected those liberties until the socialist Left took over.) And there's unambiguous evidence that the Framers drafted the Constitution to protect economic rights—unlike, say, the "rights" to abort an unborn child, to engage in anal sex, and to discriminate against certain races to ensure "diversity" in elite law schools.

Yes, it's tempting to go with those arguments—but there's a better way. Look, nobody respects the Founding Fathers more than I do, but the sad truth is that in the legal system we're forced to deal with, those kinds of arguments would fall on many deaf ears. The Right should frame legal arguments in language understandable to sitting judges— not make a case that is persuasive only in a classroom or intellectual vacuum. As you know by now, this book is all about addressing the world as it really is, not as we'd like it to look. And the way to deal with the modern-day legal system is, once again, to turn liberals' own weapons against them.

The Left wants American law to reflect the notion of the "living Constitution" and to change as society "evolves"? Let's let the Left win this intellectual point—because both national and international trends show that society is "evolving" in our direction on economic matters.

Liberals want their Supreme Court decisions to be "settled law"? No problem. Let's concede the point. Why? Because existing liberal precedents provide the basis for advancing free markets and robustly defending economic freedoms.

Left-wing activists chant "Get your laws off my body"? Hey, we're with you—because our right to property, properly understood, is inextricably linked to our right to life and our right to liberty, and we can't stand by while the government tramples all over it.

We'll follow all the Left's mantras and legal assumptions—and by doing so we'll push back against the liberals' decades-old big-government assault. We'll get rid of zany economic laws and negate the effects of dangerous court rulings such as *Kelo*. And the end result will be to ensure the constitutional right to be secure in one's property, to

keep the fruits of one's labor, and to engage in legitimate, socially productive economic activities—just as the Framers intended.

"CONTROLLED IN EVERYTHING"

VIGOROUSLY DEFENDING FREE MARKETS and economic freedoms is completely consistent with the conservative worldview. Most Americans
just want to be left alone to live their lives as they see fit; they don't
want to bear the burden of government intrusions into their lives. Yet
liberals want to use government as a means to tell us how to live, how
much of our money we can keep, what we can pay employees, with
whom we can or cannot do business, and the types of homes we can
live in.

Democrats purport to be the defenders of minorities, workers, and
the poor. But they oppose the policies by which these people can really
be helped. The helpful policies opposed by the Left are, of course, free
market policies. For example, liberals oppose tax relief, saying that
such reductions "help the rich on the backs of the poor." It's true that
tax cuts can help the rich—because the top earners in this country bear
the overwhelming burden of income taxes: The top 5 percent of income
earners in the United States pay more than half of all federal income
taxes, and the top 10 percent pay 65 percent of federal income taxes.[3]
But the poor benefit from tax cuts, too. The economist Henry Hazlitt
explained how higher taxes hurt everyone, all the way down to the
poor: "old employers do not give more employment, or not as much
more as they might have; and others decide not to become employers at
all. Improved machinery and better-equipped factories come into existence much more slowly than they otherwise would. The result in the
long run is that consumers are prevented from getting better and
cheaper products to the extent that they otherwise would, and that real
wages are held down, compared with what they might have been."[4] In
contrast, tax cuts spur economic growth, which creates more jobs and
higher wages, benefiting everyone—rich, poor, and middle-class. And,
for better or worse, even the government benefits from tax cuts, as tax
revenues increase whenever tax cuts are implemented—which is precisely what has happened after the enactment of President George W.
Bush's supposed help-the-rich-and-hurt-the-poor tax cuts.[5]

Instead of free market measures, liberals champion government interferences such as a minimum-wage law. Minimum-wage laws have been around since 1938, but they haven't ended poverty. In fact, they harm lower-income workers. How so? Basic economics: Anytime you raise the price of something, the demand falls. As economist Walter Williams explains, this principle holds true for labor services. "When labor's price exceeds its value—what it can produce—employers will buy less of it and seek substitutes," Williams wrote. "Among those substitutes are automation, moving to a lower-wage country, and customer self-service."[6]

Summarizing Williams's arguments, economist Stephen Moore makes a larger, indeed moral, point about government interference in the economy: "[Williams] says that if slavery was someone else's owning *all* of a man's output, then government's taking ownership of 50 percent of GDP means all Americans are half slaves and half free. Depressing but true. The economic impact of this spending path is not hard to envision. We know what happens when a nation becomes half Socialist. It begins to look like Old Europe—France, Germany, Italy. These nations, with their obese welfare states, confiscatory tax systems, government ownership of industry, and stifling regulations, are economically catatonic. They are not growing. They are not creating jobs. They are rusting. They have twice the rate of unemployment we have in the U.S. today."[7]

As Williams suggests—and as John Adams and other Founders knew—economic freedom is as important as, if not more important than, political freedom. Though getting a job, earning money, buying food and clothes, going to a restaurant, owning property, and renting or buying a home may seem a bit pedestrian to many head-in-the-clouds political and philosophical thinkers today, in reality these are the most important human freedoms. The Supreme Court at one point recognized this, even if it doesn't now. "Without doubt," the Court ruled in 1923, "[liberty] denotes not merely freedom from bodily restraint but also the right of the individual to contract, to engage in any of the common occupations in life, to acquire useful knowledge, to marry, establish a home, and bring up children, to worship God according to the dictates of his own conscience, and generally to enjoy those privileges long recognized at common law as essential to the orderly pursuit of happiness by free men."[8] This freedom is essentially the freedom to choose how to live one's life without meddlesome interference from others. It was this freedom—American freedom—that the nation's Founders wanted to protect.

In fact, economic liberty is a prerequisite to political freedom. As the Nobel Prize–winning economist Friedrich Hayek put it, "To be controlled in our economic pursuits means to be . . . controlled in everything."[9]

Liberals who discount the importance of economic liberties should remember that were it not for those freedoms, they could never even fight for new political freedoms and social causes. Think about it: Without economic rights, how does George Soros fund MoveOn.org or Jon Corzine spend his fortune in pursuit of his personal dream of holding elected office? What good is the right to abortion to a woman if she can't pay the abortionist? Even the right to vote—an essential right, without a doubt—is not, at the end of the day, as important as the freedom to go about our daily lives. Saddam Hussein held elections, as did the Soviet Union; the right to vote did not do much for Iraqis or people under the yoke of Communism. And ask yourself this: How many Americans would give up their right to vote (many Americans don't vote in the first place) if doing so allowed them to keep the 30 to 50 percent of their income that now is confiscated by the government in taxes? (In fact, my guess is that many Americans would willingly give up their right to vote in exchange for a free iPod!) The point is this: Economic rights are exercised every day, by everyone. Why, then, do the courts allow politicians and government basically to run roughshod over these vital rights?

It's simple, really. The Left doesn't care about them, so liberal judges don't protect them. The Right cares about them, but conservative judges engage in judicial restraint, so they defer to the politicians who pass laws that harm the economy.

ROE-ING TO ECONOMIC FREEDOM

OKAY, SO WE WANT to turn the Left's legal weapons against them to reclaim our economic liberties from rapacious governments. What's the best way to do this? How about starting with one of the Left's favorite Supreme Court decisions, *Roe v. Wade?*

In *Roe,* the Court said, "Where certain 'fundamental rights' are involved, the Court has held that regulation limiting these rights may be

justified only by a 'compelling state interest' . . . and that legislative en-
actments must be narrowly drawn to express only the legitimate state
interests at stake."[10] As we've seen, few if any rights are as fundamental as economic rights. Conservatives must throw the Left's beloved
rulings, including *Roe,* right back in the Court's face. Liberals want to
defend the rights they deem precious, such as the "right" to abortion?
Then by their own rationale, they must recognize and defend with
equal vigor economic rights as well—which are *truly* fundamental, not
invented. Relatively few Americans exercise their right to an abortion
while virtually all exercise their economic rights every single day. Is a
right rarely exercised as fundamental as one used daily?

With the *Roe* decision, the court was reaffirming a point it had made
a year earlier, when its liberal justices invalidated a law banning the
distribution of contraceptives to unmarried people. The Court wrote
then: "If the right of privacy means anything, it is the right of the individual, married or single, to be free from unwarranted governmental
intrusion into matters so fundamentally affecting a person as the decision whether to bear or beget a child."[11] Does the constitutional right
of a free and consenting adult to make economic decisions about his
well-being carry less weight than the right of a single man to buy a condom (or, for that matter, less weight than the right of a fifteen-year-old
boy to buy a condom—another "right" the court upheld, in 1977)?[12]
Wouldn't you love, say, Chief Justice John Roberts to write a majority
opinion in favor of economic freedoms that echoes that *Roe* ruling? "If
the right to contract means anything," the Court could say, "it is the
right of the individual to be free from unwarranted governmental intrusion into matters so fundamentally affecting a person as the decision
to choose how to spend his money, to sell his time and effort, to buy or
sell a home, to buy or sell a car, to take a job, or to save, invest, or donate money he has earned. We upheld the right to abort an unwanted
fetus in *Roe* and in subsequent decisions because of the need to respect
one's personal autonomy over critical life choices. By logical extension,
we think that the constitutional rights envisioned by *Roe* extend
equally to the economic realm and all the fundamental life choices
falling within that realm."

Or how about using a more recent landmark decision, the Court's
2003 ruling, in *Lawrence v. Texas,* that struck down laws banning
same-sex sodomy? In *Lawrence,* the Supreme Court explained that

laws forbidding same-sex sodomy were unconstitutional because the individuals who committed sodomy "were free as adults to engage in the private conduct."

Why couldn't a court extend the *Lawrence* case beyond the particular context of buggery to encompass the right of consenting adults to enter into voluntary private contracts? After all, the Supreme Court recognized economic rights long before it recognized the "right" to engage in same-sex sodomy. Economic rights weren't significantly curtailed until about seventy years ago; surely the courts could toss aside a mere seventy years of legal precedents in the name of contracts, free markets, and property, given that the Supreme Court trampled on hundreds (if not thousands) of years of precedents to overturn bans on homosexual sodomy. And no matter how strongly one values the freedom to engage in sodomy, it is difficult to make the case that this "right" is more valuable than the right to engage in the basic economic transactions necessary to live—a right that affects *all* Americans (even those who spend money to take out personal ads in the *Village Voice* seeking a GWM interested in such conjugal relations—handcuffs optional). While sodomy may be a critical personal liberty entitled to vigorous protection by the Supreme Court, certainly the Court should afford the same level of protection to the right to contract, which is actually mentioned in the Constitution.

The *Lawrence* decision also provides us with ammunition to make a "living Constitution" case in favor of economic rights. In *Lawrence,* the Supreme Court emphasized that whereas twenty-five states had prohibited the relevant conduct in 1986, by 2003 only thirteen states had such restrictive laws, and only four of those states enforced them. The Court added, "In all events we think that our laws and traditions in the past half century are of most relevance here. These references show an emerging awareness that liberty gives substantial protection to adult persons in deciding how to conduct their private lives in matters pertaining to sex" (emphasis added).

Obviously, the Supreme Court is tracking social trends in the law and how societal attitudes are changing or emerging. Why can't the court track economic trends as well and state that there is an emerging awareness that free markets and economic rights are critical to the success of people and the nation? Americans have finally turned away from the New Deal/Great Society drive toward government solutions for every problem under the sun, which meant higher taxes and more government interference with the free market. During the 1990s we torpedoed Hillary Clinton's horrifying health care plan that would have nationalized one-seventh of the economy, then secured landmark welfare reform that finally acknowledged that government handouts can't win a "war on poverty." Then the 1990s boom engendered a new respect for the American entrepreneur and made most Americans familiar with the opportunities in stock-market investing. (Now about 50 percent of Americans own some form of stock.)[13] These trends helped George W. Bush prevail as a business candidate over the quintessential lawyer, policy wonk, and bureaucrat Al "Let's Abolish the Internal Combustion Engine" Gore. Now Americans have moved from investing in the stock market to real estate, with over 68 percent of Americans owning their own homes.[14]

Lawrence also teaches us that we should look to foreign precedent. Specifically, the Supreme Court cited the experiences of the European Court of Human Rights in dealing with gay rights. So we should look overseas as well. After all, in recent years people around the world have developed a deep appreciation for capitalism and free markets. First we saw the collapse of the Soviet Union, after which, of course, we learned the horrible truth about how badly Communism had ravaged the economies of Eastern Europe, left the people destitute, and devastated the natural environment. In the few Communist holdouts remaining today, despair and poverty are common. For instance, in North Korea—which ranked dead last in the Index of Economic Freedom—a devastating famine in the mid-1990s killed an estimated three million people, and as recently as the summer of 2005 the United Nations World Food Program was responsible for feeding one-third of North Korea's twenty-two million people.[15] Now, Japan is awakening from its long economic slumber, thanks to free market reforms, and has started to experience economic growth and falling unemployment for the first time in over a decade.[16] Clearly there is an emerging awareness, both here and overseas, that free markets and economic liberties are essential.

And there's even better news for conservatives concerned about fundamental economic rights: We can cite other prominent Supreme Court decisions besides *Lawrence* to bolster our "living Constitution" case for economic rights.

THE *BROWN-CASEY* TAG TEAM

IN SOME OF ITS most important decisions, the Supreme Court has championed the view that we must adjust the law as society "evolves." Look at the landmark ruling in *Brown v. Board of Education* (1954), which repudiated (properly) the notion of "separate but equal." To reject the "separate but equal" doctrine, of course, the Court had to make a 180-degree turn, explicitly rejecting its 1896 ruling in *Plessy v. Ferguson*. So the court said, in effect, that times have changed. The ruling stated that the *Brown* decision was made "not on the basis of conditions existing when the Fourteenth Amendment was adopted, but in the light of the full development of public education and its present place in American life throughout the Nation."

Come 1992, the Supreme Court looked back to *Brown* when it upheld the "right" to abortion in the case of *Planned Parenthood v. Casey.* Summarizing the Court's reversal in *Brown,* the *Casey* decision explained, "Society's understanding of the facts upon which a constitutional ruling was sought in 1954 was thus fundamentally different from the basis claimed for the [*Plessy*] decision in 1896." The *Casey* ruling added, "In constitutional adjudication as elsewhere in life, changed circumstances may impose new obligations, and the thoughtful part of the Nation could accept each decision to overrule a prior case as a response to the Court's constitutional duty."[17]

"Changed circumstances" impose "new obligations" on the courts to "overrule" prior cases? Great! Then it's time the changed circumstances and the clear evidence of the power of free markets obligate us to overturn precedents that impinge on economic rights.

Interestingly, the Supreme Court touched on economic liberties (and its refusal to enforce them) in the *Casey* decision. The court admitted that in the 1937 case of *West Coast Hotel Co. v. Parrish* it had thrown aside "the theory of *laissez-faire*" and the idea of a "constitutionally protected liberty of contract." Why? Because, the *Casey* opinion noted, "the Depression had come and, with it, the lesson that *seemed unmistakable* to most people by 1937, that the interpretation of contractual freedom protected in [previous decisions] *rested on fundamentally false factual assumptions about the capacity of a relatively unregulated market to satisfy minimal levels of human welfare*" (emphasis added). In short, the Supreme Court was saying that it had been *required* to overturn free-market-friendly rulings because the facts on which the Court had made those decisions "had proven to be untrue."

Hold on a second . . . *proven* to be untrue? Actually, the idea that the government needed to intervene in the economy might have *seemed unmistakable* in 1937—at a time when socialist thought was so prevalent in world capitals, including Washington, D.C.—but it was dead wrong. Remember, the empirical and historical evidence now available proves conclusively that while President Franklin Roosevelt claimed government was the solution to the economic collapse, the reality was that government was the *problem.* All that intervention prolonged and greatly exacerbated the Great Depression. In other words, government leaders overreacted, thus turning a "momentary breakdown into an international cataclysm," as author Jean-François Revel put it.[18]

But that's okay, because there we have our solution to the problem, straight from the Supreme Court's *Planned Parenthood v. Casey* decision (this being the decision liberals like so much for upholding *Roe v. Wade*). *Casey* tells us that when the Supreme Court issues rulings based on assumptions ultimately proven false, the Court can—indeed, should—repudiate those decisions in favor of new decisions more in accord with the reality of American economic, social, and political life. By this logic, the Court should repudiate the 1937 ruling that supported government interference in the free market. Sorry, liberals—"changed circumstances."

Courts have always been allowed to take into account certain virtually indisputable facts even if the evidence isn't specifically submitted into the record. This is called taking "judicial notice" of something. For example, a court could take "judicial notice" of the fact that terrorists attacked the United States on September 11, 2001, or that Christmas Day 2006 falls on a Monday. More relevant for our purposes, courts have taken judicial notice of economic theories at the national and international levels. That, in fact, is exactly what the Supreme Court did in the 1937 *West Coast Hotel* case. The majority opinion explained, "We may take judicial notice of the unparalleled demands for [economic] relief which arose during the recent period of depression and still continue to an alarming extent despite the degree of economic recovery which has been achieved. . . . The community may direct its law-making power to correct the abuse which springs from [unconscionable employers'] selfish disregard of the public interest."[19] Now the Supreme Court must take judicial notice of the lessons of the past seventy years, which reflect the wonders of the free market and the mistakes of government interference in those free markets.

Keep in mind that when the Supreme Court in *Lawrence v. Texas* overruled its decision in *Bowers v. Hardwick* (1986), it said the earlier opinion had been based on assumptions that recent scholarship had exposed as questionable. The *Lawrence* ruling criticized the "assumptions about history" Justice Byron White articulated in his opinion, and it also stated that "scholarship casts some doubt on the sweeping nature of the statement by Chief Justice [Warren] Burger as it pertains to private homosexual conduct between consenting adults."

Of course, scholarship and history also cast some doubt (to say no more) on the efficacy of government interventions in the economy.

HOISTING LIBERALS ON THEIR OWN PETARD

SO THERE YOU HAVE it—a few examples of how we can use liberals' favorite Supreme Court rulings to push the law back to the right and to preserve fundamental economic liberties. There are other ways to hoist liberals on their own petard. For instance, we could cite the line of precedents involving the freedom of association, arguing that courts fiercely protect the right to get together to protest logging companies in the name of the spotted owl but don't do as much to protect the right to get together to form a business. Or we could mention Justice Ruth Bader Ginsburg's concerns over the constitutionality of laws forbidding prostitution when consenting adults want nothing more than for our laws to be kept off their bodies.

But the key point is this: We conservatives *must* stop relying on the losing arguments we always use. Of course we must respect the Constitution and the intentions of the Founders, but we actually betray that cause when we put forward arguments that courts respectful of left-wing precedents won't listen to. Stubbornly clinging to outmoded methods won't do anything to preserve the Constitution and the American way of life.

We've got a secret weapon. Let's use it.

And when the Left objects, we have the perfect retort: *These are your precedents, theories, and arguments. See, you were right all along!*

THIRTEEN

ANCHOR BABIES AWEIGH!

A Ready Response to the Illegal Immigration Crisis

Today, thanks to the U.S. Supreme Court, if a wife of Osama bin Laden gave birth to a child on American soil while traveling through the country on the way to bomb Chicago, that child would—guess what—automatically be an American citizen.

That's right—if an illegal (or legal) alien has a child while on American soil, then Whammo!—the kid is an American citizen entitled to all the rights and privileges of citizenship. That child not only will be eligible for American welfare benefits and other government handouts but also, upon reaching eighteen years of age, will be eligible to vote . . . for liberal Democrats. Illegal aliens who have children here in the United States are rarely deported. The newly born American citizen thus serves as an "anchor baby"—that is, he anchors his family squarely in America. And not just the parents are anchored; our nation's family unification laws allow the family to start bringing other family members into this country, legally.

The immigration debate has reached a fever pitch over the past few years as illegal immigrants steal across the American border—perhaps as many as three million per year, according to the Federation for American Immigration Reform (FAIR). Few serious observers oppose legal immigration—after all, the United States has always been a nation of immigrants, and we should continue to welcome lawful immigrants who come to this country to work hard, support themselves, and help America prosper. But illegal immigration imposes serious costs on American society. Liberals wring their hands over the effects of poor immigrants who drive gas-guzzling vehicles and "overpopulate" areas while conservatives fret over illegal immigrants enjoying taxpayer-funded welfare rolls without even trying to assimilate to the American culture. (And if you think a failure to assimilate is no big deal, then look at the riots that erupted in France in the fall of 2005, led mostly by second-generation Muslim immigrants who never assimilated to France's Brie-and-wine culture.)

As FAIR explains, "Unlike many other countries, the United States has an immigration policy that does little to ensure that annual immigration is beneficial to society." Indeed, unchecked immigration requires American taxpayers to subsidize all kinds of public benefits programs. According to FAIR, "immigrants are nearly twice as likely to be on welfare as natives, and the annual cost of public benefits to recent immigrants is estimated at $75 billion a year."[1] Cato Institute scholar Michael Tanner agrees that many immigrants rely on welfare; almost a quarter of immigrant families, he says, have had "at least one member who has used a welfare program at some time."[2] And welfare is not the only immigrant benefit taxpayers must pay for. The Center for Immigration Studies reports that in 2002, there were 9.7 million children of immigrant families in American schools.[3] And the Federal Bureau of Prisons reveals that 29 percent of the inmates in federal prisons are aliens.[4]

Not surprisingly, the courts have contributed to the immigration problem. In particular, two Supreme Court decisions, described in the next section, issued nearly eighty years apart, have ensured that the costs of immigration to American society are as great as they are today.

But there's good news for conservatives: The secret weapon of conservative judicial activism can help win this political battle over immigration, by making sure those two critical decisions are overturned. Just as the Supreme Court nudged American society away from government-sanctioned race discrimination in *Brown v. Board of Education,* so too should courts nudge the nation away from open borders and taxpayer-subsidized incentives for illegal immigration. And conservatives can ensure that they do.

THE COURT GETS IT ALL *WONG*

MANY OF THE FAILINGS of today's immigration policy can be traced to the unfortunate decision by the U.S. Supreme Court to bestow citizenship on any baby born in the United States, no matter how or why his or her parents came to be on American soil (the only exception being for children of foreign diplomats). This rule has been in place for more than a century, ever since the Supreme Court ruling in *United States v. Wong Kim Ark* in 1898. Since then, American courts have upheld the ruling that anyone born on American soil is automatically an American citizen, no matter how tenuous the child's or the parents' connection to the nation.

The Supreme Court reached this conclusion by misinterpreting the Fourteenth Amendment's citizenship clause, which provides that "all persons born or naturalized in the United States and *subject to the jurisdiction thereof,* are citizens of the United States and of the State wherein they reside" (emphasis added). In *Wong Kim Ark,* the court dismissed the phrase "subject to the jurisdiction thereof" in concluding that birth on American soil alone suffices to earn all the rights and freedoms associated with American citizenship.

Unfortunately, subsequent decisions have ensured that the hypothetical scenario involving Osama bin Laden's child isn't far-fetched. One of the absurd real-world implications of the erroneous interpretation of the citizenship clause was reflected in the Supreme Court's 2004 ruling in *Hamdi v. Rumsfeld.* After capturing Yaser Esam Hamdi fighting for the Taliban against U.S. forces in Afghanistan, the Bush administration declared Hamdi an enemy combatant. Hamdi, a Saudi citizen, claimed American citizenship by virtue of being born in the United States to Saudi parents who were temporarily working here. Hamdi left the United States as an infant, not to return until after his capture.

Why on earth should a dude be considered an American citizen when he was born in the United States only because his parents were here on a temporary work visa? He left America as a baby, later declared himself a citizen of Saudi Arabia, took up arms against U.S. soldiers for a bunch of anti-Western terrorists, and showed zero allegiance to the United States. Does this sound like an American to you? (Okay, maybe it does sound a little bit like a liberal American once you remove the arms reference.)

How should *Hamdi* have been decided? Hamdi, though born in America, never showed allegiance to the United States, as required by a proper reading of the jurisdiction requirement of the citizenship clause. Hamdi may have been born in the United States, but he was not "subject to the jurisdiction" of the United States, as that phrase was understood by the framers of the Fourteenth Amendment. Yaser Hamdi's parents had no intention of becoming American citizens and never demonstrated any attachment to the United States. They were not fully "subject to the jurisdiction" of the United States. For example, Mr. Hamdi senior could not be drafted into the United States military. Nor could Mr. and Mrs. Hamdi be guilty of treason—they owed no allegiance to the United States.[5]

What can we do to fix this silliness? Well, if Congress exercised its power under section 5 of the Fourteenth Amendment ("The Congress shall have power to enforce, by appropriate legislation, the provisions of this article"), it could change the law so bin Laden's kid would not become an automatic American just by being born here. Or, an even easier path, the U.S. Supreme Court could change course and reverse its decision in *Wong Kim Ark*.

And why not overrule *Wong Kim Ark?* No American citizen voted on the question. Those Americans alive in 1898 are now long dead. That decision—rendered a mere two years after the notorious *Plessy v. Ferguson* decision approved a segregation policy for America's schools ("separate but equal")—conveniently ignored a critical aspect of the Fourteenth Amendment's citizenship clause. Remember, liberals love to tell us that the Fourteenth Amendment's equal protection clause is too important to be bound by the Supreme Court's outdated *Plessy* decision from 1896. As left-wing judicial activists never fail to remind us, America has "evolved" greatly since then and, thus, so should the Constitution "evolve," too. Despite the absence of supporting legal authority, prominent liberal legal scholars have even argued that the equal protection clause should evolve, through judicial interpretation, to require the government to provide a minimum wage to the poor.[6] If the U.S. Supreme Court can reverse its 1896 decision in *Plessy v. Ferguson* (as it did in *Brown v. Board of Education* in 1954), it can certainly reverse its 1898 decision in *Wong Kim Ark* to protect citizenship and the future of America.

The reversal of *Wong Kim Ark* would be fully justified under the rule of law. It would, first of all, be correct under the contemporary notion of the "living Constitution"; indeed, today's Supreme Court is no more bound by the misguided decision in *Wong Kim Ark* than the *Brown v. Board of Education* court was by the misguided *Plessy* decision. Moreover, the reversal would be correct under the original understanding of the equal protection clause. The lawmakers responsible for the Fourteenth Amendment did not intend for the children of anti-American terrorists to secure citizenship merely by being born on American soil. Yet this result is exactly one implication from the Supreme Court's current view. The framers of the amendment clearly thought that an allegiance to the United States beyond merely being born on American soil was necessary to be an American citizen. That's why the Framers made a point to include the phrase "subject to the jurisdiction thereof."

The meaning and purpose of the "jurisdiction" language becomes quite clear when viewed in the context of the congressional debates leading up to the passage of the citizenship clause. The author of the citizenship clause, Senator Jacob Merritt Howard of Michigan, explained that the "jurisdiction" language meant that a person cannot owe an "allegiance to anybody else, and still be an American." Senator Howard added:

> In one sense, all persons born within the geographical limits of the United States are subject to the jurisdiction of the United States, but they are not subject to the jurisdiction of the United States in every sense. Take the child of an ambassador. In one sense, that child born in the United States is subject to the jurisdiction of the United States, because if that child commits the crime of murder, or commits any other crime against the laws of the country, to a certain extent he is subject to the jurisdiction of the United States, but not in every respect; and so with these Indians. . . . I understand the words here "subject to the jurisdiction of the United States," to mean fully and completely subject to the jurisdiction of the United States.[7]

Another senator, Illinois's Lyman Trumbull, chairman of the Judiciary Committee, affirmed the importance of the additional language. Senator Trumbull declared that any person who owes even "partial allegiance" to a foreign government should be disqualified from being an American citizen under the jurisdiction requirement of the citizenship clause.

Despite all of that, the U.S. Supreme Court for more than a century has stood by its tortured reading of the citizenship clause. This confusion is not merely an academic issue—it has substantial real-world

implications. One harmful effect is the so-called anchor baby phenomenon. Unfortunately, the anchor baby problem extends beyond the oft-
cited scenario of illegal immigrants racing across the Mexican border
only to birth their children in Los Angeles hospitals with health care
covered by American taxpayers. Foreign nationals now even utilize
businesses that offer "pregnancy tours," wherein a pregnant woman
flies to the United States as part of a vacation package just to give birth
to an American—an American who can years from now serve as an anchor to bring the parents into the United States to benefit from social
programs for the elderly. Foreign companies actually arrange for travel,
food, lodging, and health care until the mother births an American.[8]

Conservative judicial activism can fix this problem and set the law
back in line with what the creators of the law intended.

STOP DEBATING, START FIXING

UNFORTUNATELY, GIVING AUTOMATIC AMERICAN citizenship to any
child born in America is not the only misbegotten legal conclusion the
U.S. Supreme Court foisted on the nation, exacerbating the effects of
illegal immigration. Thanks to the Supreme Court, American taxpayers
are now overtaxed by being forced to pay for the free education of
not only American children but also the children of illegal immigrants. That's because the Court erred in deciding the 1982 case
Plyler v. Doe. In one of those closely divided 5–4 decisions that automatically becomes "well established" and unchallengeable because the
Left likes it, the Supreme Court ruled that states may not "discriminate" against the school-age children of illegal aliens living in America
by denying them a free public education on the backs of American taxpayers. In the process the Court rejected the State of Texas's position
that its taxpayers had no obligation to pay for the children of illegal
aliens and that the state had a substantial state interest not only in
preserving its educational funds for the children of tax-paying American citizens but also in discouraging the flood of illegal aliens into the
state. The Court's decision should not have come as a surprise, though,
given that in 1971 it found that states may not deny welfare benefits to
legal resident aliens.[9]

The mere notion of Americans paying for the children of illegal
aliens to attend American public schools is absurd. This education is

expensive and should not have to be borne by American taxpayers. Families of illegal aliens should return to their home countries, where the children can receive an education. (Liberals had no problem using armed SWAT teams to rip Elián González away from his family to ensure his proper education in Communist Cuba.) If they develop valuable skills and abilities, they can then move *legally* to the United States. Of course, Democrats don't care if you have more illiterate voters that are dependent on social services, because that just means more Democratic voters.

Just as with the Supreme Court's 1898 decision in *Wong Kim Ark,* conservatives should use the weapon of judicial activism to overturn *Plyler v. Doe.* Simply overturning those two decisions—one a misguided judgment from the nineteenth century, the other a highly controversial ruling decided by a razor-thin 5–4 margin ("highly controversial" and "razor-thin" being the descriptions liberals like to apply to 5–4 decisions they disagree with)—would help solve America's illegal immigrant crisis. Those two steps would minimize the anchor baby problem and allow states to refuse to pay for the education of the school-age children of illegal aliens.

As with so many other political issues, conservatives have tried to address illegal immigration through legislation, political referenda, and other democratic efforts. They have generally ignored the courts. But here as in so many other areas, conservative judicial activism can be the secret to achieving elusive victories.

PART V

LAYING SIEGE TO THE LEFT'S INDOCTRINATION CAMPS

FOURTEEN

"DO YOU SODOMIZE YOUR WIFE?"

The Liberal Lunacy of America's Law Schools

> I know conservative students here feel isolated, marginalized, and angry. They feel that NYU Law is full of insensitive, liberal lemmings led by the nose by the partisan *New York Times* and *The New Yorker*. And to a certain extent, they're right. . . . Conservatives are clearly in the super-minority.
> —A New York University law student, quoted in the NYU School of Law student paper

> Madmen in authority, who hear voices in the air, are distilling their frenzy from some academic scribbler of a few years back.
> —John Maynard Keynes

Supreme Court justice Antonin Scalia is a brilliant jurist whose legal mind is respected even by his intellectual foes. Scalia's opinions are renowned for their intelligence and flair, his dissents for their clarity. But none of that prevented students privileged to attend an elite law school from giving him a rude greeting in 2005.

When Scalia visited New York University School of Law, one of the nation's best, that spring, an NYU student used the question-and-answer session to reaffirm the Left's fetish for all things below the belt. The student asked the Supreme Court justice, "Do you sodomize your wife?"[1]

This intellectually vapid query, better suited for reality TV than a prestigious law school, topped off a day of protests against Justice Scalia. What had Scalia done to provoke such outrage? Had he started a war against a rape-room-infatuated tyrant? Called into question the

Religion of Peace? Used Michael Moore's name in the same sentence as Krispy Kreme? No. He simply refused to swallow the liberal legal theology that dominates today's law schools. The student's question reflected the intolerance of conservative dissent among so many of today's legal elites. After all, Justice Scalia does not argue that sodomy is good or bad, fun or unfun, moral or immoral, or anything of the kind. He instead believes only that such questions should be resolved through the democratic process, not by a small cadre of unelected judges.

And NYU Law (my alma mater) is only one of several law schools that has seen student-led protests against Scalia. Other institutions include Northwestern University, Lewis and Clark, the University of Michigan, and the University of Chicago. The outbursts should come as no surprise. While America's elite law schools pay lip service to notions of free speech and diversity, the evidence clearly shows that political correctness reigns and liberal nostrums must remain unchallenged. Many liberals not only defended the "do you sodomize your wife" question to Scalia, but even expressed outrage at the Supreme Court justice's visits to these schools.

Stories like this one boil many conservatives' blood. But should we really care about the liberal dominance of law schools? Does it really matter at the end of the day?

Does it matter? You betcha!

Many Americans think law school is only about producing attorneys capable of handling ordinary day-to-day legal problems such as preparing wills, negotiating contracts, and closing home purchases. Or perhaps when you think of law schools you imagine diploma mills that produce the stars of those late-night commercials featuring short, balding men wearing shiny suits and earnestly asking, "Have you been injured?" (or perhaps "*¿Ha sido lastimado?*"). And law schools do produce plenty of attorneys to handle relatively routine legal matters. But among the assembly line of attorneys rolling out the doors of academia each year, many young legal eagles are destined—for better or worse—for more prestigious futures. Far too many of today's law students will become tomorrow's ruling elites—judges, politicians, professors, business owners, and even (gulp) authors. And whether tomorrow's elites embrace conservative or left-wing visions, especially in regard to the role of law in society, may depend on their lessons in law school.

If many at America's elite law schools regard Antonin Scalia, one of the nation's finest legal minds, as a fringe lunatic, what does this say about the future of conservatism in the law? Our law schools are, unfortunately, breeding grounds for tomorrow's liberal leaders.

The liberalism of elite law schools does not simply portend a problem for the future but represents a clear and present danger now. Today, elite faculty members exert extraordinary influence in the legal culture, not just within the academic cocoon. Northwestern University law professor John McGinnis explains,

> Through their submissions to the public and to the courts, law professors have attempted to shape many of the nation's most important recent legal decisions—the impeachment of President Clinton, judicial review of the 2000 presidential election, affirmative action, terrorism policy, and homosexual rights. Moreover, law professors regularly offer theories and ideas for other lawyers and judges to use in reforming and transforming the law. As Alexis de Tocqueville first observed almost two hundred years ago, lawyers are the 'aristocrats' of American democracy—far more politically influential than any other profession. Law professors play an important role in sustaining this "aristocracy," acting as both its gatekeepers and its theorists.[2]

When you realize how many of these legal "aristocrats" tilt left, you start to see why conservatives can't ignore the conditions festering in America's law schools.

HOTHOUSES OF LIBERALISM

DOG BREEDERS OFTEN OBSERVE that a spoiled, undisciplined Chihuahua is simply annoying, but a spoiled, undisciplined pit bull is truly dangerous. Similarly, a silly sociology professor wearing a French beret, toking on a marijuana joint, and spouting off about Noam Chomsky may be a cute cliché, but an elite law professor of the same intellectual and political bent wields great prestige and influence. The silly sociology professor may pollute young, forming minds, but a law professor may pollute the rule of law and the society it governs.

A comprehensive academic survey published in 2005 by the National

Association of Scholars found that among college humanities and social-science professors nationwide, the ratio of Democrats to Republicans is at least 7 to 1, and probably more like 9 to 1. It's not just liberal arts professors that are predominantly Democrats, either. Another survey by the same lead scholar covered twenty-three different academic departments at Stanford University and Berkeley, spanning the humanities, the social sciences, the hard sciences, math, engineering, journalism, medicine, law, and business. At Stanford the ratio of Democrats to Republicans was 7.6 to 1; at Berkeley it was 9.9 to 1.[3]

That colleges are liberal constitutes "dog-bites-man" news. A 2004 study by the *Chronicle of Higher Education* found that nine out of ten college professors identified themselves as liberals. A 2005 survey produced similar results, showing that 87 percent of professors at elite colleges identify themselves as liberals, while only 13 percent admit to being conservative. Of the professors surveyed, 84 percent supported abortion, 88 percent wanted more environmental protection even if it raised prices or cost jobs, 67 percent considered homosexuality acceptable, and 65 percent wanted government to guarantee full employment.[4] And if surveyed, they probably would trust Al Jazeera TV over Fox News. Liberal bias on college campuses is like gravity—it's a given.

But few recognize the more insidious form of liberal domination in higher education—the domination of law school campuses by liberal professors. The liberal leanings of America's law faculties is also dog-bites-man news. In 2005, the *Georgetown Law Journal* published an expansive study tracking campaign contributions over many years by law professors at America's top law schools. The study covered eleven years of records and professors at the top twenty-one law schools in America (using *U.S. News & World Report* rankings). Of the law professors who contributed $200 or more to campaigns, fully 81 percent gave their money "wholly or mostly to Democrats"; only 15 percent made their contributions "wholly or mostly to Republicans."

The most prestigious schools were even more liberal: at Harvard, 91 percent of professors gave to Democrats; at Yale, 92 percent; at Stanford, 94 percent.[5] In fact, at Yale Law School, the ratio of Democrat to Republican law professors among those contributing $200 or more to politicians was a whopping twenty to one—that's right, twenty to one in favor of Democrats.[6] Talk about a blowout. The study's conclusion? No surprise: "The ideological composition of politically active law professors . . . is clear: they are overwhelmingly Democratic."[7]

To what degree do the political views of these legal elites differ from those of their countrymen? As the *New York Times* reported, nationwide, people with similar credentials and incomes gave far, far less to Democrats. In the 2000 election cycle, "34 percent of people with advanced degrees and 44 percent of those earning $95,000 to $200,000 gave exclusively to Democratic candidates," the *Times* wrote. In contrast, 78 percent of law professors donated exclusively to Democrats.[8]

Political contributions alone do not tell the full story. According to author and Harvard Law School graduate Andrew Peyton Thomas, a 2003 survey of Harvard Law professors showed that "conservative views were almost never expressed by faculty members." The survey revealed that "not a single professor advocated originalism, the conservative philosophy of constitutional interpretation holding that judges must interpret the Constitution in light of the intentions of the framers of that document. Throughout American history, this judicial philosophy guided major Supreme Court rulings, with a small number of notable exceptions, until the activism inaugurated by the Warren court. Originalism was the preferred legal philosophy for the nation's leading conservatives, including Justices Antonin Scalia and Clarence Thomas."[9]

Harvard law professor Charles Fried, a former Massachusetts Supreme Court justice, lent support to the survey's conclusions. When asked to name an originalist on the Harvard Law faculty, Fried replied candidly, "I can't think of one." As noted, he said, "I think such a person would have a hard time getting appointed" to the faculty, for a belief in originalism would make an applicant seem like "a Flat Earther in a geography department."[10]

So if the Harvard Law School faculty lacks a constitutional law professor who subscribes to the judicial philosophy of at least two of the most influential Supreme Court justices of the era, how are Scalia and Thomas's views taught to students? Or think of this: Do you believe liberal senator Barack Obama taught his University of Chicago law students about the law in a "fair and balanced" way when he was on the faculty there? Of course, one could posit that a liberal law professor could convey conservative perspectives on the law in an unbiased fashion while personally supporting the Welfare, Abortion, and Surrender Now Party. Didn't Dan Rather, Walter Cronkite, and the rest of the mainstream media present "both sides" of the news? Isn't Madonna's British accent authentic?

It's really not surprising that law school faculties house mostly liberals. They are mainly a product of the 1960s and include many former
law clerks to liberal Supreme Court justices. For example, the majority
of former law clerks to *Roe v. Wade* author Harry Blackmun pursued
positions in academia, "public interest law," and government rather
than with for-profit law firms competing in the economic marketplace.
As to those Blackmun clerks who are professors now, is there any doubt
that they are teaching about the glorious legacy of their former boss
and mentor, the great liberal hero? Who, after all, would admit to working for a dud?

While it requires no rocket science degree to understand the effect
of wall-to-wall liberalism on the intellectual climate of law schools
or the teaching slant of polarizing subjects such as constitutional law,
one illustration may help. Most Americans believe that they have
the right to carry and use guns for self-defense.[11] In fact, Bill Clinton
and other political observers believe Al Gore lost the 2000 election
largely because of the NRA's campaign to highlight Gore's anti-gun positions, which cost the Democrat several states with large pro-gun elec-
torates.[12] Nevertheless, America's elite law schools generally treat the
Second Amendment as "dead letter law." Whereas the core constitutional law curriculum at most law schools deals in depth with abortion
rights, free speech rights, and other rights popular with the liberal
elites, the Second Amendment does not earn such esteemed treatment.
With perhaps rare exceptions, elective classes are the most we can hope
for when it comes to teaching about gun laws and gun rights. Consider,
for instance, that the reputable, widely used law student study guides
Gilbert Law Summaries: Constitutional Law and *Emmanuel's Constitutional Law* do not include any significant discussion of the Second
Amendment. Apparently the books' editors do not believe enough constitutional law professors require their students to learn about the
topic, so they see no need to include it in a study guide.

SHAPING "SOCIALLY CONSCIOUS THINKERS AND DOERS"

AND JUST WHAT ARE all these liberal institutions trying to do with the
students they educate? Once again, we cannot view law schools as
merely vocational schools. Charles Whitebread, a law professor at the
University of Southern California, explains that "since law orders society in so many different ways, legal education draws more and more

upon other disciplines to illuminate the policies underlying social and legal choice. Public policy issues and principles of other disciplines such as economics, history, philosophy, and the behavioral sciences may be far more important in your legal education than the pat black-letter formulations nonlawyers associate with the law."[13]

More important, to view legal education as glorified trade school grossly underestimates law schools' influence on American society. That influence is beyond debate. The Association of American Law Schools (AALS) told the Supreme Court in 2003 that legal training is a "formal prerequisite" or a "practical path" for those seeking to "participate directly in the formulations, execution, or review of broad public policy."[14] Consider the evidence the AALS presented: Lawyers and judges "constitute barely one-half of 1 percent of the population of the United States between the ages of 25 and 84," but people with law degrees hold "virtually every judgeship, roughly half of the governorships, more than half of the United States Senate, and more than a third of the United States House of Representatives." Moreover, the AALS noted, "Three of the last seven Presidents of the United States had law degrees."[15]

This is no accident. The nation's elite law schools expressly admit that they try to breed politically active attorneys to reshape American society. Here's a sampling:

- Harvard Law School claims that "through its faculty, students, and alumni, Harvard Law School is able to contribute to the world's most complex legal and social challenges."[16]

- Yale Law School brags that its "tradition of emphasizing public as well as private law proved ever more prescient as events of the twentieth century increased the role of public affairs in the life of the law. Yale graduates found themselves uniquely well prepared to play important roles in the rise of the administrative state, the internationalization following the World Wars, and the domestic civil rights movement."[17]

- The University of Michigan Law School boasts that its faculty members "shape the world of law and policy in concrete ways, influencing governmental decision makers and frequently doing stints as such decision makers themselves," and that its graduates "are leaders in court rooms and board rooms across the land . . . [and] champions for underserved peoples and causes both domestically and internationally."[18]

- New York University School of Law calls itself "the preeminent global law school," comprising "legal scholars and practitioners, economists, social scientists, and representatives of the innovation industries. Working side-by-side with our students, these leaders shape the debate on the issues of the day."[19]

- The University of Chicago Law School says that its "graduates lead and innovate in government, activism, academia, and business, as well as law. For this reason, Chicago aims not to merely certify lawyers, but to train well-rounded, critical, and socially conscious thinkers and doers."[20]

Get the picture? Lawyers graduating from these schools don't just draft a will bequeathing Grandma Bertha's heirloom rocking chair to your ingrate cousin; they also can (and do) rock your political, social, and economic world. The descriptions of what graduates of these schools can accomplish in modern America beckons thoughts of the 1970s commercial ditty "I can bring home the bacon, fry it up in a pan, and never let you forget you're a man"—they can do it all and have it all.

The schools are not issuing empty boasts, either. The law is an elitist profession, one that places a premium on credentials—attending a prestigious school, receiving honors such as Phi Beta Kappa, earning a federal judicial clerkship, working for a top law firm, and so on. Simply put, if a person did not go to a top law school, he has little chance to join an elite national law firm, win a prestigious clerkship, or become a professor at a top law school—which are natural (though not the only) ways to advance in the law biz. Author and attorney Richard Montauk explains, "Some parts of the legal profession are virtually off limits to graduates of lesser law schools. These include the major corporate law firms and high-profile government jobs as well as public interest organizations. The most desirable employers would no more think of recruiting at 'Acme' Law School than they would of giving this year's profits to the Flat Earth Society."[21] Note that all of the sitting Supreme Court justices since the early 1990s, including Samuel Alito (Yale), John Roberts (Harvard), William Rehnquist (Stanford), and Sandra Day O'Connor (Stanford), attended one of the nation's elite law schools.

CLIMBING OUT OF THE IVORY TOWER

BEYOND TRAINING YOUNG PEOPLE to think like liberal lawyers, law professors inevitably exploit their own prestigious professional positions and credentials to try to change society. Notably, Laurence Tribe and Alan Dershowitz use their perches at Harvard to argue for all sorts of liberal positions. They can do so because they have the protection of tenure and because their affiliation with Harvard gives the liberal views they express added prestige. As Andrew Peyton Thomas pointed out, "Professorships at Harvard Law also were positions of power, and as such were a great boon to the Left. Tenured professors enjoyed safe positions from which to advocate authoritatively all manner of causes to the rest of the nation."[22]

Indeed, law professors at the most prestigious schools are not confined to the ivory tower. Their writings, lectures, and media appearances allow them to extend their influence throughout society. When the media or politicians seek guidance on critical issues, they often seek out those with elite credentials for comment. (Think Bill O'Reilly: "What say you, counselor?") And professors often play a direct role in high-profile legal cases. For instance, in November 1998 hundreds of law professors signed a letter condemning the impeachment of Bill Clinton as wrongheaded and unwarranted. The president's attorneys then wielded this letter, even quoting from it, in defending Clinton from impeachment before Congress.[23] The letter provided Clinton not only with a useful legal defense before the U.S. Senate, which ultimately voted not to convict him, but also with a forceful political weapon. During one press conference during the impeachment fight, Clinton used the letter to great effect to dodge pointed questions from reporters. "I believe that it's not necessary for me to comment further than our brief," he said. "The important thing that I think you should be asking yourself is why did nearly 900 constitutional experts say that they strongly felt that this matter was not the subject of impeachment? My opinion is not important here."[24] (Clinton never could quite manage the truth: The letter had been signed by about 430 "constitutional experts," not 900.)

Law professors use their academic bully pulpit not simply to defend philandering perjurers. In 2004, Harvard Law faculty members led a group of more than 450 professors who sent a letter asking Congress to consider impeaching President Bush and others in connection with the Abu Ghraib scandal.[25] And in 2000, there were 445 law professors representing 104 American law schools who were enraged that the U.S. Supreme Court scolded the Florida Supreme Court's endorsement of a chaotic, standardless recount of paper ballots by Democratic political operatives holding dimpled chads up to the sun to discover more Gore votes. Their letter argued that by halting the recount of ballots, the Supreme Court (don't laugh too hard now) had taken "power from the voters" and "tarnished its own legitimacy." In a greater hoot, the law professors whined, "As teachers whose lives have been dedicated to the rule of law, we protest."[26] One wonders why these same law professors supposedly "dedicated to the rule of law" weren't also writing letters protesting how the Supreme Court "tarnished its own legitimacy by taking power from the voters" on issues such as partial-birth abortion, the death penalty, same-sex marriage, or homosexual sodomy.

The law school elites have also petitioned the Supreme Court to protest the U.S. military's policies on homosexuality—and to keep the military from infiltrating their ivory tower. For years many law schools had blocked military recruiters from their campuses, objecting to the military's supposedly discriminatory "don't ask, don't tell" policy. Michael Barone of *U.S. News and World Report* put it well when he wrote that the law schools "preen themselves on opposing the evil military for giving homosexuals no harsher a penalty than a general discharge."[27] When Congress passed the Solomon Amendment, a law cutting federal financing to universities that barred military recruiters, a consortium of law schools challenged the law, claiming it violated the schools' First Amendment rights. The case went to the U.S. Supreme Court, and the law schools received support from "900 law professors" and "a dozen top law firms," according to the law schools' attorney, E. Joshua Rosencranz. Fortunately, all of the efforts of these out-of-touch legal elites did not persuade the Supreme Court; the justices unanimously upheld the Solomon Amendment.[28]

LEFT-WING INDOCTRINATION CAMPS

FOR ALL THE EVIDENCE of rampant liberalism on law school campuses, some will still ask whether surrounding young and impressionable minds with liberal views influences those students. Well, does Bill Clinton enjoy interns and cigars?

As law schools are educating future leaders in an environment of wall-to-wall liberalism, how can they not inundate students with liberal legal doctrine and, more broadly, a liberal worldview? A student who spends four years earning an undergraduate degree at an elite (and liberal) college and then experiences three more years of liberal indoctrination at law school will probably lean leftward. True, many conservative legal elites, including conservative Supreme Court justices, attended Ivy League law schools. But most if not all of these people were rock-solid right-wingers before they set foot in law school. What about those students who are largely apolitical, who went to law school because they hated the sight of blood but wanted a job with indoor work and light lifting? It's as simple as that. Many students, because of their training— indeed, indoctrination—at the hands of liberal professors, emerge from law school with a skewed view of the role of law and courts in society. Think of a lawyer's time at an elite college and a prestigious law school as seven years of the most expensive North Korean–style "reeducation" money can buy.

To understand the influence of these left-wing indoctrination camps, look no further than the personal story of Hillary Rodham Clinton. Before matriculating at Wellesley College, Hillary Rodham was a "Goldwater girl." After moving from Illinois and attending Wellesley and then Yale Law School, she began defending the Black Panthers, studying with radical Saul Alinsky, and thinking it takes a socialist village, not a family, to raise a child.

Liberals keep telling us that a child's educational environment matters. Indeed, one of the frequent arguments we hear from the Left to justify an ever-expanding nanny state is that all of these government activities are undertaken in the name of the children. Improving the learning environment is the justification for just about every liberal argument for free school breakfasts, school lunch, after-school programs, more money for teachers, and the like.

So why would liberals doubt that the overwhelming liberalism on elite law school campuses profoundly influences the views of students?

For sure, law students are not children. But if they are not seriously taught conservative legal perspectives, how can they reasonably assess, let alone critique or disagree with, liberal doctrine? Students pay more than $100,000 to receive a law degree from an elite school and to "learn the law." People do not wake up one day and just understand how the First Amendment, civil procedure, or rule against perpetuities works—they have to be taught. The narrow worldview of so many professors significantly curtails what students learn. And as discussed earlier, the law at its highest and most politicized levels is frequently subject to multiple reasonable interpretations. If conservative legal perspectives are given short shrift in schools, then they will be at a distinct disadvantage in the marketplace of legal ideas.

Some argue that the liberalism of America's elite law schools will not necessarily produce liberal lawyers and judges. Richard A. Posner, a renowned federal appeals court judge who also teaches at the University of Chicago, said, "I don't think the liberal bias of law school faculties has much impact on the students. Law students are careerists, and for them law school is career preparation, not Sunday chapel."[29]

Posner is wrong. If a student is a careerist, he will seek high grades and professor recommendations to advance professionally, earn a clerkship, land a job at a fancy law firm, and so forth. Such a student will not naturally seek to challenge professors' views any more than a dog would bite the hand that feeds him. Rather, the careerist will try to regurgitate the professors' liberal pap. Demonstrating that you "listened" in class and "learned" from the assigned materials by parroting back is rarely a bad game plan for high academic marks. After all, one critical lesson taught to young lawyers and lawyer wannabes is to adapt your arguments to your audience. Charles H. Whitebread, a nationally recognized legal scholar and law professor, wrote a book designed specifically to help law students score high grades. Professor Whitebread asks, "Wouldn't it be great to know *exactly* what your professor's looking for on your exam? To find out everything that is expected of you, so that you don't waste your time doing anything other than maximizing your grades?"[30] Need I say more?

FIGHTING BACK

AMERICA'S LAW SCHOOLS have taught generations of America's best and brightest law graduates that law and politics are the same and that using the courts and unelected judges to effect positive social change is not just admirable but downright heroic. Americans need to realize that these schools are propagandizing the men and women who will eventually become judges, politicians, elite attorneys, legal scholars, authors, lobbyists, and businesspeople. Thus, the prejudices and pet doctrines taught as "mainstream" in America's law schools today stand a good chance of becoming or remaining law tomorrow.

This book, of course, is about fighting back. And the first step in fighting back is taking a clear-eyed look at the situation as it really is. The situation in our law schools may seem depressing, but conservatives must accept this reality. That's the only way we will learn to deal with a judiciary that for decades has been siding with the Left.

How do we fight back on law campuses? To be honest, it's doubtful that conservatives could ever come to dominate America's law school faculties. The real goal on law school campuses should not be to rid them of liberals (though the prospect of being able to learn about liberals only in a museum has a certain appeal) but to achieve a critical mass of conservatives in prominent positions in the legal academy. The next chapter discusses one legal step we can take toward achieving that goal—and in fact toward achieving critical mass throughout all of academia.

FIFTEEN

AFFIRMATIVE ACTION FOR CONSERVATIVES

Suing for True Diversity

L iberalism is rampant not just among law school faculties but throughout academia. When the *New York Times* ran a headline reading "Republicans Outnumbered in Academia, Studies Find," George Will said
it perfectly when he wrote, "The great secret is out: liberals dominate
campuses. Coming soon: 'Moon Implicated in Tides, Studies Find.' "[1]
You know you've got a problem when there's a nine-to-one ratio of liberals to conservatives among college professors.

Is the preponderance of liberals a function of chance? Or is it just a
reflection of the fact that liberals are more inclined than conservatives
to pursue careers in the academy? Or perhaps liberals are more intellectual than conservatives? Well, it seems something more invidious might
be at play. After recounting the overwhelming number of registered
Democrats teaching on America's college campuses, *National Review*'s
John Miller noted, "It defies belief to suggest that these political alle-
giances play no part in hiring and promotion." John Tierney of the
New York Times agrees, writing that alternate explanations can't account for the fact that "there are so many more liberal professors now
than there used to be."[2]

Miller and Tierney are right. The truth is, colleges and universities
punish rising academic stars of the vast right-wing conspiracy for
being, well, conservative. Feminists want to talk about "glass ceilings"
(you know, those glass ceilings that Oprah, Martha Stewart, and Barbra
Streisand keep bumping into on their way to more multimillion-dollar
paydays), but the real barriers are those keeping far too many talented
conservatives out of the academy, unable to teach college students
and law students. Even National Public Radio has aired stories on the
possible discrimination against Republicans, and some Republican

members of Congress wish to enact an Academic Bill of Rights that would call on professors to include dissenting views in class.

There are legions of horror stories of academics expressing conservative—nay, just mainstream—political and economic views and finding themselves on the outside of the academy with their noses pressed against glass, asking, "What happened?"

Take the story of Smith College economist James Miller. In 2002 Miller was denied tenure in part because he occasionally wrote for *National Review Online*.[3] Horror of horrors! That sin is certainly far worse than, say, spouting off about how the World Trade Center victims on 9/11 were "little Eichmanns," as tenured University of Colorado professor Ward Churchill has done, or declaring, "The only true heroes are those who find ways that help defeat the U.S. military," as Columbia University professor Nicholas De Genova did.[4]

Miller eventually did gain tenure at Smith, thanks in part to the publicity generated when Bill O'Reilly of Fox News picked up the story. But that was a rarity. John Miller accurately characterized academia as "an impenetrable fortress of liberalism." In fact, said Miller, "many young conservatives who might otherwise be drawn to a career in higher education don't consider it an option."[5] Or those who are committed to a career in academia might well try to tailor their views in order to become a more appealing candidate to overwhelmingly liberal hiring committees. So much for academic freedom. Conservative academics who want to get hired or gain tenure are virtually forced to toe the liberal line.

It's not just conservative professors who suffer from this discrimination. In a nation where conservatism has been ascending and liberalism has been waning, it constitutes educational malpractice to deny college kids an explanation of the basic tenets of conservatism. As the group Students for Academic Freedom observes, "You can't get a good education if they're only telling you half the story."[6] The Left pays lip service to the importance of diversity in education but generally ignores the only diversity that really matters when it comes to educating people—diversity of opinions and viewpoints. Diversity of viewpoints is certainly not the same as diversity of skin pigmentation. If you think ethnic diversity alone can provide diversity of opinion, ask yourself this: How many different viewpoints do you think you'd get in a room full of *New York Times* editorial writers, all of different races but all educated at Ivy League schools and all living on Manhattan's Upper West Side?

When complaining about racial discrimination, liberals invariably talk about the "disparate impact" of a policy—how something falls more harshly on one group than on another. For example, to show that the United States is racist and discriminatory, the Left frequently points to statistics showing that while blacks make up roughly 13 percent of the American population, they commit more than 10 percent of the crimes and make up more than 10 percent of the criminals on death row. Or they complain that there aren't enough minority coaches in professional sports. Looking at such statistical disparities, liberals maintain that racial discrimination exists even when no direct proof of discrimination can be shown. The Left does not care whether there was evil intent or ill motive behind a particular policy; all that matters to them is the disparate impact.

Liberals love to encourage lawsuits based on disparate-impact theories. For example, Ted Kennedy and John Kerry wholeheartedly support the FAIRNESS (Fairness and Individual Rights Necessary to Ensure a Stronger Society) Act, which would expand opportunities for individuals to sue under disparate-impact theories. And during the Supreme Court nomination hearings for Samuel Alito in January 2006, Democrat Joe Biden lectured the nominee on why the law must pay close attention to disparate impact: "Discrimination has become very sophisticated. It's become very, very sophisticated, very much more subtle than it was when I got here 34 years ago or 50 years ago. . . . It's harder to make a case of discrimination even though there's no doubt that it still exists."[7] Typical liberal—claiming something exists despite a lack of reliable proof.

So let's assume you have members of a discrete and insular minority group who are repeatedly denied jobs readily available to others with comparable job qualifications. And let's say the percentage of the group in a particular profession lags by orders of magnitude behind its representation in the population at large, and even in every state in the union. Let's say, further, that this disparity has existed for many decades—and in fact is far greater today than it was in previous eras. You may be on your way to a pretty good discrimination case.

Well, at most universities, conservatives are that discrete and insular minority group. If it's discriminatory for, say, 6 percent of a college faculty to be African-American when approximately 13 percent of the American population is black, it seems even more discriminatory that only 10 percent of professors lean to the right when conservatives represent half the population. Given the skewed (non)representation of conservatives on university faculties, the Right has loads of ammunition to wage a legal battle against ideological discrimination on campuses. As UCLA law professor Stephen Bainbridge observes, the statistical evidence "makes out a prima facie case that university hiring practices are having a disparate impact. The burden of proof is therefore on the university to show why this disparity exists."[8]

THE LEGAL REMEDY:
AFFIRMATIVE ACTION FOR CONSERVATIVES

SO HOW DO WE fix the ideological imbalance in higher education? Embrace the Left's tactics. How about a policy of affirmative action for conservatives?

In the 1960s and the 1970s, universities began using affirmative action programs to recruit minority students and faculty members to their schools. Affirmative action, of course, provides extra advantages for individuals falling into a minority group that has historically been discriminated against. The policy encourages (or requires) companies and universities to increase the hiring and promotion of candidates from certain favored minority groups. Proponents of affirmative action typically claim that these hiring practices will better society as a whole, even if some individuals suffer because of the policy.

The justification for affirmative action policies comes from the Fourteenth Amendment to the Constitution, or laws inspired by the ideals of the Fourteenth Amendment. The amendment's equal protection clause generally prohibits government from affording the full protection of the law to one group but not to another. Historically the equal protection clause has been interpreted to help protect racial minorities, women, and now homosexuals from discrimination. Yet there is no reason why it cannot be applied to cover diversity of viewpoints as well. Indeed, the text of the Fourteenth Amendment speaks neither to race nor sex nor sexual orientation; it merely provides that no *person* shall be deprived of the equal protection of the laws. Contrary to what some liberals might think, conservatives are people, too. Keep in mind as well that public universities are government entities, as they are paid for by taxpayers. (And in fact, many if not most private universities receive federal funding—think science and humanities grants.)

Why not have courts step in and rectify the consequences of liberal academics' ideological discrimination against conservatives? Certainly universities aren't fixing the problem on their own; given all the past discrimination against conservatives, right-leaning academics don't have a strong presence on hiring committees, so the discrimination is likely to endure. As John Tierney observes, "Once liberals dominate a department, they can increase their majority by voting to award tenure to like-minded scholars. As liberals dominate a field, conservatives' work comes to be seen as fringe scholarship."[9] So how else can conservatives overcome the effects of such long-standing ideological discrimination?

One way to achieve this goal of affirmative action for conservatives is to seek a court directive requiring state colleges to hire a certain percentage of conservatives over the next few decades. Certainly courts have broad powers to order sweeping remedies to undo the effects of past government discrimination or to approve consent decrees in cases when there has been ample evidence of past unlawful discrimination against a disadvantaged group. If courts have the power to order school busing, the building of swimming pools at public magnet schools, the creation of civil unions and gay marriage, and the raising of taxes, then surely they have the power to order affirmative action for conservatives.

Think it's crazy for a court to monitor hiring processes? Think again. The Berkeley, California, school system has come under judicial supervision for disciplining black and Hispanic students disproportionately to their representation in the population.[10] Courts have taken over homeless shelters, prisons, and schools. Why can't they supervise this, too?

USING LIBERAL PRECEDENTS AGAINST THE LEFT

In pursuing the goal of affirmative action for conservatives, the Right should loudly herald its reliance on Supreme Court precedents—precedents loved by liberals.

The Supreme Court has clearly announced that maintaining educational diversity in universities is "a compelling state interest." This was the Court's conclusion in the case of *Grutter v. Bollinger* (2003), which upheld the University of Michigan Law School's use of racially discriminatory policies in admitting students.

A compelling state interest? That's a big deal. Another time when the Supreme Court thought it acceptable for the government to discriminate on the basis of race was when it approved the internment of Japanese-Americans in World War II. So apparently the Supreme Court thinks admitting the sons of Colin Powell and Jesse Jackson to fancy law schools advances a "compelling state interest" on a par with winning World War II. This academic diversity thing must be pretty gosh darn important.

Sure, we conservatives don't like the ruling in the Michigan case, but let's exploit this precedent to advance our own cause. If diversity in higher education is important enough to be considered a "compelling state interest," it would seem obvious that a public university must also consider the ideology of the educators themselves to advance the same goal of diversity. The argument for racial preferences in university admissions holds that admitting students from different ethnic backgrounds allows the sharing of different perspectives, which enhances everyone's education. But by that rationale, shouldn't students also be exposed to different perspectives from professors, something more than just Marxist theories and other left-wing ideas? Let's think about this—who will have more of an influence on your education, the student sitting next to you or the professor who gives the lectures, gives you grades, and writes your recommendations?

Beyond the *Grutter* decision, conservatives have no shortage of Supreme Court rulings we can cite to make the case for ideological diversity in universities. In fact, let's use some of the Left's favorite First Amendment cases involving free speech.

In deciding *Keyishian v. Board of Regents* (1967), liberal hero Justice William Brennan stated, "Our Nation is deeply committed to safeguarding academic freedom, which is of transcendent value to all of us and not merely to the teachers concerned. That freedom . . . does not tolerate laws that cast a pall of orthodoxy over the classroom. . . . The classroom is peculiarly the 'marketplace of ideas.' The Nation's future depends upon leaders trained through wide exposure to that robust exchange of ideas which discovers truth 'out of a multitude of tongues, [rather] than through any kind of authoritative selection.'" I couldn't have made the case for ideological diversity better myself!

And in fact, the Supreme Court has expressly stated that government entities cannot discriminate against Republicans in hiring. Since the 1947 case of *United Public Workers v. Mitchell,* the high court has held that "Congress may not 'enact a regulation providing that no Republican, Jew or Negro shall be appointed to federal office.'"

And in the case of *Perry v. Sindermann* (1972), the Supreme Court explained, "For if the government could deny a benefit to a person because of his constitutionally protected speech or associations, his exercise of those freedoms would in effect be penalized and inhibited. This would allow the government to 'produce a result which [it] could not command directly. . . . Such interference with constitutional rights is impermissible."

There's more. In the case of *Elrod v. Burns* (1976), the Supreme Court stated that "political belief and association constitute the core of those activities protected by the First Amendment. . . . [W]hether it be by the denial of public employment or . . . by the influence of a teacher over students, '[i]f there is any fixed star in our constitutional constellation, it is that no official, high or petty, can prescribe what shall be orthodox in politics, nationalism, religion, or other matters of opinion or force citizens to confess by word or act their faith therein.' And, though freedom of belief is central, '[t]he First Amendment protects political association as well as political expression.'"[11] In that same decision, the court explained that "the threat of dismissal for failure to provide [support for the favored political party] unquestionably inhibits protected belief and association, and dismissal for failure to provide support only penalizes its exercise").[12]

And then there was the case of *Sweezy v. New Hampshire* (1957), in which the Supreme Court recognized a right of "academic freedom." Protecting the right of a professor to refuse to disclose his political affiliations, the *Sweezy* plurality referred to the "vital role" higher education played in a democracy and warned against imposing "any strait jacket upon the intellectual leaders in our colleges and universities." The Supreme Court worried then that requiring professors to disclose political affiliations might harm higher education, our intellectual leaders, and democracy. Sounds like a compelling state interest to me!

By seeking legal redress against liberal universities, faculty members, and administrators, and citing these and other Supreme Court precedents, conservatives will not only highlight the problems of ideological intolerance but also hoist liberals on their own petard.

FOLLOW THE COMMIES

THE LAST CASE CITED, *Sweezy v. New Hampshire,* highlights a string of court rulings that would be particularly enjoyable for conservatives to rely on: cases upholding the rights of academics not to disavow or disclose their membership in or association with the Communist Party. In the *Sweezy* case, the court held that punishing a college professor for contempt because of his refusal to answer the state government's questions concerning the content of his lectures and his knowledge of the Communist Party abridged the professor's right to free speech and academic freedom without due process of law.

Today, conservative professors can follow in the footsteps of their mortal enemy—Marxist Communism. In other cases besides *Sweezy,* such as *Keyishian v. Board of Regents,* courts ruled that states could not penalize professors who had connections to the Communist Party. For example, as Justice William Douglas explained in a 1972 dissenting opinion, "no more direct assault on academic freedom can be imagined than for school authorities to refuse to hire a teacher because of his or her political, philosophical, or ideological beliefs."[13] And as if doing our work for us, the U.S. Supreme Court has already looked back on its rulings in Communist cases to make a direct comparison to membership in the Republican Party. "Though those cases involved affiliation with the Communist Party," the Court said, "we do not 'consider these [respondents'] interest in freely associating with members of the [Republican] Party less worthy of protection than [other] employees' interest in associating with Communists or former Communists.' "[14]

Isn't it fun tossing all these rulings back in the Left's face? It's good strategy, too.

STOP THE LEFTIES

CAN WE REALLY SUE to eat into the liberal dominance of our universities and law schools? Why not? Think about it: Some of the most famous victories for civil rights arose from lawsuits involving educational institutions, from *Brown v. Board of Education* to busing cases to cases challenging the University of Michigan's admission policies to school financing litigations. And suing for ideological diversity will, if nothing else, draw attention to the Left's ideological monopoly on college and law school campuses. The more Americans recognize the link between the liberal views taught in elite institutions and the leftward tilt of the elite legal culture, the better. After all, ultimately the American taxpayer pays for public universities. Start angering taxpayers and parents, and we can help cut the money supply to lefties on campus.

What we really want, though, is to see real gains in representation of conservatives on university and law school faculties. To paraphrase Justice Sandra Day O'Connor's comments about her desire to phase out affirmative action, we hope that twenty-five years from now the use of affirmative action for ideological conservatives will no longer be necessary.

STORMING THE COURTS

President Franklin D. Roosevelt sat listening to a group of activists make an impassioned plea for their cause. When they finished, he responded, "You've convinced me—now go out and put pressure on me."[1]

There's a lesson in this for conservatives today. In the fight for our rights, our individual liberties, and the American way of life, we must apply pressure. And we do that by going on the offensive. We don't need to watch helplessly as unelected judges enact the left-wing agenda, and as elected politicians do little to thwart the liberal legal assault. We can push for, and achieve, real results.

Don't think ordinary Red State Americans can effect serious change in the courts? Just ask Supreme Court justice . . . whoops, *White House counsel* Harriet Miers. Samuel Alito sits on the Supreme Court today not because of politicians in Washington but because rank-and-file conservatives expressed their outrage about the Miers selection. It was the Right who stopped Miers, not the Left. The grass roots put pressure on President Bush, and Bush responded.

Conservatives can't rest easy now that Alito and John Roberts have secured seats on the Supreme Court. Our work has barely begun. The highest court in the land will, to be sure, play an essential part in the campaign to defeat the left-wing legal assault on fundamental American values. But fighting liberalism is like a high-stakes Whack-a-Mole game: You can knock down the loony Left in one place, but its ugly head will pop right up somewhere else. We must fight the Left at all levels of the legal system, federal, state, and local. The substantial victories conservatism has achieved elsewhere must be translated into success in the courts, where the Left still maintains a stranglehold.

Fortunately we have the weapons, and the battle plan, with which to fight the Left. Better still, the battle plan enables all of us—ordinary taxpaying Americans—to contribute. We're engaged in a political struggle over the most fundamental issues in our lives, not a legalistic debate over obscure theoretical concepts. Conservatives can't leave the fighting to cloistered judges and Beltway lawyers, bureaucrats, and politicians.

It is essential, then, to demystify the courts. Once we accept courts for what they really are—political bodies—we realize that it's not just legal elites who can talk about the law and how it shapes our lives. Massive numbers of Americans actually play a *direct* role in shaping the courts and thus the law, since thirty-nine different states hold some form of judicial elections. At a time when Republicans control federal and state governments and when there are twice as many self-identified conservatives as there are self-identified liberals in the United States, we have a glorious opportunity to push for real change.[2]

So what should conservatives do, first and foremost?

Ask for exactly what we want.

It's that simple. Conservatives support free markets, the right to own a gun and use it in self-defense, the right to life for the unborn, freedom of religion, strong criminal laws, and a strong national defense, and recognize the fact that the nation was founded on the notion that unalienable individual rights are derived from the Creator, not from government know-it-alls. We must demand that courts protect and advance these essential American values. Conservatives can't continue to describe judges and courts using technical jargon that means almost nothing to nonlawyers—terms like "strict constructionism," "originalism," and the vague "judicial restraint." Clinging to such nondescript language will fail the conservative movement. An individual need not be able to explain, say, why the doctrine of incorporation comports with the views expressed in the Federalist Papers to understand that the courts should protect key individual freedoms and limit the reach and power of the government.

For too long the Left has exploited conservatives' failure to define precise objectives and devise effective strategies for the courts. Liberals have also taken advantage of the Right's utopian view of the courts. While conservatives naively insist that judges operate at a distance from the political arena, liberals have long recognized that American law at the upper levels is highly politicized. We can't let liberals exploit our mistakes any longer.

If the Left can demand pro-choice judges who never met a lefty cause that lacked merit, why should conservatives continue to emphasize vague notions such as exercising judicial restraint and upholding the rule of law? Instead we must insist on appointing and electing strong conservatives who will use the judiciary to protect gun rights, free markets, the rights of the unborn, and the American way of life. We need, at long last, principled conservatives on the bench who consider not just arcane processes but real-world results as well.

The battle plan laid out in these pages can work, because the weapons and strategies already exist and have worked time and again—*against* us. The Left has deployed these very strategies to advance values and principles antithetical to the American way of life. Slowing or even halting the left-wing campaign is not good enough. Conservatives can, by finally going on the offensive in the courts, actually overturn many of the Left's legal victories from the past seven decades. Unabashed conservative judicial activism will prevent liberal legal precedents from remaining welded to the body politic. And more important, it will *advance* conservatism.

WHAT WE'VE LOST—AND WHAT WE STAND TO GAIN

SINCE THE LEFT HAS a stranglehold on American law, it's easy for conservatives to view the courts as the enemy. But we must recall that the liberal domination of the American legal system is a relatively recent phenomenon. Remember that in 1923—a decade before liberals hijacked the courts to advance their radical agenda—the U.S. Supreme Court defined the term *liberty* this way: "Without doubt, it denotes not merely freedom from bodily restraint but also the right of the individual to contract, to engage in any of the common occupations of life, to acquire useful knowledge, to marry, establish a home and bring up children, to worship God according to the dictates of his own conscience, and generally to enjoy those privileges long recognized at common law as essential to the orderly pursuit of happiness by free men."[3]

Yes, believe it or not, Supreme Court rulings actually read like that at one point in the not-so-distant past. It's a testament to how much we've lost as a result of the loony Left's sustained legal assault that we're surprised to learn the Court ever spoke so forcefully in defense of liberty. (These days courts usually employ such powerful rhetoric only when discussing sex.) But the 1923 ruling also serves as a reminder that the courts can actively defend the principles that the Founders built this nation around and that now represent the bedrock values of the conservative movement.

To advance those values and principles, conservatives must first cast aside the failed tactics, strategies, and rhetoric we rely on when approaching the courts. That's why we need new weapons and a new battle plan. The weapons and strategies the Left used to take over the American legal system are not inherently liberal or anti-American. They can just as easily be deployed by the Right—for the good of conservatism and America.

Still, many conservatives want us to keep using the same old tactics, even though it is clear that liberals have utterly dominated the Right in the courts. These conservatives tend to cite the Framers, and the Constitution they drafted, as our greatest guide. But we must always remember that the first priority of the Framers was defending the freedoms and principles on which this country was founded. Indeed, they saw no problem in tossing aside our nation's first governing constitution—the Articles of Confederation—when it proved inadequate to protect the "unalienable rights" and liberties mentioned in the Declaration of Independence. It was a daring move, but it was absolutely essential to preserving what made this nation great.

Two centuries later, Ronald Reagan took another bold step. He launched the Reagan Revolution, challenging the conventional wisdom that Americans must learn to live with a stagnant economy, accept big government, accommodate the Communists, and in general be pessimistic about the future. As Reagan reminded the American people in his 1989 farewell address, pundits initially said his administration's "programs would result in catastrophe," its "views on foreign affairs would cause war," and its "plans for the economy would cause inflation to soar and bring about economic collapse." But, Reagan said, those opinion leaders were wrong. "The fact is, what they called 'radical' was really 'right.' What they called 'dangerous' was just 'desperately needed.' "[4]

And so today Americans must take yet another bold step, this time to reclaim the courts from the Left and advance the rights and values the Founders bequeathed to us. And we hope that like Ronald Reagan's revolution, our seemingly radical battle plan will in time be affirmed as not only right but desperately needed.

Indeed, by taking swift action now, we might someday look back on our efforts in the courts just as Reagan reflected on the work Americans did in the 1980s to reclaim the "shining city upon a hill": "We made a difference. We made the city stronger. We made the city freer, and we left her in good hands. All in all, not bad, not bad at all."

NOTES

ONE: "IS THIS IT?"

1. Note to readers who wear Imperial Stormtrooper apparel to *Star Wars* premieres or debate whether Captain Jean-Luc Picard could take Captain James T. Kirk: I am aware that under the rules of Quidditch, certain instances may arise where the team capturing the Golden Snitch could still lose the match, as reflected in *Harry Potter and the Goblet of Fire.*

2. Thomas Sowell, *A Conflict of Visions: Ideological Origins of Political Struggles* (New York: William Morrow, 1987).

3. See, for example, "Major Rulings of the 2004–2005 Term," *New York Times,* July 3, 2005.

4. Harvey C. Mansfield Jr., "Friends and Founders," *The New Criterion,* vol. 13, no. 9, (May 1995), available at http://www.newcriterion.com/archive/13/may95/mans.htm.

5. Erwin Chemerinsky and Catherine Fisk, "Judges Do Make Law—It's Their Job," *USA Today,* August 24, 2005.

6. Quoted in Abner Mikva, "What Justice Brennan Gave Us to Keep," 32 *Loyola of Los Angeles Law Review* 655 (April 1999).

TWO: BLUE COURTS, RED STATES, AND JUDGES GONE WILD

1. Mark Kozlowski, *The Myth of the Imperial Judiciary,* (New York: New York University Press, 2003), p. 20, citing Mary Ann Glendon, *Rights Talk* (New York: Free Press, 1991).

2. Tunku Varadarajan, "Judges or Priests," *Wall Street Journal,* May 11, 2001.

3. Grant Gilmore, *The Ages of American Law* (New Haven: Yale University Press, 1979), p. 35.

4. Mark Levin, *Men in Black: How the Supreme Court Is Destroying America* (Washington, D.C.: Regnery, 2005).

5. "Queer Eye on '04," *Mother Jones,* November 20, 2003, available at www.motherjones.org/news/dailymojo/2003/11/we_606_04a.html.

6. Patrick J. Buchanan, "Miers' Qualifications Are 'Non-Existent,'" Human Events Online, October 3, 2005, available at www.humaneventsonline.com/article.php?id=9444.

7. Sean Hannity, *Hannity & Colmes,* Fox News Channel, July 1, 2005, and November 1, 2005.

8. Alexis de Tocqueville, *Democracy in America* (1889; reprint, Washington, D.C.: Regnery, 2002), p. 221.

9. Antonin Scalia, speech at the Woodrow Wilson International Center for Scholars,

Washington, D.C., March 14, 2005, available at http://www.cfif.org/htdocs/legal_issues/legal_updates/us_supreme_court/scalia-constitutional-speech.htm.

10. Ronald Reagan, reprinted in "Abortion and the Conscience of the Nation: Ronald Reagan's Pro-Life Tract," *National Review Online*, June 10, 2004, available at www.nationalreview.com/script/printpage.p?ref=/document/reagan200406101030.asp (President Reagan's article was originally published in the *Human Life Review*'s Spring 1983 issue).

11. "The Court Rules for Mr. Bush," *New York Times*, December 13, 2000; "A Gay Rights Landmark," *New York Times*, June 27, 2003.

12. *Grutter v. Bollinger et al.*, 539 U.S. 306 (2003). The VMI case was *United States v. Virginia*, 518 U.S. 515 (1996).

13. See Mark W. Smith, "A Congressional Call to Arms: The Time Has Come for Congress to Enforce the Fifth Amendment's Takings Clause," 49 *Oklahoma Law Review* 295 (Summer 1996), pp. 301–2, 312.

14. *Lingle v. Chevron, USA,* 125 S. Ct. 2074 (2005).

15. Quoted in Marcia Coyle, "Takings Decision Alters Landscape," *National Law Journal,* May 30, 2005.

16. Quoted in Ramesh Ponnuru, "The End of the Federalism Revolution," *National Review,* July 4, 2005.

17. I am indebted to many authors, scholars, attorneys, and friends for their analyses of how the U.S. government, courts, and law have changed over time. There are far too many to cite here, but worth special mention is a series of lectures I attended in 2005 while visiting the Cato Institute in Washington, D.C., that helped shape my perspective on these issues. Especially influential were the reflections of Roger Pilon, Cato's vice president for legal affairs, and Jim Powell, author of *FDR's Folly: How FDR and His New Deal Prolonged the Great Depression* (New York: Crown Forum, 2003). Equally important was Pilon's October 2005 testimony before the U.S. Senate regarding the history of the Constitution. See Statement of Roger Pilon, Cato Institute, before the Committee on Homeland Security and Governmental Affairs Subcommittee on Federal Financial Management, Government Information, and International Security, October 25, 2005, available at http://hsgac.senate.gov/_files/102505Pilon.pdf.

18. Mark Pollot, *Grand Theft and Petit Larceny: Property Rights in America* (San Francisco: Pacific Research Institute, 1993), p. 11.

19. Judith S. Kaye, "Safeguarding a Crown Jewel: Judicial Independence and Lawyer Criticism of Courts," 25 *Hofstra Law Review* 703 (Spring 1997).

20. Justice George Sutherland, speech before the New York State Bar Association, January 21, 1921, quoted in "Quote of the Week," *Madison Policy Digest,* March 28, 2005.

21. U.S. Supreme Court, 1895, *Pollock v. Farmers' Loan & Trust Co.*

22. Statement of Roger Pilon, pp. 56–67.

23. Ibid., endnotes 20 and 22.

24. Ibid., p. 7.

25. The different "standards of review" played out as follows. If a case involved property rights or economic liberties, then the courts would apply a "rational basis" test, which meant that the legislation would be upheld as constitutional if there was any conceivable rational reason for enacting the legislation—even if the law harmed the economic interests of individual Americans. In contrast, if a law affected a "personal right" such as speech, the only way the courts could allow it to stand would be if the government could satisfy the heavy legal burden of proving that the law satisfied "strict scrutiny," i.e., that the law advanced a "compelling state interest" and was "narrowly tailored."

26. Janice Rogers Brown, "A Whiter Shade of Pale: Sense and Nonsense—the Pursuit of

Perfection in Law and Politics," speech to the Federalist Society chapter of the University of Chicago Law School, April 20, 2000.

27. Bernard Schwartz, "How Justic Brennan Changed America," in E. Joshua Rosenkrantz and Bernard Schwartz, eds., *Reason and Passion: Justice Brennan's Enduring Influence* (New York: W. W. Norton, 1997), pp. 32–33.

28. Robert Bork, *"A Country I Do Not Recognize": The Legal Assault on American Values* (Stanford, Calif.: Hoover Institution Press, 2005), pp. ix–x.

29. James R. Kelly and Christopher Kudlac, "Pro-Life, Anti–Death Penalty?" *America Magazine,* April 1, 2000, available at http://www.americamagazine.org/gettext.cfm?article TypeID=1&textID=650&issueID=286#.

30. *Abington School District v. Schempp,* 374 U.S. 203, 225 (1963).

31. *Board of County Commissioners v. Umhehr,* 518 U.S. 668, 688–89 (1996).

THREE: SHOGUN

1. Note to history buffs: Historians cannot agree whether the Polish cavalry actually charged Nazi tanks at the Battle of Krojanty in 1939. Still, the illustration here is apt regardless of its historical accuracy. Personally, whatever story the Poles want to tell about Krojanty is fine with me—after all, we need them to operate our secret CIA prisons for Islamo-fascists.

2. U.S. Reports, November 15, 1993, *"Proceedings in the Supreme Court of the United States in Memory of Justice Marshall."*

3. Tribute to Harry Blackmun, *Historical Society News,* vol. 7 (1999).

4. *Plyler v. Doe,* 457 U.S. 202 (1982).

5. Senate Judiciary Hearings, Transcript, September 14, 2005, available at www.pbs.org/weta/washingtonweek/transcripts/transcript050914.html.

6. *Plyler v. Doe,* 457 U.S. 202 (1982) (Burger, C. J., dissenting) (citations omitted).

7. Legal scholars have identified a number of types of constitutional argument. For example, constitutional arguments can be based on (1) the Constitution's text, (2) the history surrounding the creation of the Constitution, or the intent of the Founding Fathers, (3) the structures created by the Constitution, such as the three branches of government or the separate state and federal governments, (4) earlier decisions, or precedents, by the U.S. Supreme Court, (5) what the policy implications of a particular legal decision might be, or (6) the limited-government "ethos" that many argue is central to America' political culture. See Sanford Levinson, "The Embarrassing Second Amendment," *Yale Law Journal,* vol. 99, p. 637 (1989), citing to Philip Bobbitt, *Constitutional Fate: Theory of the Constitution* (New York: Oxford University Press, 1984).

8. Senator John Thune, Remarks on the Nomination of Judge John Roberts to Be Chief Justice of the United States Supreme Court, September 28, 2005, available at http://thune. senate.gov/public/index.cfm?FuseAction=Speeches.Detail&Speech_id=8&Month=9& Year=2005.

9. Quoted in "Judicial Misconduct and Discipline," Statement of Roger Pilon, Ph.D., J.D., Senior Fellow and Director, Center for Constitutional Studies, Cato Institute Testimony Before the Subcommittee on Courts and Intellectual Property, Committee on the Judiciary United States House of Representatives, May 15, 1997, available at http://www. cato.org/testimony/ct-rpo51597.html.

10. Alan Dershowitz, "What Kind of Justice Will Alito Be?" *Forbes,* January 13, 2006.

11. Robert Bork, *The Tempting of America: The Political Seduction of the Law* (New York: Touchstone Books, 1990), p. 16.

12. *Lawrence v. Texas,* 539 U.S. 558 (2003) (Scalia, J., dissenting).

13. Thomas Jefferson to William C. Jarvis, 1820, available at www.landmarkcases.org/marbury/jefferson.html.

14. Laurence Tribe, *God Save This Honorable Court: How the Choice of Supreme Court Justices Shapes Our History* (New York: Mentor, 1985), p. 23.

15. Robert Bork described the Madisonian dilemma as a conflict between two fundamental principles of American political life: "The first principle is self-government, which means that in wide areas of life majorities are entitled to rule, if they wish, simply because they are majorities." The second principle is "that there are nonetheless some things majorities must not do to minorities, some areas of life in which the individual must be free of majority rule." See *The Tempting of America*, p. 139.

16. Erwin Chemerinsky and Catherine Fisk, "Judges Do Make Law—It's Their Job," *USA Today*, August 24, 2005.

17. E. Joshua Rosenkrantz and Bernard Schwartz, eds. *Reason and Passion: Justice Brennan's Enduring Influence* (New York: W. W. Norton, 1997), p. 9.

18. Quoted in Abner Mikva, "What Justice Brennan Gave Us to Keep," 32 *Loyola of Los Angeles Law Review* 655 (April 1999).

19. Kevin Ring, ed., *Scalia Dissents: Writings of the Supreme Court's Wittiest, Most Outspoken Justice* (Washington, D.C.: Regnery, 2004).

FOUR: JUDICIAL ACTIVISM IS NOT A FOUR-LETTER WORD

1. Scott Douglas Gerber, *To Secure These Rights: The Declaration of Independence and Constitutional Interpretation* (New York: NYU Press, 1995), p. 15.

2. Erwin Chemerinsky and Catherine Fisk, "Judges Do Make Law—It's Their Job," *USA Today*, August 24, 2005.

3. Thomas Jefferson to W. H. Torrance, 1815, available at www.landmarkcases.org/marbury/jefferson.html.

4. Mark Kozlowski, *The Myth of the Imperial Judiciary: Why the Right Is Wrong About the Courts* (New York: NYU Press, 2003).

5. *McCulloch v. Maryland*, 17 U.S. 316 (1819).

6. Theodore Sky, *To Provide for the General Welfare: A History of the Federal Spending Power* (Cranbury, N.J.: Associated University Press, 2003), p. 115.

7. Kenneth Starr, *The Supreme Court in American Life* (New York: Warner Books, 2002).

8. Richard Epstein, "Written in Stone," *Wall Street Journal*, September 17–18, 2005.

9. Antonin Scalia, speech at the Woodrow Wilson International Center for Scholars, Washington, D.C., March 14, 2005, available at http://www.cfif.org/htdocs/legal_issues/legal_updates/us_supreme_court/scalia-constitutional-speech.htm.

10. Andrew Peyton Thomas, *The People v. Harvard Law: How America's Oldest Law School Turned Its Back on Free Speech* (San Francisco: Encounter Books, 2005), p. 127.

11. Ruth Bader Ginsburg, "Speaking in a Judicial Voice," 67 *New York University Law Review* 1185 (December 1992)

12. "Questioning Continues for Supreme Court Nominee Samuel Alito," CNN.com, January 10, 2006.

13. Abner Mikva, "What Justice Brennan Gave Us to Keep," 32 *Loyola of Los Angeles Law Review* 655 (April 1999).

14. Lino A. Graglia, "Constitutional Law Without the Constitution: The Supreme Court's Remaking of America," in Robert H. Bork, ed., *"A Country I Do Not Recognize": The Legal Assault on American Values* (Stanford, Calif.: Hoover Institution Press, 2005).

FIVE: "LET'S HUG IT OUT"

1. Sandra Froman, "The President's Column," *America's First Freedom,* December 2005, available at http://webwonks.org/Extra/NRA/nraarchive/2005/dec_05.html.

2. Saul Alinsky, *Rules for Radicals: A Pragmatic Primer for Realistic Radicals* (New York: Vintage Books, 1989), p. 14.

3. Ibid., p. xix.

4. "Fate and Roe v. Wade," *Washington Times,* January 25, 2005, available at http://www.washtimes.com/op-ed/20050124-091843-2176r.htm.

5. Linda Greenhouse, "The Supreme Court: Affirmative Action: Justices, 5 to 4, Cast Doubts on U.S. Programs That Give Preferences Based on Race," *New York Times,* June 13, 1995.

6. "The Right Kind of Justice," *New York Times,* July 17, 2005.

7. *Lawrence v. Texas,* 539 U.S. 558 (2003).

8. Jeffrey Rosen, "So, Do You Believe in 'Superprecedent'?" *New York Times,* October 30, 2005.

9. *Coker v. Georgia,* 433 U.S. 584 (1977).

10. *Boy Scouts of America v. Dale,* 530 U.S. 640 (2000).

11. "The Supreme Court's Overruling of Precedent: An Overview," CRS Report for Congress, November 29, 2005, available at http://digital.library.unt.edu/govdocs/crs//data/2005/upl-meta-crs-8231/RL33172_2005Nov29.pdf?PHPSESSID=dd2d40cd858b799d9occcocbdd5e5b558.

12. Erwin Chemerinsky and Catherine Fisk, "Judges Do Make Law—It's Their Job," *USA Today,* August 24, 2005.

13. George F. Will, "Damaging 'Deference,'" *Washington Post,* June 24, 2005.

14. Lori Aratani and Daniel de Vise, "Montgomery Blindsided Over Sex-Ed: Program Backers Blame Conservative Movement," *Washington Post,* May 7, 2005.

SIX: LEARNING TO LOVE THE LIVING CONSTITUTION

1. Liberal legal scholars are now working out rationales for this change of position, in what respected law professor Erwin Chemerinsky calls the "trendiest development in constitutional scholarship." Progressive scholars, he explains, are "turning against the courts" and arguing for "people—not judges—interpreting the Constitution." This school of interpretation goes by the name "popular constitutionalism." See Erwin Chemerinsky, "In Defense of Judicial Review: The Perils of Popular Constitutionalism," *University of Illinois Law Review 673,* December 6, 2004, p. 675.

2. Quoted in Jonah Goldberg, "It's Alive: Why the Constitution Should Remain Dead," National Review Online, July 8, 2003.

3. Antonin Scalia, speech at the Woodrow Wilson International Center for Scholars, Washington, D.C., March 14, 2005, available at http://www.cfif.org/htdocs/legal_issues/legal_updates/us_supreme_court/scalia-constitutional-speech.htm.

4. *Lawrence v. Texas,* 539 U.S. 558 (2003).

5. See, e.g., Linda Greenhouse, "Will the Court Move Right? It Already Has," *New York Times,* June 22, 2003, available at http://www.cnn.com/2003/US/06/22/nyt.greenhouse/.

6. Walter E. Williams, "The Law or Good Ideas?" Townhall.com, March 30, 2005, available at http://www.townhall.com/opinion/columns/walterwilliams/2005/03/30/14951.html.

7. Goldberg, "It's Alive."

8. *Shaffer v. Heitner,* 433 U.S. 186 (1977).

9. U.S. Reports, vol. 510 November 15, 1993, "Proceedings in the Supreme Court of the United States in Memory of Justice Marshall."

10. "Excerpts of Brennan's Speech on the Constitution," *New York Times,* October 13, 1985.

11. Remarks of Thurgood Marshall, Annual Seminar of the San Francisco Patent and Trademark Law Association, May 6, 1987, available at http://www.thurgoodmarshall.com/speeches/constitutional_speech.htm.

12. Remarks of Justice David H. Souter at the funeral mass for Justice Brennan, July 29, 1997, http://www.breannancenter.org/programs/programs_cele_eulogy.html.

13. Saul Alinsky, *Rules for Radicals: A Pragmatic Primer for Realistic Radicals* (New York: Vintage Books, 1989), p. 22.

SEVEN: DESPERATELY SEEKING JUDICIAL REAGANS

1. Emily Bazelon and David Newman, "A Different Shortlist: How About an Old-Style Conservative Supreme Court Nominee?" *Slate,* July 6, 2005, available at http://www.slate.com/id/2122079/.

2. Jeffrey Rosen, "Worst Choice," *New Republic,* February 24, 2003.

3. Laurence Tribe, "The Supreme Court, 1972 Term—Foreword: Toward a Model of Roles in the Due Process of Life and Law," 87 *Harvard Law Review* 1, 7 (1973).

4. Edward Lazarus, "The Lingering Problems with *Roe v. Wade,* and Why the Recent Senate Hearings on Michael McConnell's Nomination Only Underlined Them," FindLaw Legal Commentary, October 3, 2002.

5. Ruth Bader Ginsburg, "Speaking in a Judicial Voice," 67 *New York University Law Review* 1185 (December 1992).

6. See Roger Pilon, "Foreword: Restoring Constitutional Government," *Cato Supreme Court Review,* 2002, available at http://www.cato.org/pubs/scr/docs/2002/forward.pdf.

7. James Zagel and Adam Winkler, "Federal Judicial Independence Symposium: The Independence of Judges," 46 *Mercer Law Review* 795 (Winter 1995).

8. Linda Greenhouse, "Under the Microscope Longer Than Most," *New York Times,* July 10, 2005.

9. Robert H. Bork, "Their Will Be Done: How the Supreme Courts Sows Moral Anarchy," *Wall Street Journal,* July 10, 2005.

10. Linda Greenhouse, "Will the Court Move Right? It Already Has," *New York Times,* June 22, 2003.

11. *Sex Bias in the U.S. Code: A Report of the United States Commission on Civil Rights,* April 1977, pp. 93, 97, 100, 146, 195–96, 215–16, 218, 219–20, 225. See also Phyllis Schlafly, "Isn't Turnabout Fair Play?" www.eagleforum.org, August 24, 2005.

12. *Republican Party of Minnesota v. White,* 536 U.S 765 (2002).

13. Jeffrey Rosen, "We Hardly Know It When We See It: Obscenity and the Problem of Unprotected Speech," in E. Joshua Rosenkrantz and Bernard Schwartz, eds., *Reason and Passion: Justice Brennan's Enduring Influence* (New York: W. W. Norton, 1997), p. 72.

14. Kerry spokeswoman Stephanie Cutter was quoted as saying that "George Bush has been the steward of the worst economy since the Great Depression" in Richard W. Stevenson, "Bush Aide Sees $1 Trillion Gap in Kerry's Plans," *New York Times,* March 22, 2004.

15. Bradley Brooks, "U.S. Nears 1,000th Execution Since 1977," Associated Press, November 25, 2005. Table, "Estimated Number and Rate (Per 100,000 Inhabitants of Offenses Known to Police," *Sourcebook of Criminal Justice Statistics 2003* (Washington, D.C.: USGPO, 2003), available at http://www.albany.edu/sourcebook/pdf/t3106.pdf.

16. *Missouri v. Jenkins*, 515 U.S. 70, 1995 (quoting *Missouri v. Jenkins*, 495 U.S. 33, 77) (Kennedy, J., concurring in part and concurring in judgment).

17. Compare Justice Antonin Scalia, Speech at the Gregorian University, June 13, 1996, available at http://www.learnedhand.com/scalia.htm, with Jeffrey Sikkenga, "Lest We Forget: Clarence Thomas and the Meaning of the Constitution," *On Principle*, vol. 6, no. 6, December 1998, available at http://www.ashbrook.org/publicat/onprin/v6n6/sikkenga.html.

18. Tom Krannawitter, "Defending Thomas," *Precepts*, December 13, 2004, available at http://www.claremont.org/writings/precepts/041213.html.

19. Senator Charles Schumer to President George W. Bush, June 10, 2003, available at http://www.senate.gov/~schumer/SchumerWebsite/pressroom/press_releases/PR01772.html.

20. Antonin Scalia, speech at the Woodrow Wilson International Center for Scholars, Washington, D.C., March 14, 2005, available at http://www.cfif.org/htdocs/legal_issues/legal_updates/us_supreme_court/scalia-constitutional-speech.htm.

21. Alito's job application can be found at http://news.findlaw.com/usatoday/docs/alito/11158 5stmnt2.html.

22. These attacks on Souter are all quoted in David Skinner, "A Souter They Should've Spurned: Whoever Bush Names, the Left Will Pitch a Fit," *Weekly Standard*, July 25, 2005.

EIGHT: NO MORE SOUTERS

1. Laurence Tribe, *God Save This Honorable Court: How the Choice of Supreme Court Justices Shapes Our History* (New York: Mentor, 1985), pp. 74, 82, 92, 94.

2. Commission on Presidential Debates, Debate Transcript, Third Bush-Kerry Presidential Debate, October 13, 2004, Arizona State University, Tempe, Arizona, available at http://www.debates.org/pages/trans2004d.html.

3. Kimberly Strassel, "This Land Is Not Your Land," *Wall Street Journal*, December 15, 2005.

4. Linda Greenhouse, "Under the Microscope Longer Than Most," *New York Times*, July 10, 2005.

5. Tribe, *God Save This Honorable Court*, pp. 111, 108.

6. Manuel Miranda, "The Original Borking: Lessons from a Supreme Court Nominee's Defeat," *Wall Street Journal*, August 24, 2005.

7. John M. Broder, "Have a Seat, Your Honor (Presidents Wish It Were That Easy)," *New York Times*, July 10, 2005.

8. Adam Nagourney, "Glum Democrats Can't See Halting Bush on Courts," *New York Times*, January 15, 2006.

9. Senator Charles Schumer, quoted in Ronald Brownstein and Richard B. Schmitt, "Battle Lines Are Drawn for Fight Over Supreme Court Nominee," *Los Angeles Times*, July 4, 2005.

10. " 'Far Right Dream Judge' Janice Rogers Brown Joins Lineup of Extremist Appeals Court Nominees," press release, People For the American Way, August 28, 2003, available at http://www.pfaw.org/pfaw/general/default.aspx?oId=11894.

11. Ann Coulter, "Fool Me Eight Times, Shame on Me," *Human Events*, July 28, 2005.

NINE: JUDICIAL DARWINISM

1. Dahlia Lithwick, "The Souter Factor: What Makes Tough Conservative Justices Go Soft?" *Slate*, August 3, 2005.

2. Larry Sabato, "Supreme Questions: The Draft Lottery for a Chance to Ride the Bench," July 7, 2005, available at http://www.centerforpolitics.org/crystalball/article.php?id=LJS2005070601.

3. Stuart Taylor Jr., "Leftward Ho! Cry the Justices: Why Do So Many Republican Appointees to the Supreme Court Turn Liberal on the Bench?" *National Journal,* July 7, 2003.

4. John C. Jeffries, *"Bakke* Revisited," *UVA Lawyer,* Fall 2004, available at http://www.law.virginia.edu/home2002/html/alumni/uvalawyer/fo4/bakke.htm.

5. Taylor, "Leftward Ho! Cry the Justices."

6. "The Right Kind of Justice," *New York Times,* July 17, 2005.

7. C. Boyden Gray, "Four Democratic Myths About Confirming Judges," Human Events Online, May 13, 2005.

8. See http://www.ehow.com/how_12356_become-judge.html.

9. Alex Kozinski, "The Appearance of Propriety," *Legal Affairs,* January/February 2005.

10. Ibid.

11. "Two Norwegian public relations executives and one member of the Norwegian parliament tell Fox News that they have been contacted by the White House, or those working on behalf of the White House, to help campaign for President Clinton to receive this year's Nobel Peace Prize for his work in trying to negotiate peace in the Middle East. . . . It is considered highly unethical in Norway to actively campaign for a peace prize candidate." Rita Cosby, *Special Report with Brit Hume,* Fox News Channel, October 12, 2000.

12. Mark Levin, "Death by Privacy: Emanations, Penumbras, and Bad Law," National Review Online, March 14, 2005, available at http://www.nationalreview.com/levin/levin200503140754.asp.

13. Tony Mauro, "O'Connor Fires Back on Judicial Independence," *Legal Times,* November 28, 2005, available at http://www.law.com/jsp/article.jsp?id=1132740311603; Linda Greenhouse, "Justice Weighs Desire vs. Duty (Duty Prevails)," *New York Times,* August 24, 2005.

14. Martin Tolchin, "Press Is Condemned by a Federal Judge for Court Coverage," *New York Times,* June 15, 1992.

15. "William J. Brennan Jr.," *Washington Post,* July 26, 1997.

16. Taylor, "Leftward Ho! Cry the Justices."

17. Richard Posner, "What Do Judges Maximize? (The Same Thing Everybody Else Does)," available at http://www.law.uchicago.edu/Lawecon/WkngPprs_0125/15.RAP.Judges.pdf.

18. John O. McGinnis et al., "The Patterns and Implications of Political Contributions by Elite Law School Faculty," 93 *Georgetown Law Journal* 1167 (2005).

19. David E. Bernstein, "Affirmative Blackmail: The ABA Orders Law Schools to Practice Racial Preference—Even If They Have to Break the Law," *Wall Street Journal,* February 15, 2006, available at http://www.opinionjournal.com/extra/?id=110007954.

20. Adam Nagourney, "Glum Democrats Can't See Halting Bush on Courts," *New York Times,* January 15, 2006.

21. I heard this remark in a Dirksen Office Building elevator immediately before the U.S. Senate vote on the nomination of John Roberts to become chief justice of the United States, September 29, 2005.

22. Steve Kraske, "GOP Trend Likely to Continue in Kansas," *Kansas City Star,* October 6, 2003.

23. Karen Tumulty, "A One-Man Earthquake: Jim Jeffords' Defection from the G.O.P. Turned Washington Upside Down," *Time,* June 4, 2001.

24. Jeffrey Rosen, "A Majority of One," *New York Times,* June 3, 2001.

25. Wilson Ring, "Vermont Judge Imposes 3–10 Year Sentence for Sex Offender," Associated Press, January 26, 2006.

26. David J. Garrow, "The Brains Behind Blackmun," *Legal Affairs*, May/June 2005, p. 28.

27. Adam Liptak, "If the Law Is an Ass, the Law Professor Is a Donkey," *New York Times*, August 28, 2005.

28. Charles Lane, "Alito Hires as a Clerk Former Ashcroft Aide," *Washington Post*, February 15, 2006.

29. Thomas Jefferson to Spencer Roane, September 6, 1819, available at http://press-pubs.uchicago.edu/founders/documents/a1_8_18s16.html.

30. *Republican Party of Minnesota v. White*, 536 U.S. 765 (2002).

TEN: UNLEASHING THE RAPACIOUS VELOCI-LAWYERS ON THE LEFT

1. Heather MacDonald, "Clinical, Cynical," *Wall Street Journal*, January 11, 2006.

2. Jim Carlton, "Rancher Turns the Table," *Wall Street Journal*, August 19, 2005, B1.

3. Barbara Hinkson Craig, *Courting Change: The Story of the Public Citizen Litigation Group* (Washington, D.C.: Public Citizen Press, 2004), p. i.

4. *NYU Review of Law and Social Change*, Volume 8, Number 3, 1978–1979.

5. Genna Rae McNeil, "Groundwork," in Deborah L. Rhode and Charles J. Ogletree Jr., eds., *Brown at 50: The Unfinished Legacy* (Chicago: American Bar Association, 2004).

6. Lino A. Graglia, "Constitutional Law without the Constitution: The Supreme Court's Remaking of America," in Robert H. Bork, ed., *"A Country I Do Not Recognize": The Legal Assault on American Values* (Stanford, Calif.: Hoover Institution Press, 2005), pp. 27–28.

7. Tony Mauro, "Voucher Advocates Plan Next Push to High Court," Law.com, August 5, 2002, available at http://www.law.com/jsp/law/LawArticleFriendly.jsp?id=1024079086859.

8. Craig, *Courting Change*, p. xx.

9. Ibid., pp. 31–32.

10. Kate Zernike, "Iowa Governor Will Give Felons the Right to Vote," *New York Times*, June 18, 2005.

11. Craig, *Courting Change*, p. 27.

12. Ibid., p. 8.

13. Kieran Crowley and Marsha Kranes, "Hamptons Warpath," *New York Post*, June 16, 2005, p. 3.

14. Kevin Freking, "Judge Throws Out Drug Benefit Challenge," Associated Press, December 30, 2005.

15. Jennifer Sullivan, "Police: Tapes Show Bestiality," *Seattle Times*, July 16, 2005.

16. Paul Weyrich, *Q&A*, C-SPAN, March 27, 2005.

17. Craig, *Courting Change*, p. 44.

18. In February 2006, the *New York Times* reported, "In a rare display of unanimity that cuts across partisan and geographic lines, lawmakers in virtually every statehouse across the country are advancing bills and constitutional amendments to limit use of the government's power of eminent domain to seize private property for economic development purposes. The measures are in direct response to the United States Supreme Court's 5-to-4 decision last June in a landmark property rights case from Connecticut, upholding the authority of the City of New London to condemn homes in an aging neighborhood to make way for a private development of offices, condominiums and a hotel. It was a decision that one justice, who had written for the majority, later all but apologized for." See John M. Broder, "States Curbing Right to Seize Private Homes," *New York Times*, February 21, 2006.

19. Rhode and Ogletree, eds., *Brown at 50*.

20. Democratic National Committee, "Bush and Cheney's Energy Task Force," available at http://www.grandoldpetroleum.com/a/2005/10/bush_and_cheney_1.php.

21. Ibid.

22. "ACLU Calls Abu Ghraib Scandal 'Predictable Result' of U.S. Detention Policies; Asks Government to Comply with Information Request on Torture," press release, May 11, 2004, available at http://www.aclu.org//safefree/general/17405prs20040511.html.

23. "ACLU Threat Drives Scouts out of Schools," *WorldNetDaily,* March 11, 2005.

24. Thomas Sowell, *Affirmative Action Around the World: An Empirical Study* (New Haven: Yale University Press, 2004).

25. Roberta Cooper Ramo, "A Yardstick for us all," in E. Joshua Rosenkrantz and Bernard Schwartz, eds., *Reason and Passion: Justice Brennan's Enduring Influence* (New York: W. W. Norton, 1997), pp. 312–13.

26. A logical template for an Academic Bill of Rights would be the proposal by David Horowitz of the Center for the Study of Popular Culture, which can be viewed at www.cspc.org.

ELEVEN: WHAT A DIFFERENCE A GUN MAKES

1. Jack Sullivan and Franci Richardson, "Records Show Dartmouth Probe Drew Thousands of Tips," *Boston Herald,* June 29, 2002. See also Kathryn Marchocki, "Tulloch Gets Life Terms,'" *Manchester Union Leader* (New Hampshire), April 5, 2002, available at http://www.keepandbeararms.com/information/xcibviewitem.asp?id=3291.

2. John R. Lott Jr., *More Guns, Less Crime: Understanding Crime and Gun Control Laws,* 2d ed. (Chicago: University of Chicago Press, 2000), p. 1.

3. *United States v. Miller,* 307 U.S. 174 (1939).

4. "Witnesses Appraise Supreme Court Nominee's Approach to Law," *New York Times,* January 14, 2006, p. A10.

5. Barbara Vobejda, Cheryl W. Thompson, and David B. Ottaway, "Response in Littleton Was Swift, But Unsure," *Washington Post,* May 12, 1999.

6. Robert B. Bluey, "Republican Senator Wants to Scrap DC Gun Ban," *CNSNews,* July 17, 2003, available at http://www.cnsnews.com/ViewCulture.asp?Page=%5CCulture%5Carchive%5C200307%5CCUL20030717b.html.

7. John R. Lott Jr. and David B. Mustard, "Crime, Deterrence, and Right-to-Carry Concealed Handguns," *Journal of Legal Studies,* January 1997.

8. Jim Burns, "Survey: Top Cops Favor Concealed Carry Laws," *CNSNews,* November 30, 2001, available at http://www.cnsnews.com/ViewCulture.asp?Page=culture/archive/200011/cul20001113.

9. Jennifer Lee and Colin Moynihan, "Brooklyn Man Is Beaten in Bias Attack, Police Say," *New York Times,* June 11, 2005.

10. John R. Lott Jr., *The Bias Against Guns: Why Almost Everything You've Heard About Gun Control Is Wrong* (Washington: Regnery, 2003), pp. 83–84.

11. Steven D. Levitt and Stephen J. Dubner, *Freakonomics: A Rogue Economist Explores the Hidden Side of Everything* (New York: William Morrow, 2005).

12. See *U.S. v. Verdugo-Urquidez,* 494 U.S. 259 (1990).

13. Amicus curiae brief of Firearms Civil Rights Legal Defense Fund submitted in *Perpich v. U.S.,* U.S. Supreme Court, 496 U.S. 334 (1990).

14. *United States v. Emerson,* 270 F. 3d 203 (5th Cir. 2001), cert denied 122 5. Ct. 2362 (2002).

15. Memorandum opinion for the Attorney General, "Whether the Second Amendment

Secures an Individual Right," U.S. Department of Justice, August 24, 2004, available at http://www.usdoj.gov/olc/secondamendment2.htm.

TWELVE: KEEP YOUR ECONOMIC LAWS OFF MY BODY!

1. Marc A. Miles, Kim R. Holmes, and Mary Anastasia O'Grady, *Index of Economic Freedom* (Washington, D.C.: Heritage Foundation/*Wall Street Journal,* 2006), available at http://www.heritage.org/research/features/index/chapters/htm/index2006_excsum.cfm.

2. John Adams, "A Defence of the Constitutions of Government of the United States," in Charles Francis Adams, ed., *The Works of John Adams* (1787), vol. 6, pp. 8–9, as quoted in Philip B. Kurland and Ralph Lerner, *The Founders' Constitution,* available at http://press-pubs.uchicago.edu/founders/documents/v1ch16s15.html.

3. William Ahern and Gerald Prante, "Summary of Federal Individual Income Tax Data," TaxFoundation.org, October 11, 2005, available at http://www.taxfoundation.org/taxdata/show/250.html.

4. Henry Hazlitt, *Economics in One Lesson* (1966; reprint, San Francisco: Laissez Faire Books, 1996), p. 26.

5. Ahern and Prante, "Summary of Federal Individual Income Tax Data ("In sum, 2003 combined a rapidly growing economy, higher incomes, lower average tax cuts, and increased government tax revenue").

6. Walter E. Williams, *More Liberty Means Less Government: Our Founders Knew This Well* (Stanford, Calif.: Hoover Institution Press, 1999), pp. 57–58.

7. Stephen Moore, "Is U.S. in Slow Motion to Socialism?" Human Events Online, May 6, 2005, available at http://www.humaneventsonline.com/article.php?print=yes&id=7373.

8. *Meyer v. Nebraska,* 262 U.S. 390 (1923).

9. Friedrich August von Hayek, *The Road to Serfdom* (1944; reprint, Chicago: University of Chicago Press, 1994), p. 100.

10. *Roe v. Wade,* 410 U.S. 113 (1973). Of course, just to be accurate, in *Planned Parenthood v. Casey* (1992), the Supreme Court concluded that abortion was not a fundamental right but still found that the right to abortion existed and could not be regulated where the regulation imposed an undue burden upon the woman's right to choose. Liberals, however, view the right to abortion to be a fully fundamental constitutional right. See, e.g., *Planned Parenthood v. Casey,* 505 U.S. 833 (1992) (Blackmun, J., concurring in part, and dissenting in part).

11. *Eisenstadt v. Baird,* 405 U.S. 438, 453 (1972).

12. *Carey v. Population Services Int'l,* 431 U.S. 678 (1977).

13. Martin Fackler, "As Japan Roars Back, Who Will Be in Charge?" *New York Times,* January 15, 2006, available at http://www.cato.org/special/ownership_society/boaz.html.

14. Ibid.

15. "North Korea 'Loses 3 Million to Famine,'" BBC News, February 17, 1999; James Brooke, "By Order of North Korea, UN Halts Food Assistance There," *New York Times,* January 6, 2005.

16. David Boaz, "Defining an Ownership Society," available at http://www.iht.com/articles/2006/01/13/business/wbpolicy.php.

17. *Planned Parenthood v. Casey,* 505 U.S. 833 (1992).

18. Jean-François Revel, *The Flight from Truth* (New York: Random House, 1991), p. xxxvii, quoted in Janice Rogers Brown, " 'A Whiter Shade of Pale': Sense and Nonsense— The Pursuit of Perfection in Law and Politics," speech to the Federalist Society chapter of the University of Chicago Law School, April 20, 2000. For the most thorough recounting of the overwhelming evidence showing that President Franklin Roosevelt's New Deal made

the Depression worse, see Jim Powell, *FDR's Folly: How Roosevelt and His New Deal Prolonged the Great Depression* (New York: Crown Forum, 2003).

19. *West Coast Hotel Co. v. Parrish,* 300 U.S. 379 (1937).

THIRTEEN: ANCHOR BABIES AWEIGH!

1. "Overview of Annual Immigration," Federation for American Immigration Reform, October 2002, available at http://www.fairus.org/site/PageServer?pagename=research_research16b2.

2. Michael D. Tanner, *The Poverty of Welfare: Helping Others in Civil Society* (Washington, D.C.: CATO Institute, 2003), p. 7.

3. Steven A. Camarota, Center for Immigration Studies, "Immigrants in the United States—2002: A Snapshot of America's Foreign-Born Population," November 2002, available at http://www.cis.org/articles/2002/back1302.html.

4. Federation for American Immigration Reform, citing statistics from the National Institute of Corrections, Federal Bureau of Prisons, June 2003, available at http://www.fairus.org/site/PageServer?pagename=iic_immigrationissuecentersob9c.

5. See remarks by Edith Hakola, vice president, Center for American Unity, Capitol Hill Club Press Luncheon, March 25, 2004, available at http://www.cfau.org/hamdi/hakola_remarks.htm.

6. Frank I. Michelman, "The Supreme Court, 1968 Term—Foreword: On Protecting the Poor Through the Fourteenth Amendment," 83 *Harvard Law Review* 7 (1969).

7. *Hamdi v. Rumsfeld,* 542 U.S. 507 (2004), amicus brief of the Center for American Unity et al., available at http://www.cfau.org/hamdi/amicusmerits.htm

8. Ibid., (citing *Los Angeles Times* article).

9. *Graham v. Richardson,* 403 U.S. 365 (1971).

FOURTEEN: "DO YOU SODOMIZE YOUR WIFE?"

1. Joe Alonzo, "Protests Mark Scalia's Visit," *The Commentator,* April 22, 2005, p. 1.

2. John O. McGinnis et al., "The Patterns and Implications of Political Contributions by Elite Law School Faculty," *Georgetown Law Journal,* vol. 93 (2005), p. 1168.

3. Daniel B. Klein and Charlotta Stern, "How Politically Diverse Are the Social Sciences and Humanities? Survey Evidence from Six Fields" (working paper), and Daniel B. Klein and Andrew Western, "How Many Democrats per Republican at UC-Berkeley and Stanford? Voter Registration Data Across 23 Academic Departments" (working paper), both available http://www.nas.org/aa/klein_launch.htm.

4. Howard Kurtz, "College Faculties a Most Liberal Lot, Study Finds," *Washington Post,* March 29, 2005.

5. Adam Liptak, "If the Law Is an Ass, the Law Professor Is a Donkey," *New York Times,* August 28, 2005.

6. *The Patterns and Implications,* p. 1170.

7. Ibid.

8. Liptak, "If the Law Is an Ass."

9. Andrew Peyton Thomas, *The People v. Harvard Law: How America's Oldest Law School Turned Its Back on Free Speech* (San Francisco: Encounter Books, 2005), p. 112.

10. Ibid., p. 213.

11. Lawrence Research, National Survey of Registered Voters, 1988, available at www.nraila.org/issues/factsheets/read.aspx?ID=83.

12. Joanne Kenen, "NRA Victims on Killing Gun Ban, Now Targets Elections," Reuters, September 12, 2004.

13. Charles Whitebread, *The Eight Secrets of Top Exam Performance in Law School* (New York: Harcourt Legal and Professional Publications, 1997), p. 6.

14. *Sugarman v. Dougall*, 413 U.S. 634, 647 (1973); amicus curiae brief by Association of American Law Schools in support of respondents, *Grutter v. Bollinger*, 539 U.S. 306 (2003), p. 4.

15. Amicus curiae brief by Association of American Law Schools in support of respondents, *Grutter v. Bollinger*, p. 5.

16. Harvard Law School website, http://www.law.harvard.edu/about/.

17. Yale Law School website, http://www.yale.edu/bulletin/html/law/study.html.

18. Message from Dean Evan H. Caminker, University of Michigan, http://www.law.umich.edu/propectivestudents/welcome/dean.htm.

19. NYU School of Law website, http://www.law.nyu.edu/prospective.

20. University of Chicago Law School website, http://www.law.uchicago.edu/Life/culture.html.

21. Richard Montauk, *How to Get into the Top Law Schools* (New York: Berkeley Publishing Group, 2004), p. 4.

22. Thomas, *The People v. Harvard Law*, p. 125.

23. Trial memorandum of President William Jefferson Clinton, in re impeachment of William Jefferson Clinton, President of the United States, January 13, 1999, available at http://www.law.umkc.edu/faculty/projects/ftrials/clinton/clintonbrief.html.

24. "Clinton Answers Questions About Senate Impeachment Trial," CNN.com, January 13, 1999, available at http://www.cnn.com/ALLPOLITICS/stories/1999/01/13/clinton.transcript.

25. "Harvard Law Professors Urge Congress to Review Interrogation Policy and Hold Executive Branch Accountable," Harvard Law School website, June 16, 2004, available at http://www.law.harvard.edu/news/2004/06/16_congressletter.php.

26. The jointly signed letter by 585 law professors was published as an advertisement in the *New York Times* in early January 2001; it is located at http://archive.democrats.com/view.cfm?id=966.

27. Michael Barone, "The Supreme Court on Military Recruiters," USNews.com, March 7, 2006, available at http://www.usnews.com/usnews/opinion/baroneblog/archives/060307/the_supreme_cou.htm?track=rss.

28. Linda Greenhouse, "U.S. Wins Ruling Over Recruiting at Universities," *New York Times,* March 7, 2006.

29. Liptak, "If the Law Is an Ass." See Jon Dougherty, "Law Profs Protest High-Court Recount Decision: Claim Five Justices Acted as 'Political Proponents for Candidate Bush,' " WorldNetDaily.com, January 27, 2001, available at http://ads.wnd.com/news/article.asp?ARTICLE_ID=21502.

30. Whitebread, *The Eight Secrets*, p. 52.

FIFTEEN: AFFIRMATIVE ACTION FOR CONSERVATIVES

1. George F. Will, "Academia, Stuck to the Left," *Washington Post,* November 28, 2004.

2. John J. Miller, "Pariahs, Martyrs—and Fighters Back," *National Review,* October 24, 2005; John Tierney, "Why Righties Can't Teach," *New York Times,* October 15, 2003.

3. Andrew Varnon, "Smith's Young Republican: Professor James Miller Pushes the Liberal Campus as the Republicans' Next Big Wedge Issue," *Valley Advocate,* February 10, 2005, available at http://www.valleyadvocate.com/gbase/News/content?oid=oid:99647.

4. David Horowitz, "Moment of Truth (For the Anti-American Left)," FrontPage Magazine.com, March 31, 2003, available at http://www.frontpagemag.com/Articles/Read Article.asp?ID=6962.

5. Miller, "Pariahs, Martyrs."

6. See http://www.studentsforacademicfreedom.org.

7. Senator Joseph Biden, Hearing of Senate Judiciary Committee, January 10, 2006.

8. Stephen Bainbridge, "Disparate Impact in Academic Hiring," www.professor bainbridge.com, January 22, 2006.

9. Tierney, "Why Righties Can't Teach."

10. "Agreement Sends Wrongfully Expelled Minority Students Back to Berkeley High," Youth and Education Law Clinic, Stanford Law School, available at http://www.law. stanford.edu/clinics/yelc.

11. *Elrod v. Burns,* 1976, 427 U.S. 347 (1976).

12. 427 U.S., 347, 375 (Stewart, J., concurring in judgment).

13. *Board of Regents v. Roth,* 408 U.S. 564 (1972) (Douglas, J., dissenting).

14. *Elrod v. Burns,* 427 U.S. 347 (1976).

CONCLUSION: STORMING THE COURTS

1. This story is told, with slight variations, in George Embrey, "Democrats Urged to Get to Work," *Columbus Dispatch,* January 22, 1993; Susan Eng, "It's Time to Turn on Pressure," *Toronto Star,* June 12, 1995; and Bruce Shapiro, "Rethinking the Death Penalty," *The Nation,* July 22, 2002.

2. Frank Newport, "Most Americans Identify as Either Conservative or Moderate," Gallup Poll, November 11, 2003.

3. *Meyer v. Nebraska,* 262 U.S. 390 (1923).

4. Ronald Reagan, Farewell Address, January 11, 1989, available at http://www.national review.com/document/reagan200406052132.asp.

ACKNOWLEDGMENTS

I want to mention only a few individuals here, thereby limiting the number who may be asked by Congress about their association with me.

To begin, I want to thank my friends Joseph Giganti, Joseph Gehring Jr., Kellyanne Conway, Noelle Kowalczyk, Robert Hornak, and Phil Davis for their critical contributions to this book.

Thanks also to George Conway, Ann Coulter, and Lucianne Goldberg—without whom there might not be a vast right-wing conspiracy.

Researchers Lisa De Pasquale and Ceyda Savasli performed admirably, tracking down the most obscure references with skill, diligence, and enthusiasm.

I can never say enough good things about my literary agent, Gene Brissie, and my attorneys, Frank Martinez, J. Mark Lane, and Sal Calabrese—friends all. Each is always ready to answer yet another "one last question."

Finally, a special debt of gratitude must go out to Jed Donahue, Crown Forum's editor extraordinaire, for his outstanding editing, hard work, and wise guidance.

INDEX